Power, Justice, and the Environment

Urban and Industrial Environments
Series editor: Robert Gottlieb, Henry R. Luce Professor of Urban and Environmental Policy, Occidental College

For a list of the series, see page 333.

Power, Justice, and the Environment
A Critical Appraisal of the Environmental Justice
Movement

edited by David Naguib Pellow and Robert J. Brulle

The MIT Press
Cambridge, Massachusetts
London, England

MIT Press books may be purchased at special quantity discounts for business or sales promotional use. For information, please email special_sales@mitpress.mit.edu or write to Special Sales Department, The MIT Press, 55 Hayward Street, Cambridge, MA 02142.

Set in Sabon by The MIT Press. Printed and bound in the United States of America. Printed on recycled paper.

Library of Congress Cataloging-in-Publication Data

Power, justice, and the environment : a critical appraisal of the environmental justice movement / edited by David Naguib Pellow and Robert J. Brulle.
    p. cm. — (Urban and industrial environments)
Includes bibliographical references and index.
ISBN 0-262-16233-4 (alk. paper) — ISBN 0-262-66193-4 (pbk. : alk. paper)
1. Environmental justice—United States. I. Pellow, David N., 1969– II. Brulle, Robert J. III. Series.
GE180.P686   2005
363.7'00973—dc22   2005045105

10 9 8 7 6 5 4 3 2 1

Contents

Acknowledgments

This book has been in the works since 2001, when the two of us hatched the idea of having a panel at the 2002 American Sociological Association meeting entitled "From Environmental Injustice to Environmental Justice: A Critical Appraisal of the Environmental Justice Movement." At that event, Rob Benford, Sherry Cable, Donald Hastings, Tamara Mix, and Bunyan Bryant presented outstanding papers in front of a standing-room-only audience. We owe each of them special thanks for that. We then gained the confidence of our wonderful editors, Clay Morgan and Robert Gottlieb, who gave us the authority to bring together a larger group of scholars and activists to publish a book on this topic. Many others were involved, and we owe them our gratitude. Thanks to Kamala Kempadoo, Kathryn Mutz, and Nancy Naples, for sharing their great wisdom on editing books that reach academic and activist audiences; to our wonderful research assistants Miya Saika Chen, Katrina Behrend, Sabrina Kandwhalla, and Anthony Kim, for putting in countless hours transcribing interviews and doing literature searches; and to Robert Bullard, Lois Gibbs, and Ted Smith for inspiring us to raise critical questions while keeping the faith in the cause. Finally, we wish to thank the many activists working for environmental justice around the world—particularly those who first raised the critical questions we address in this book.

Power, Justice, and the Environment

1

Power, Justice, and the Environment: Toward Critical Environmental Justice Studies

David Naguib Pellow and Robert J. Brulle

Man's attitude toward nature is today critically important simply because we have now acquired a fateful power to alter and destroy nature. But man is a part of nature and his war against nature is inevitably a war against himself. Now, I truly believe that we in this generation must come to terms with nature, and I think we're challenged as mankind has never been challenged before to prove our maturity and our mastery, not of nature, but of ourselves.

—Rachel Carson, "CBS Reports: The Silent Spring of Rachel Carson," broadcast April 3, 1963

Since Rachel Carson spoke these words, our war on nature, and thus ourselves, has continued to accelerate. Despite numerous warnings, the United States continues to act as if the global environment has an unlimited capacity to provide its citizenry with natural resources and to absorb the continued production of toxic materials. Nearly a decade after Rachel Carson's warning, the famous book *The Limits to Growth* was published. "If the present growth trends in world population, industrialization, pollution, food production, and resource depletion continue unchanged," the authors predicted, "the limits to growth on this planet will be reached sometime within the next 100 years." (Meadows et al. 1972) The authors of *The Limits to Growth* updated their analysis 20 years later in *Beyond the Limits* (Meadows et al. 1992). That study maintains that "human use of many essential resources and generation of many kinds of pollutants has already surpassed rates that are physically sustainable."

At the beginning of the twenty-first century, it is clear that we have gone beyond the carrying capacity of Earth's environmental systems. In addition, the experience of these limits to growth is not equally shared. Those who have the resources and political and economic power can reduce their exposure to these limits. Resource shortages are experienced as increasing prices for basic commodities (housing, food, energy). The affluent can better absorb these price increases than can the poor, working-class, people-of-color, and immigrant populations. Access to a healthy and clean environment is increasingly distributed by power, class, and race. Where one can afford to live has a major effect on the nature and extent of one's exposure to toxic pollutants. Within this dynamic, elites can move from polluted industrial areas to less polluted suburban neighborhoods (Pulido et al. 1996) and locations featuring natural amenities, such as Aspen, Pebble Beach, or the Hamptons. The poor and powerless cannot. They are confined to national environmental sacrifice areas, such as Navajo or Western Shoshone lands, Chester, Pennsylvania, or Cancer Alley, Louisiana. In fact, certain neighborhoods and regions of the United States are defined as "undesirable" not only because of the level of pollution in these places, but also because of the type of persons who occupy these spaces. "Bad" neighborhoods, for example, are as much about the type of ecological disamenities found in these areas as about the type of people found there. Hence, where we find social inequalities we also find environmental and health inequalities.

Limits to growth are thus first and most consequentially experienced by the less powerful of the Earth. The "other" of society—those outside of the dominant cultural, political, and economic elite classes—experience the brunt of the "bads" of industrial production and of the limits to growth. As limits to growth are exceeded, we can expect the experience of a clean and unpolluted environment to become less and less possible for everyone. But since poor and people-of-color communities are the first to feel the adverse consequences of growing ecological degradation, they have also been among the first communities to mount a political challenge to these conditions. Beginning in the late 1970s and the early 1980s, a powerful social force—the environmental justice movement—emerged from within communities of color and poor and working-class white communities around the United States that have been inundated with air, water, and soil pollution (Bullard 2000; Gottlieb 1993). The neighborhoods where these populations "live, work, and play" (Alston 1990) have been disproportionately burdened with a range of toxic and hazardous pollution and other environmental harms. The environmental justice (EJ) movement is a political response to the deterioration of the conditions of everyday life as society reinforces existing social inequalities while exceeding the limits to growth. As environmental degradation expands, we can expect that more and more communities will suffer a similar fate and will join in this effort. Thus the EJ movement has laid a foundation for environmental and social justice politics in the twenty-first century.

The EJ movement is viewed as distinct from the larger mainstream environmental movement that has been active in the United States for 120 years (Taylor 1997). Even so, the degree to which the broader environmental movement has fared is in many ways instructive for the EJ movement's prospects. For example, despite the continued development of the environmental movement, environmental degradation and social inequalities continue to increase in the United States and globally. As Blühdorn (2000) notes, despite a vast amount of empirical research and advocacy for environmental issues, this movement has failed to gain sufficient political adherents or strength to effect a transition to a sustainable society, and it has failed "to reach its central aim of changing the most fundamental principles of the capitalist growth economy and the industrial consumer society." Because of this failure, the environmental movement is undergoing a historical transition. In this situation, Blühdorn maintains, there is a need to rethink the movement's tactical and ideological basis and to develop a more self-critical and politically efficacious environmental movement.

It is within this political and cultural space that the environmental justice movement has emerged. The EJ movement has sought to redefine environmentalism as much more integrated with the social needs of human populations, and, in contrast with the more eco-centric environmental movement, its fundamental goals include challenging the capitalist growth economy as well. Despite its numerous successes, this quarter-century-old effort has also confronted the harsh reality that the political economic structures on which the United States operates have not been significantly altered with regard to ecological protection and social justice. If the movement and scholars are to have any possibility of creating an ecologically sustainable and socially just society, we must understand this social movement and critically assess which strategies have worked and which have not.

We start with a theoretical discussion of the social dynamics of environmental degradation through the application of the "risk society" concept (Beck 1986). This perspective is then amplified by summarizing the empirical work regarding inequality and environmental degradation. Impacted communities have sought to redress this situation through the creation of a number of movements that seek environmental justice. In the second section of the chapter we describe the various components of these movements and offer an assessment of their effects. In the third section we discuss the state of the environmental justice movement today. We outline some of the main political and ideological issues within this movement and discuss the need for the movement to become more self-reflexive in developing a more efficacious political practice. The contribution that academics can make to this project is what we define as "critical environmental justice studies." We conclude with an overview of the chapters in this book that seek to initiate such a dialogue. While many of these topics are controversial and have remained hidden from public and scholarly discussion, we believe it is imperative to openly examine them with the goal of building a stronger environmental justice movement.

Environmental Justice in the Risk Society

The first step toward understanding the origins of and prospects for the environmental justice struggle is to situate the EJ movement within a larger social dynamic of the social production of inequality and environmental degradation. We agree with Ulrich Beck that "environmental problems are fundamentally based in how human society is organized" (1986: 81). Thus, exploitation of the environment and exploitation of human populations are linked. In order to understand and develop meaningful measures to mitigate ecological degradation, this analysis begins with the development of a theoretical perspective on the social processes by which these problems originate.

A well-developed literature locates the origin of environmental problems in the political economy of advanced capitalist economies (Schnaiberg 1980; Schnaiberg and Gould 1994; O'Connor 1973, 1984, 1987). This perspective maintains that the capitalist economy forms a "treadmill of production" that continues to create ecological problems through a self-reinforcing mechanism of ever more production and consumption. The logic of the treadmill of production is an ever-growing need for capital investment in order to generate goods for sale on the market. From the environment, it requires growing inputs of energy and material. When resources are constrained, the treadmill of production searches for alternative sources rather than conserving resources and restructuring production. The treadmill operates in this way to maintain a positive rate of return on investments. In theory, the state is responsible for reconciling disparities between the treadmill and society's social needs. In practice the state has often acted to accelerate the treadmill in the hope of avoiding political conflict (Schnaiberg 1980: 418). The ecological result of this process is that the use of natural resources continues to increase, regardless of the consequences on the sustainability of the ecosystem. The social result is that inequalities increase and working-class populations receive less and less material benefit from their labor. Thus, both ecological disorganization and race and class inequalities are inherent by-products of the social order.

This perspective has been further expanded by the work of Beck (1986, 1995), who provides a model of the interaction among technology, social dynamics, and the process of ecological degradation. For Beck, the continued development of industrial production is based on the dynamic of modernization and industrialization. These processes are "blind and deaf to consequences and dangers" (1986: 28). At the center of the process of modernization is the application of scientific research and knowledge to expand economic growth. The power to define technological development, and thus our future, becomes concentrated in the private corporate power that controls and directs much of research and development. This results in a shift in the locus of power from the nation state to the corporations and their control over the scientific agenda.

There arise winners and losers in the politics of the distribution of environmental degradation, favoring more powerful communities over others (Beck 1986: 53). "What is denied collects itself into geographical areas, into 'loser regions' which have to pay with their economic existence for the damage and its unaccountability." (Beck 1995: 29). Beck defines the idea of "risk positions," which characterize the levels and nature of technological risk to which people are exposed (1986: 23). He goes on to characterize the distribution of risk positions in which "like wealth, risks adhere to the class pattern, only inversely; wealth accumulates at the top, risks at the bottom" (ibid.: 35).

This "class pattern" is also complemented by a "race pattern" that afflicts neighborhoods, regions, and nations with large concentrations of people of color. In view of the strong statistical correlation between race and class, this should not be surprising. The research on environmental inequality dates back to the 1970s, when scholars were reporting significant correlations between socioeconomic status and air pollution in US urban centers (Asch and Seneca 1978; Berry 1977; Burch 1976; CEQ 1971; Freeman 1972). In the 1980s, researchers began to focus more directly on the links between pollution and race, via studies of the proximity of hazardous waste sites to communities of color (United Church of Christ 1987; US GAO 1983). This research found that a community's racial composition was the best predictor of where hazardous waste sites would be located in the United States, prompting the use of the term "environmental racism" to characterize these disparities. In the 1990s and the 2000s this body of work was followed by an explosion of studies on a host of questions, including analyses of the relationship between race, class, and environmental hazards (Anderton et al. 1994; Bryant and Mohai 1992; Krieg 1998), the social forces driving and influencing environmental inequalities (Boone and Moddares 1998; Lavelle and Coyle 1992; Maher 1998), the historical trajectory of environmental injustices in particular geographic contexts (Been 1994; Bullard 1996; Pastor, Sadd, and Hipp 2001; Pulido, Sidawi, and Vos 1996), the spread of environmental inequalities and environmental racism beyond the United States to the global South (Adeola 2000; Mpanya 1992), and the emergence of the EJ movement via case studies of community resistance against toxics (Bryant 1995; Bullard 1993, 1994, 2000; Hofrichter 1993).

Advanced capitalism creates wealth for some and imposes risks on others. The problem of ecological destruction, however, ends up returning to impact its creators in a boomerang effect. The risks of modernization catch up with those who create them. This generalization of risks that are not limited in space or time creates a phenomenon labeled by Beck "the End of the Other." In the course of human history, one group of people inflicted violence on the "other," whether in the form of an enemy, a scapegoat, or a dissident. Now the harm caused by global environmental problems, such as global climate disruption or ozone depletion, is inflicted on all persons, regardless of social class or ethnicity (Beck 1995: 27). Property becomes devalued as a result of ecological destruction (ibid.: 60). Ozone depletion creates skin cancers among all classes. Sea levels rise due to global climate change and flood rich and poor alike. The politics of a risk society thus has the potential to challenge the fundamental premises on which industrial society is constructed. According to Beck (1986: 40), what is at stake in these conflicts is the question of whether "our concepts of 'progress,' 'prosperity,' 'economic growth,' or 'scientific rationality' are still correct. In this sense, the conflicts that erupt here take on the character of doctrinal struggles within civilization over the proper road for modernity."

In view of the potentially explosive political threat posed by environmental risks, Beck argues that these threats must be continually repressed and denied. There is the development of an entire politics that either denies or minimizes the extent and nature of environmental degradation (Beck 1995: 140–142). The environmental justice movement, composed of the representatives of the most marginal communities, is ill equipped at present to overcome this type of entrenched resistance. As a result, not only does the market fail to take into account the ecological consequences of its actions; the state also fails to control the market. Janicke (1990) has developed the concept of "state failure" to explain the inability of states to address the problem of ecological degradation. Janicke maintains that the evidence for state failure is "the inability of governmental reform policies to replace the outmoded postwar pattern of industrialism" (ibid.: x), which he maintains lies at the basis of the problem of ecological degradation. "State failure" results from the tight relationships that develop between the government bureaucracies and industries and from the relative exclusion of the public institutions that are supposed to hold the bureaucracies accountable (ibid.: 14–30). As a result, the response to ecological degradation takes the form of symbolic post facto responses rather than anticipatory and preventive action (ibid.: 41–54).

Movements for Environmental Justice

In the late 1970s and the early 1980s, local EJ groups began to form throughout the United States. These groups originated in working-class neighborhoods and communities of color that were experiencing high levels of environmental degradation, primarily in the form of toxic waste pollution (Freudenberg and Steinsapir 1992). As Bullard (1993: 8) argues, "in many instances, grassroots leaders emerged from groups of concerned citizens (many of them women) who see their families, homes, and communities threatened by some type of polluting industry or government policy." These groups originated in two different communities. In the white working-class community, it took the form of a "citizen-worker" or "anti-toxics" movement (Gould, Schnaiberg, and Weinberg 1996: 2; Levine 1982; Cable and Cable 1995: 75–84). In communities of color, it took the form of the "People of Color Environmental Movement." Unlike previous environmental movements, the People of Color Environmental Movement was not just characterized by the formation of new groups. While there has been an expansion of new groups articulating the EJ discourse, a significant component of this movement involved the reformulation of the goals of existing civil rights and community organizations to include environmental concerns (Taylor 1993; Bullard and Wright 1993: 47).

Thus the environmental justice movement began in small towns and counties like Love Canal, New York and Warren County, North Carolina and addressed the unequal toxic burdens of working-class and people-of-color communities head on. The movement grew in the 1980s as particular struggles built on lessons learned from previous conflicts (Roberts and Toffolon-Weiss 2001) and as activists convened regional and national gatherings to exchange ideas, tactics, and strategies. By the early 1990s the term "environmental racism" had caught fire in social-movement, scholarly, policy, and media networks and the call for environmental justice had galvanized one of the most exciting and hopeful social causes of the twentieth century. EJ advocates were regularly engaging polluting corporations, regulators, the courts, and elected officials in city councils, in state legislatures, in Congress, and in the White House.

Realizing Environmental Justice?

Since the mid 1980s the anti-toxics and EJ movements have made it extremely difficult for waste-management firms to locate incinerators and landfills anywhere in the United States without a political struggle. Efforts to expand existing polluting facilities have also caused considerable controversy across the nation. The movement has successfully challenged American society to redefine, broaden, and deepen its conception of what constitutes "the environment" and, no less important, which populations exhibit environmental concerns (Taylor 1989). Through numerous participatory research ventures and the emergence of lay experts on a host of environmental issues, EJ activists and their allies have challenged the very foundation of the scientific method and the positivist paradigm of the science community (Brown and Mikkelsen 1990). These are significant accomplishments in the movement's short history. That the EJ movement has significantly affected the direction of environmental policy, research, and activism in the United States is unquestionable. However, several dimensions of the movement's influence on society remain unclear. What is the nature and extent of the movement's effects on the United States and other societies? To what degree has the movement achieved its goals? There are four areas of focus.

Local Struggles

Without a doubt, it is at the level of local community struggles that the EJ movement has had its clearest victories. While there may be questions about the indirect effects of a particular victory (i.e., displacing a locally unwanted land use onto another community), the movement has had significant influence at the local scale. Examples include shutting down major incinerators and landfills in Connecticut, California, and Illinois; preventing polluting operations from being built or expanding (such as the plant proposed by Shintech); and relocating and/or buying out residents of polluted areas. If "all politics is local," then the EJ movement has certainly been successful at engaging environmental justice politics where it matters most. People in the above-mentioned communities across the United States have benefited directly from the power of the movement to focus its strength and energy in a local context, a definable space.

Legal Gains and Losses

The litigated cases emerging from EJ conflicts in communities have produced a much less promising record than activists had hoped for (see Gordon and Harley, this volume). The courts have systematically refused to challenge polluters based on Title VI of the 1964 Civil Rights Act without direct evidence of a discriminatory intent. Administrative relief via the US Environmental Protection Agency has also had little effect. Since 1994, when the USEPA began accepting Title VI claims, more than 110 have been filed and none has been resolved. Only one federal agency has thus far invoked environmental justice to protect a community in a major decision. In May 2001, the Nuclear Regulatory Commission denied a permit for a uranium-enrichment plant in Louisiana, citing its findings that environmental justice issues had been ignored.

National Environmental Policy

Despite a dismal court record, sparse legislative and governmental policy impacts, and little national visibility among mass publics, the EJ movement has succeeded in capturing the attention of high-level elected officials. Most prominent among these successes was President Clinton's signing of Executive Order 12898, mandating all federal agencies to ensure environmental justice in their operations. Less visible on the public radar are more modest and perhaps more meaningful victories. These include Paul Mohai's (2002) finding that the Congressional Black Caucus has one of the strongest environmental voting records of any other group in the US Congress and the passage (or expected passage) of EJ laws and rules in Massachusetts (Carey 2001), Florida (Nicholson-Choice 2000), and California (Keith 2001). More problematic are the participatory schemes that a neoliberal USEPA hatched during the 1990s to address EJ demands. As much as activists and scholars would like to celebrate the development of the National Environmental Justice Advisory Council (NEJAC) and other high-level advisory committees and task forces, because they represent an acknowledgement of the issue by decision makers, these entities are so rife with problems (lack of political power, inequalities among participants, a drain on energy away from grassroots issues) that they are unlikely to bear much fruit. Even the vaunted Executive Order on Environmental Justice has had a very limited effect (Lazaroff 2000). As was noted in March 2004 by the Inspector General of the EPA (EPA 2004), the agency is not doing an effective job of enforcing environmental justice. The Inspector General noted that the EPA has no strategic plans, goals, or performance measurements designed to advance the intent of this Executive Order.

Globalization and Environmental Justice

The evaluation of the EJ movement is of significance because, as economic globalization continues at an unchecked pace, as the United States and other industrialized nations continue to produce greater volumes of hazardous waste, and as the level of social inequality in these societies also increases, the frequency and intensity of environmental justice conflicts will also rise. These conflicts will become more routine in the United States and in the global South as global North nations continue dumping waste in both domestic and global "pollution havens" where the cost of doing business is much cheaper, regulation is virtually non-existent, and residents do not hold much formal political power. In some cases, these practices have nearly led to military confrontations among nations, threatening geopolitical stability. Impressively, much of the leadership of the EJ movement has been cognizant of the trends toward economic globalization and the trans-national corporate move toward the path of least resistance with regard to dumping and polluting wastes. There are numerous instances of communications, information sharing, coalition building, and solidarity work between EJ groups in the global North and South. Since the 1990s, EJ activists and delegates have made high-profile visits to Rio de Janeiro, Durban, Johannesburg, the Hague, Beijing, Istanbul, and Cairo (Environmental Justice Timeline-Milestones, October 2002). However, these efforts have been sporadic and have had meager resource support. Paralleling the hierarchical dynamics between the US mainstream environmental movement and the US environmental justice movement, we often see mainstream global North groups facilitating and dominating transnational discussions and actions around global EJ issues. What is clear is that if the EJ movement cannot curb the excesses of capital and the government inside the United States, it surely will be ill equipped to challenge global corporations on unfamiliar turf in the global South. Furthermore, and most troubling, as the mainstream environmental movement and white communities are partly responsible for influencing the shift in waste dumping into communities of color in the United States and abroad (through anti-toxics mobilizations and the passage of more stringent and costly environmental regulations), the EJ movement may contribute to the globalization of environmental inequality in the same manner.

After this brief overview, what can be said about the state of the movement for environmental justice? The outlook is not positive. The production of toxic chemical waste continues to increase exponentially; the level of cancers, reproductive disorders, and respiratory illnesses is on the rise in communities of color; environmental inequalities in urban and rural areas have remained steady or increased during the 1990s and the 2000s; the gap between the wealthy and the poor is the greatest seen in several decades; and the labor movement continues to lose ground as corporate power has usurped the ability of ordinary citizens and politicians to ensure that basic sovereignty remains intact in the United States. Moreover, political and economic forces in the African-American community in particular, such as the National Black Chamber of Commerce, have organized nationally to oppose the EJ movement, claiming that the movement seeks to prevent all economic development in communities of color. How the EJ movement understands, analyzes, and challenges this intra-racial resistance and highly organized opposition will be instructive and a harbinger of the future health of the cause.

The State of the EJ Movement
The success of the environmental justice movement is mixed. It is not a case of overall success or failure. Rather, we feel that an analysis and discussion of a number of specific areas will illustrate where the movement itself has either gained or lost ground, and should guide the major themes that EJ activists must address in the coming years. Many of these are often unspoken and unacknowledged by EJ leaders in open forums because of their potentially divisive and controversial nature. But they are burning issues that exist just below the surface and have contributed to a number of setbacks and therefore must be addressed.

Cultural Hegemony and Ideology
Changes in social structures are brought about through a redefinition of what constitutes the common sense embodied in the everyday practices of society. Thus the path to the realization of power in society is through the ability to define what constitutes the common-sense reality that applies to a field of practice (Bourdieu 1985: 729). This allows us to see the symbolic dynamics of the political community as based on the interaction between the dominant worldview and its challengers. We view this as the central battlefield for the EJ movement—the struggle over the definition of environmental and social reality between social movement groups and the corporate-state structures that produce environmental inequalities. This is

a problem of "framing," and the EJ movement has succeeded in framing—redefining—environmental concerns as civil rights, social justice, and human rights issues (Montague 2002a). Because of this success, few of the major environmental organizations and governmental agencies charged with any aspect of environmental protection can ignore the issue of social equity (even if only symbolically). While the movement has gained ground in this effort, its impact on mass publics has not been as significant as would be necessary to disrupt the popular consent of the current hegemonic relations of ruling.

Ideology and Analysis: Race versus Class

So much of the EJ movement has advanced, interacted with, and been informed by social science research that, while it represents a rare level of cooperation between activists and researchers, this close association has created some strategic and ideological limitations. The "race versus class" debate has produced exceptional methodological advances in the study of environmental racism and inequality, but has missed the larger picture. While researchers argue over whether zip codes or census tracts are the most appropriate level of analysis for EJ studies, communities continue to be inundated with pollution. The fact is that environmental injustice is, and has always been, about both race and class (Faber and Krieg 2001). But since the EJ movement has had to work so hard to claim ownership over the discourse, the ideology and framing of the problem has all too often focused so heavily on environmental racism as to exclude considerations of environmental inequality by class within communities of color. The movement must address the issues of class and political hierarchies within communities of color. There are scores of environmental justice conflicts that one simply cannot explain by reducing the cause solely to racism. Some scholars (LaDuke 1999; Pellow 2002) have begun to tackle this question, but movement leaders have been slow to do so. These dynamics go to the heart of social movement theory because they underscore the need for the EJ movement to rethink the way it mobilizes resources, to re-articulate the way it frames the problem and solution, and to re-imagine the particular political opportunities it will seek to create and exploit. By restricting or expanding the vision of environmental justice, each of these strategies will change significantly.

Resource Dependence and Democratization

As much as EJ leaders have portrayed the movement as grassroots, decentralized, and focused on bottom-up decision making, these claims have yet to be evaluated systematically. Is the EJ movement truly characterized by this self-described populist, democratized power structure? We have seen evidence for and against this assertion, at the local, regional, and national levels. For example, many EJ organizations have little to no membership base, even in their own back yards. Instead, these groups have survived hand-to-mouth on grants awarded by foundations and by government agencies and through collaborative ventures with larger environmental groups. What happens in many cases is that these activists become token "representatives" for their entire communities, vested with the authority to speak not only "for themselves" but also for thousands of others. This raises the more immediate question about democratic and participatory decision making (Brulle 2000: 64–68) within EJ organizations (see Brulle and Essoka in this volume). The question of democratization of EJ organizations is closely related to the issue of resource mobilization. If much of the resource focus ('dependence' might be a more accurate word) within EJ groups is on funding from philanthropic and government sources, then there is little attention paid to—and even less accountability to—local publics (Brulle and Caniglia 2005). In view of the extraordinarily minimal funds the philanthropic sector has shared with the EJ movement (Faber and McCarthy 2001), we can only describe this state of affairs as regrettable and urgent. We contend that the EJ movement might model some of its resource-mobilization strategies after other (historical and contemporary) movements. The best example is the civil rights movement, which built its monumental human and financial resource base from within and outside the African-American community by organizing the black church, mobilizing local residents, and gaining the support of synagogues and celebrities from around the nation.

Institution Building

The EJ movement has worked successfully to build up local organizations and regional networks, and it has initiated relationships with pre-existing institutions such as churches, schools, and neighborhood groups. In view of the close association between many EJ activists and EJ researchers, perhaps it is not surprising that one of the most visible institutional settings the movement has influenced is the university. There are numerous examples of entities in higher education focusing on EJ issues. So the work of institution building with academia and select government agencies has been promising and is ongoing. But the work of institution building must also take root closer to home with a vision toward building sustainable institutions and sustainable communities. And this may be the greatest challenge for the movement—to complement its well-honed acumen for opposition to hazardous technologies and unsustainable development projects with a concrete vision and plan of action for the construction and protection of sustainable communities. A number of EJ groups have indeed taken control over community development functions in their areas and own and manage housing units, agricultural firms, job training facilities, farmer's markets, urban gardens, and restaurants (Gottlieb 2000; Medoff and Sklar 1994; Shutkin 2001). These successes should be noted and celebrated. However, they have been extremely limited in their ecological and social impacts and endurance, in comparison with the majority of business and community development ventures tied to the global market economy. EJ activists, scholars, and practitioners would do well to document these projects' trajectories and seek to replicate and adapt their best practices in other locales.

Boundaries, Parameters, and Limits

Many activists and scholars celebrate the refreshing fact that the EJ movement is one of only a few movements in the United States not founded on a "single-issue" platform. According to Faber and McCarthy (2001), they view the EJ movement as a social force with six sources: the civil rights movement; the occupational safety and health movement; the indigenous peoples' movement; the toxics movement; solidarity, human rights, and environmental movements in the global South; and the community-based movements for social and economic justice that have traditionally focused on housing, public transportation, crime and police conduct, access to jobs, etc. One observer goes even further and argues for adding the movement of persons affected by multiple chemical sensitivities, breast cancer, birth defects, diabetes, chronic fatigue syndrome, Gulf War syndrome, and other illness and the international "zero waste" and "clean production" movements, which are focused on "revolutionizing the material basis of the industrial enterprise" (Montague 2002b). However, there are limits to how much plurality a movement can embrace. On that question, the EJ movement has yet to find a balance. A flyer announcing the Second National People of Color Environmental Leadership Summit noted that potential participants should attend if they were interested in any number of topics, including biopiracy, globalization, food quality, deforestation, oil and mineral extraction, waterfront development, transportation, pesticides, human genetics, citizen participation, military toxins, and smart growth. This is an extraordinary range of issues, all of which we would agree have relevance to the overall goal of environmental justice, but taken as a whole they run the risk of diffusing the movement's focus. The difficulty in drawing boundaries for the EJ movement may stem from its multi-issue focus, its multi-ethnic and multi-racial composition, its multi-national scope, and its origins in multiple related movements. EJ activists must bound and limit the purview of their concerns. If instead they seek to explain every problem at the intersection of development and social inequality in terms of environmental injustice, surely their movement will lose its explanatory (and mobilizing) power (Benford, this volume; Getches and Pellow 2002).

These are just a few of the pressing concerns facing the EJ movement. Yet the literature on the movement is quite problematic. The majority of the literature is not only uncritical of the EJ movement, but quite celebratory. This is, perhaps, unsurprising. The movement's founding was largely premised on a challenge to the mainstream, white middle-class environmental movement and its lack of attention to the crises occurring in communities of color (Gottlieb 1993). What this means is that, while researchers have discussed the myriad contributions the EJ movement has brought to the discourse on environmentalism, only a few scholars have asked how effective the movement has been at achieving its basic goals. For example, in a study of various conflicts over waste in Chicago's communities of color, Pellow (2002) concludes that EJ activists and elected officials of color were complicit in producing or intensifying environmental inequalities in a range of cases. Reasons for this culpability include short-term political and economic gain, limited strategic vision, and historic structural inequalities that leave activists and politicians in marginal communities with constrained choices. Pellow raises serious concerns about the EJ movement's capacity to build power without also addressing these racial, class, and political divides. Other scholars have raised similar concerns. In two other major works scholars ask whether the movement should continue to put its scarce resources into legal strategies rather than developing a more coherent grassroots network of power (Camacho 1998; Cole and Foster 2001). Foreman (1998) charges that EJ scholars and advocates have mistakenly cast too broad a net around a range of issues only loosely connected to environmental and social justice concerns. Still other scholars argue that the EJ movement has not extended its reach broadly enough, whether to confront the root political economic causes of environmental racism (Faber 1998) or to take seriously the role of natural resource exploitation in the production of environmental inequalities (Mutz, Bryner, and Kenney 2002); we find merit in these critiques. Roberts and Toffolon-Weiss (2001) studied five EJ conflicts in Louisiana and carefully evaluated the degree of success achieved by local movement advocates. Their study offers a starting point for the kind of research that is needed to answer the questions driving our own effort—questions directed at the EJ movement's efficacy and capacities.

Toward Critical Environmental Justice Studies

To move the environmental justice movement forward, we believe, will require a change in the locus and the direction of environmental justice studies. Various concepts and a few theoretical models have been presented in analyses of the problems associated with environmental inequality and racism (Bullard 2000; Capek 1993; Pellow 2000; Taylor 2000). However, little theoretical effort has been exerted toward the purposes of evaluating the effectiveness of the EJ movement. While documentation of environmental injustices continues to teach us a great deal about how environmental inequalities develop and impact communities, the literature suffers from a lack of attention to the larger question of whether this movement has the efficacy or the capacity to achieve its stated goals. We propose a more critical examination of the movement's tactics, strategies, discursive frames, organizational structure, and resource base. It is imperative that we document both successes and failures in gaining political power, and both effective and ineffective rhetorical strategies and practices. Critical environmental justice studies—i.e., studies that can link theoretical models and research—

can help to increase the movement's reflexivity. By linking theory to practice, we might contribute to a more effective movement, and thus aid in the effort to create a socially just and ecologically sustainable society.

We view this volume as the first step in a wider dialogue that includes scholars, theorists, activists, and practitioners from a range of institutions working in the area of environmental justice. This dialogue began with a special panel at the American Sociological Association's annual meeting, in Chicago, on August 17, 2002, at which two social movement scholars and two environmental justice scholars presented papers appraising the EJ movement's record. The dialogue continues in this book.

We invited additional contributors from several different perspectives to submit chapters to this volume. The chapters examine the EJ movement's historical and continuing efforts to realize the goals of environmental justice. The book is divided into three parts, each focused on a major theme that raises fundamental questions about the strength and future direction of the EJ movement.

Overview of the Book

The chapters in part I examine the effectiveness of movements for environmental justice and equality. They examine a number of related themes that illustrate and analyze the EJM's progress, failures, and anticipated challenges. Bryant and Hockman compare the EJ movement with the civil rights movement and draw provocative conclusions from a range of data sources. Benford examines how EJ groups frame and tactically approach problems and solutions to environmental injustice. His analysis raises the possibility that the rhetorical structure of the environmental justice frame is a limiting factor for the success of the EJ movement. Cable, Mix, and Hasting and Toffolon-Weiss and Roberts address the complexities of collaboration between activists and allies as well as what tactical approaches achieve success or failure. Anthony reflects on his experience of more than 40 years as an advocate for civil rights and environmental justice, and on future struggles for environmental justice.

The chapters in part II focus on the development of new strategies, practices, and cultural perspectives to better realize the goals of the environmental justice movement. Sze and Williams break new ground on issues of energy activism and food security in EJ communities. Peña considers how local groups use the EJ frame to approach problems and mobilize community support; he then describes an alternative frame for local mobilization which he believes would be more effective. Gordon and Harley and Targ focus on the mixed record of the courts and legislatures in realizing environmental justice. Brown et al. discuss the rise of environmental health movements and how these movements can relate to the goals of environmental justice in two EJ conflicts, one in Boston and one in New York. Brulle and Essoka examine the governance structure of existing EJ organizations and discuss how the practices of such organizations can be modified to make the movement more efficacious. Lee's study of four communities presents a new model of collaboration and capacity building articulated in the voices of some of the most successful American EJ activists.

The chapters in part III examine the challenges presented by the processes of globalization and how globalization affects environmental inequality. The chapters in this part ask questions such as the following: What vision have leaders of the EJ movement devised to address larger questions concerning the globalization of capital, social inequality, and environmental injustice? In what ways do transnational environmental injustices present parallel or unique challenges to local and national movement efforts? What is the nature and extent of the EJ movement's effects on the United States and other societies, and how have US-based EJ advocates built alliances with advocates in other nations? Kalan critiques efforts by the US EJ movement to build coalitions with activists in the global South. Palmer and Peek discuss their work as EJ activists doing advocacy work in many different nations. Margoluis explores the complexity of attaining the goals of ecological sustainability and environmental justice. In the concluding chapter, we assess the EJ movement, using the perspectives advanced by the contributing authors.

We believe that the environmental justice movement has the potential to challenge the limits-to-growth and risk-society frameworks on which the global North operates. We are committed to the principles of environmental justice, and we seek to enter this collection of chapters into the tool kit of concerned individuals and institutions that share a vision of an ecologically sustainable and socially just future. Let us end the war against nature and ourselves.

I

Environmental Equality and Justice: Progress or Retreat?

2

A Brief Comparison of the Civil Rights Movement and the Environmental Justice Movement

Bunyan Bryant and Elaine Hockman

Growing out of the civil rights movement (CRM) and the environmental movement (EM) of the late 1950s and the 1960s, the environmental justice movement (EJM) seeks to address important issues that have remained unchanged by the pioneering efforts of those earlier movements. Although the voter registration and public accommodation campaigns of the CRM challenged and ultimately dismantled the racially segregated system of the South, multiple forms of racial discrimination still remain even to this day. Racial discrimination as evidenced in the North may be less blatant, but it is equally widespread, as shown by schools, communities, and workplaces that remain racially segregated. Legal actions and legislation such as the 1964 Civil Rights Act and the 1965 Voter Rights Act, put in place to remedy society's civil wrongs against all minorities, had positive impacts on middle-class blacks (Feagin and Sikes 1994; Landry 1987; Pattillo-McCoy 1999; Zweigenhaft and Domhoff 1991). The impoverished conditions of the vast majority of blacks, Latinos, and Native Americans, however, went basically unimproved by the movement and by civil rights legislation that was not vigorously enforced.

When we were asked to evaluate the success of the EJM, we asked ourselves "compared with what?" In the first section of this chapter we compare the CRM and the EJM from the 1950s to the present. We compare these two movements based upon certain variables that pointed to major differences and similarities. Both movements, with their integrationist and/or distributive focus, failed to confront in any meaningful way the structural underpinnings that support multiple forms of injustice. We first look at the origins and composition of the movements, and the role that students and black women played in them. We compare them based upon the normative strategies used and the role of nonviolence in the two movements. We compare the movements' access, use, and ability to retrieve information and to conduct meaningful research to advance their strategic goals. We also examine the role both movements have played internationally.

Origins of the Movements

We begin our discussion by comparing the origins of the two movements. The origins of the CRM are associated with structural changes or major social disruptions in society that resulted in migration patterns among African-Americans leaving the South for the North (Oberschall 1973; Burns 1963; Piven and Cloward 1977; Zhang 2002). These disruptions starting in the early 1900s resulted from the mechanization of the Southern textile and agricultural industries, which pushed black sharecroppers from the land to be pulled to the North by available jobs. To free themselves from an economic system rooted in the class structure of the post-Reconstruction period and to free themselves from a status of serfdom and economic controls supplemented by mob and police violence, Southern blacks migrated to cities primarily in the North. A second major black migration took place during and after World War II, when large numbers of blacks migrated to the North to work in the defense industry. Each time blacks migrated to the cities and became urbanized, they increased their political power, level of education, and economic status, laying the groundwork for the present-day CRM (Oberschall 1973; Piven and Cloward 1977; Zhang 2002). Oberschall (1973) concluded that blacks in the South were able to improve their condition only when they migrated to the cities and built their own organizations, such as black churches, the National Association for the Advancement of Colored People (NAACP), and the Congress of Racial Equality (CORE), and formed in those cities coalitions with a variety of groups in order to advance the struggle for civil rights. Burns (1963) stated that it was not only changes in the Southern economy and population structure, especially urbanization of previous rural populations, that served as an impetus for the CRM, but also the impact of World War II, the emergence of civil rights organizations, and the struggle for independence among African states. A related view is advanced by Morris (1984) and Bloom (1987), who argue it was African-Americans themselves (rather than external supporters, as many scholars had earlier argued) that brought about and drove the CRM. Changes in the black community and its organizations, particularly the black church, played a significant role in the emergence of the movement.

Broad-based historical forces that destabilized the country provided the conditions necessary for the contemporary CRM to flourish. After each social disruption, conditions for blacks improved. These eventually set the contemporary stage for nonviolent direct-action civil rights events.

Although scholars can point to other momentous struggles, a critical event was the collective action of the 1953 bus boycott in Baton Rouge, Louisiana. Today little is known about this important action that showed how mobilization of the masses to support economic boycotts could be a powerful strategy in the fight against racial segregation. The success of the Baton Rouge bus boycott was the impetus for the legendary Montgomery bus boycott and subsequent economic boycotts used in the broader CRM struggles.[1]

With regard to the EJM, the community struggle in Warren County, North Carolina reveals how the EJM grew out of the CRM more so than from the environmental movement.[2] In the early 1980s, Dollie Burwell, a member of the Oak Leaf United Church of Christ and the Southern Christian Leadership Conference (SCLC), helped to trigger the EJM in Warren County. Burwell was instrumental in getting members of the church, members of the SCLC, and other community activists to use nonviolent direct-action strategies to prevent the disposal of polychlorinated biphenyls (PCBs) in a landfill located in this predominately black community (Lathan 1993). Although this protest failed to achieve its goal, it was nonetheless a milestone for consciousness raising. But this movement, we feel, was based upon two other movements that preceded it: the civil rights and environmental movements. Many of the leaders in the Warren County struggle were members of the United Church of Christ, and this particular denomination had been involved in previous civil rights struggles. Also, because the EM and the CRM overlapped, activists in Warren County were able to combine the frames of the two movements into a "master frame" that came to be known as environmental justice (Taylor 2000).

The energy of both these movement events quickly spread to the North and other parts of the country. The black church in both instances played a significant role in their origins, but the church played a longer-term role in the CRM than in the EJM.[3]

In addition to differences in the composition of the CRM and the EJM, we also found differences in their respective emphases on top-down versus bottom-up normative strategies. One could argue that the nonviolent direct-action part of the CRM began when local black activists in the South organized indigenous protests groups in the 1950s and the 1960s to demand immediate and equal access to civic institutions (Eskew 1997). Although blacks had built many other organizations and institutions, it was in the church that most blacks felt at home. National organizations and leaders, however, often overshadowed local movement organizing and leaders.

Early in the nonviolent direct-action phase of the CRM there was a tendency to emphasize national leaders, national organizations (such as the NAACP, CORE, the SCLC, and the Student Nonviolent Coordinating Committee), court rulings (such as *Brown v. Board of Education*), or legislation (such as the 1964 Civil Rights Act and the 1965 Voting Rights Act). This focus on national, large-scale, top-down strategies of achieving social change often made it difficult to appreciate the role that local people played in igniting, fueling, and sustaining the movement at enormous personal cost (Lawson and Payne 1998).

The movement was also a top-down approach from the structural position of student activists. Oberschall (1973) reported that the CRM was basically the product of the black middle class, and that students played a prominent role. Although the grassroots played a significant role in the CRM, it was basically middle-class blacks who benefited from its outcomes. Although both national and local movements empowered each other, poor people were basically unaffected by the CRM.[4] The concentrated attack upon segregation by the middle class is often viewed as an expression of that class's interests rather than the interest of the black populace, most of whom were poor (Lomax 1962; Thompson 1963). The black masses were poor before the movement and are still poor today, almost a half-century later. The masses of the black poor could not hope to enjoy the gains of desegregation of public accommodations so long as they lacked the funds to afford them (Landry 1987).

In contrast, to examine the bottom-up strategies of the EJM, we will look at the First National People of Color Environmental Leadership Summit, held in Washington in 1991. To build an effective movement, activists at the Summit committed themselves to the social construction of diverse, egalitarian, and nonhierarchical leadership and to decentralized structures that were democratic and locally and regionally based. They developed 17 principles of environmental justice as guidelines for organizing at the local and regional levels. Summit activists rejected not only any top-down approach, but even the formation of a national organization or national leadership, because they felt such an approach was disempowering, paternalistic, and exclusive. Alston adds another important point about the building of the EJM:

I think that those of us who study the history of social movements have learned so much from other movements that we made a commitment to spend the next two years building local and inter-regional structures and to strengthen those, and to then come back together and see. . . . We didn't want one person to emerge as the "spokesperson" because we have worked too long and too hard to have the bonds between us destroyed. The media and the EPA were pushing for this spokesperson, so it's been a real struggle. I'm really glad that we have made that decision. (quoted in Di Chiro 1998)

To emphasize the importance of self-representation, the activists at the Leadership Summit developed the slogan "We speak for ourselves," which is still often voiced throughout the movement. The EJM activists seemed generally to distrust national leadership or events, and to feel that the people most affected by environmental insults should be at the table when decisions were made. Even today, there is no consensus for a national leader or strategy even though a number of activists have gained a national reputation. Today the question before the movement is "Can the EJM sustain its grassroots character, or will it eventually resort to national leaders?" The EJM continues to struggle to use bottom-up normative strategies[5] of local leadership and small-scale mobilization activities and to resist vehemently the nationalization of the struggle. And although the church played both a top-down role and a bottom-up role in the CRM and helped to trigger the EJM,[6] it no longer plays a significant role in the latter movement.

Composition of the Civil Rights and the Environmental Justice Movements

Even though white and Jewish men and women and other white ethnic groups were involved in the CRM, we want to highlight the CRM and the

EJM from the perspective of people of color. By no means does this mean we do not recognize and honor the important role that whites from all backgrounds played and the sacrifices they made in the struggle for desegregation and equality. Much of the similarity regarding composition comes from the fact that the EJM comes out of the CRM and to a more limited extent from the broad environmental movement. Many EJM activists began as civil rights activists, and they have brought with them their CRM organizing skills and experiences. Others moved to the EJM from the Chicano/Latino, Asian-American, Native American, or union movements. Issues of class struggle and racism were imported into the EJM. Yet important differences between the two movements must be acknowledged. Even though women perform the lion's share of the work, just as in the CRM, and even though they must struggle for leadership in the movement, there seems to be more acceptance and formal recognition of their leadership roles in the EJM than was the case in the CRM. Students, who played a prominent role in the CRM, have to date played less of a role in the EJM.

Although both movements came out of the black community in the South, their racial compositions are radically different.[7] The CRM was characterized as basically a black/white movement focused primarily on black/white relations. At the time Asians, blacks, Latinos, and Native Americans stood alone and apart from one another and failed to work in coalition to any significant degree. Perhaps blacks were too preoccupied with their own struggle to focus on coalescing with other groups in a broader struggle for social justice. Or perhaps they simply lacked the energy and resources needed to form coalitions beyond individuals and groups that were already willing and able to join. Historically, the working relationships among various racial and ethnic groups were often filled with distrust and lack of knowledge of each other's cultures and traditions. Dana Alston, one of the leaders of the EJM, spoke at the First National People of Color Environmental Leadership Summit on the importance and difficulty of forming multicultural coalitions:

The most important thing that came out of the Summit was the bonding. Many people think that because they're nonwhite, that they're going to come together, but the society is built on keeping people divided and we all know about the tensions between African-Americans and Asians Americans and Latinos and Native Americans, but it's the history, the culture, the society that's keeping us divided . . .

because that's how power structures stay in power, by keeping us separate, so we had to from the very beginning put together a set of principles from which we were going to relate to each other. (quoted in Di Chiro 1998)

The composition of the EJM adds another level of complexity in working effectively across cultural lines. In this movement, perhaps for one of the few times in American history, leadership by people of color—particularly at the local and regional levels—has brought together groups from a variety of racial and ethnic backgrounds to address social and environmental concerns that affected their communities. To strengthen the EJM will require a greater focus on learning about the historical and cultural backgrounds of groups that make up the EJM. We need to recognize and celebrate the uniqueness, the contribution, and the history of each culture. Within the movement there will always be conflict. The important question is whether such conflict can be used constructively and creatively.

Black women have not only been an important part of the composition of the CRM, they also played critical roles in founding it. Despite their noteworthy contributions, with the exception of Ella Baker, Fanny Lou Hamer,[8] Rosa Parks, and Daisy Bates, the names of men come more easily to mind when we think of national leaders of the CRM. Few people have heard of Mary Fair Burks, Johnnie Carr, A. W. West, Septima Clark, and Jo Ann Gibson Robinson, all of whom were members of the Women's Political Council of Montgomery—an organization that predated the work of and provided the impetus for the Montgomery Improvement Association and the Montgomery Bus Boycott (Robnett 1998; Levy 1988). Women provided leadership not only for the Bus Boycott, but also for the Freedom Rides of the early 1960s and for the Mississippi Freedom Democratic Party (which tried to unseat the all-white Mississippi delegation at the 1964 Democratic National Convention). In the South, black women served the CRM by going from door to door, speaking to their neighbors, meeting in voter registration and citizenship classes, attending mass meetings, and organizing through their churches. Often they provided the charismatic leadership that motivated people and held the movement's activities together (Blee 1998). They, too, were exposed to dangers. Women in Mississippi, for example, were clubbed at demonstrations, beaten in jail, and had their homes firebombed (Lawson and Payne 1998). Yet a large share of movement leadership came from black women who remain nameless in the annals of history. During those days, black leaders, including Martin Luther King Jr. and Malcolm X, held traditional views of the acceptable roles of women. Highlighting the role that women played in the movement does not disregard the important role that black men played. Many men were also unsung heroes.

In contrast, the composition of the leadership of the EJM varies. At the local level, EJ leadership seems to be multi-ethnic and often influenced by activist women of color (Di Chiro 1998). Many of these women are older, and many are veterans of the civil rights, labor, or farm-worker movements. Older people (particularly women) who live in proximity to hazardous waste facilities are more likely to be differentially exposed to and affected by environmental toxins. They are more likely to be poor and to lack geographic mobility or health insurance. They may also be more conscious of their mortality than are younger people, and they may have more time at their disposal to devote to the struggle. While the kinds of dangers women in the EJM face are not the traditional forms of violence that we observed during the CRM, instead they and their families are exposed to lethal pollutants and toxins that can kill and maim just the same. At the national networking meetings, leadership of the EJM seems to be shared by men and women, although there is still some gender inequality. Today, more names of women readily come to mind to people in the movement when we think of our leaders. The women's movement undoubtedly has helped bring women to the fore in the EJM. At the Environmental Justice Summit II, women were recognized for their leadership ability and outstanding work in the environmental justice arena.

While women played a significant role in the CRM, so, too, did students of both sexes. In February 1960, a major event in the CRM took place. David Richmond, Franklin McCain, Joseph McNeil, and Ezell Blair, four freshmen at North Carolina A&T, sat down to be served at a lunch counter in a Greensboro F. W. Woolworth store[9] (Fendrich 1993; Levy 1998; Newfield 1966). They refused to leave until they were served. Without prompting or guidance from any existing civil rights organization, these courageous students launched a new phase in the CRM. Their bold action inspired students all over the country to engage in nonviolent direct-action protests against the national chain of Woolworth stores. Within a year and a half, student sit-ins had spread to over 20 states and 100 cities. At least 70,000 black and white students demonstrated and picketed in actions that brought more than 36,000 arrests (Fendrich 1993). During this time, thousands of students left college campuses to work in voter registration projects in the South or to fight racial discrimination in public accommodations. Students endangered their lives by participating in nonviolent direct-action demonstrations. Students needed no prodding from adults to participate in the movement; in fact they were in its vanguard.

Yet, while both high school and college-age students were actively involved in the CRM, they are, for the most part, conspicuously absent from the EJM. And although students were very active in EJ Summit II, and claimed they were central to the future of the movement, to date they have failed to launch an effective environmental justice component of the movement. If the EJM is to survive, it must educate and recruit young people into the fold and create a new generation of leaders. While the EJM is more decentralized and has the structural ability to survive, young people must be more involved if this movement is to grow.

Strategies and Tactics

When we observe the strategies of the EJM, we see that they are similar to nonviolent direct-action strategies used in the CRM. Nonviolence is not just passive resistance, it is active resistance to violence and civil wrongs, and it can be extremely intense and powerful. To be effective in challenging racial segregation, CR activists had to use nonviolence very skillfully as the moral equivalent of war—a war of love and truth seeking. They knew that if they responded to violence with violence they would never be able to seize and maintain the moral high ground from which they could sway public opinion to support their activism and goals.[10] Thousands of CR activists were trained in the philosophy and tactics of nonviolent resistance. But when EJM leaders use nonviolent direct-action demonstrations, they seldom prepare volunteer activists in the philosophy of nonviolence beforehand.[11] If violence were to occur at a protest event, it is unclear whether EJ demonstrators would have the discipline to respond with nonviolence and thus maintain the moral high ground.

Research and data gathering can also be a critical component of movement building. All too often, however, research findings in the civil rights field have failed to serve the interests of affected communities. In the EJM, community activists are more determined to be the locus of control or at least to be a partner in determining the research agenda (see the chapter by Cable et al. in this volume).

The CRM and the EJM: Legal, Legislative, and Rule Making

History and Dilemma

Civil rights legislation passed by Congress and court decisions have had more far-reaching effects than EJ legislation. The 1964 Civil Rights Act and the 1965 Voting Rights Act had unparalleled impacts upon the nation as a whole. Taken together, these acts were two of the most important of the twentieth century. They sought to abolish discriminatory practices in voting, opened up places of public accommodation for people of color, gave the federal government tools to wage school desegregation battles, prevented the recipients of federal taxpayer dollars (such as hospitals, schools, and transportation agencies) from engaging in racial discrimination, and outlawed racial discrimination in employment as well as religious and sex discrimination. The CRA and the VRA have, of course, been overshadowed by the much more visible legal decision handed down in the 1954 *Brown v. Board of Education* case, which overruled *Plessy v. Ferguson* and the doctrine of "separate but equal" educational accommodations.

The EJM has yet to win, or indeed to argue, an environmental justice case in the Supreme Court, or to get national legislation passed in Congress. Even though a number of EJ bills have been introduced in Congress and in state legislatures, most have not been made into law because of the strong opposition of the Chamber of Commerce and other business groups. Most EJM regulation or legislation has been at the state and local levels. The track record for grassroots EJ victories in court cases has been mixed. In Houston, a federal district court awarded the black community a modest amount of money after it was shown that the city's black children had unacceptable levels of lead in their blood. In Flint, Michigan, a decision against a wood-burning plant was reversed because the state felt that its removal would be a disincentive to economic investment.

Even if they are rarely successful in court, EJ advocates continue to make their voices heard in local governments and at the federal level. There have been some tangible results. Because of the 1990 Michigan Conference and the 1991 First National People of Color Environmental Leadership Conference, the US Environmental Protection Agency, under William Reilly of the George H. W. Bush administration, created the Office of Environmental Equity and later produced a report titled "Environmental Equity: Reducing Risks for All Communities." The report, issued in 1992, outlined the EPA's strengths and weaknesses in addressing environmental equity. In addition, EJ activists pushed EPA Administrator Carol Browner to create the National Environmental Justice Advisory Council (NEJAC) and President Clinton to sign Executive Order 12898, which directed federal departments to take stock of themselves and to plan and implement an EJ strategy. Perhaps the EJM's activities in this area will increase, particularly if current government policies fail to improve environmental conditions.

The CR and EJ Movements at the International Level

In the 1960s, while the civil rights struggle was taking place in the United States, African nations were liberating themselves from their colonial oppressors. International events such as the 1961 assassination of Patrice Lumumba in the fledgling Democratic Republic of the Congo and the escalating war in Vietnam, where blacks fought and died, increased the overall global awareness of black Americans.[12] Identification with the African liberation struggles was manifested by SNCC's reception for and tour of the American South with Oginga Odinga, vice president (1964–1969) of the newly independent country of Kenya. Martin Luther King Jr. was the first black leader to speak out publicly on the connection between the war in Vietnam, civil rights, and the poor people's struggle in the United States. Malcolm X did the same with regard to the black struggle in the United States and the liberation struggles taking place in Africa during the 1950s and the 1960s. Even though black Americans supported and identified with these liberation struggles, at least in dress and speech, and even though they in many instances quietly questioned the war in Vietnam, they were not able to move much beyond that. They were, perhaps, too occupied with their own struggles to seek help beyond the borders of the United States or to make a meaningful contribution to the international community (Lewis and Dorso 1998).

The EJM was a different story. In the 1990s and the 2000s, EJM representatives attended a number of international conferences, where they made the connections between the environmental struggles back home and the oppressed peoples of the world. At the 1992 Rio Conference[13] (the first major international conference in which EJ activists and thousands of others participated) the Agenda 21 Declaration was adopted. Social and environmental conditions, however, continued to deteriorate. The 1997 Environmental Justice and Global Ethics for the Twenty-First Century Conference, held in Melbourne, was the first international conference to include "Environmental Justice" in its title. EJ activists have made their mark at numerous other international events since that time.

What might strengthen this international presence even more is the grassroots connection through the "climate justice" frame. More specifically, this frame incorporates the perspective that not only people in developing countries will suffer more if the threat of climatic change is ignored, but so too will people in the United States suffer—some disproportionately more than others.[14] The predicted impacts of climate change include not only the exacerbation of hunger and poverty the world over, but also mass migration of people in search of food, potable water, arable land, and jobs. Such an upheaval would lead to social and political conflict and regional wars (Climate Change: State of Knowledge, no date). Environmental justice activists are speaking out at international conferences, but also working in communities across the country to educate people about the harmful impacts of pollutants and greenhouse gases, particularly from oil- and coal-fired power plants. These plants are disproportionately affecting the health of people who live in their vicinity and significantly contributing to global warming. An international connection is finally being successfully made, and it will carry the movement above and beyond the international work done during the CRM.[15] It is within the context of climate justice that activists can make an impact that could surpass the impact of the CRM.

Notes

1. For more on the history of the CRM, see Morris 1984.
2. The EJM grew out of the CRM more so than the environmental movement. Although the number of blacks active in the environmental movement was small,

activists were able to use environmental concepts to further their aims of civil rights and justice.

3. Although Love Canal was not viewed as the impetus for the EJM, it played a significant role in raising the consciousness of people to the dangers of chemicals inadequately disposed. Activists in Warren County were able to construct a movement frame that combined civil rights with environmental concerns and protection.

4. Intense class conflict was in evidence when the Mississippi Freedom Democratic Party attended the 1964 Democratic Convention in Atlantic City to unseat an all-white delegation elected under Jim Crow laws.

5. During the First National Environmental Justice Leadership Summit, participants consciously decided not to build a national organization, deciding instead to take the 17 Principles of Environmental Justice back to their regions and local communities to be used for organizing.

6. Morris (1984) argues that the black church and other organizations played an indigenous resource mobilization role. But the leadership of the movement came mostly from middle-class blacks, supported by the mass of poor blacks, who have enjoyed few fruits of the movement.

7. We recognize the work of Charles Lee of the United Church of Christ Commission for Racial Justice. A Chinese-American, he used his leadership to bring together a racially diverse group of people at the First People of Color Environmental Justice Leadership Summit, held in Washington in 1991.

8. Women did emerge as charismatic leaders in the movement, but they were excluded from positions of formal leadership.

9. In many instances students working at the local level were tied to national organizations such as SNCC. However, the student sit-in at F.W. Woolworth in Greensboro was started by local students.

10. Two books that illuminate the role and importance of nonviolence in social transformation and change are Lynd and Lynd 1995 and Sharp 1980.

11. The exception to this would be the 1982 struggle in Warren County, North Carolina, in which activists deliberately used nonviolent strategies and were arrested when they refused to let the trucks carrying soil laced with PCBs into the landfill.

12. This was not the first time African-Americans connected liberation struggles in this country with struggles of others throughout the world. Paul Robeson, W. E. B. DuBois, Marcus Garvey, Malcolm X, and the Black Panther Party did this kind of work.

13. Environmental justice scholar-activists have been at many international meetings to champion the cause of environmental justice. In addition to the 1992 Rio Conference and the one in Melbourne, they have informally participated through the NGO framework in the 1997 Kyoto Protocol, the 2000 Conference of Parties (COP6), the 2001 UN World Conference Against Racism, the 2002 UN World Summit on Sustainable Development (WSSD).

14. Power plants are the biggest industrial source of air pollution in the United States. Most African-Americans live near a power plant. Asthma attacks send African-Americans to the emergency room at three times the rate (174.3 visits per 10,000 population) of whites (59.4 visits per 10,000 population).

15. Toxic waste continues to find its way to developing countries and the American South, even though these areas lack the infrastructure or the expertise to handle such waste.

3

The Half-Life of the Environmental Justice Frame: Innovation, Diffusion, and Stagnation

Robert Benford

In this chapter, drawing on the social movement framing perspective, I critically analyze the environmental justice frame (EJF) by elaborating conceptually and empirically on its three discourse cycles: innovation, diffusion, and stagnation. I begin by offering a brief introduction to the social movement framing perspective. Next, I analyze the development and evolution of two related innovative collective action frames: environmental racism and environmental justice. I then turn to mapping the remarkable geographic and organizational diffusion of the EJF and assessing its effects. I conclude by suggesting that the EJF suffers from stagnation as a result of its defuse conceptualization, the many issues it seeks to address, the subordination of environmentalism to human justice, and its failure to embrace and articulate revolutionary solutions. One potential way to reinvigorate the EJF would be to return to its radical roots and to follow the logic of its original diagnostic framing by advocating sweeping systemic changes.

Social Movement Framing Theory[1]

Whatever else social movements do, they seek to affect how people interpret and make sense of the world around them. The interactive, contested, constructionist activities associated with such meaning work have been addressed by a number of scholars under the rubric of social movement framing theory.[2] From this perspective, social movements are not viewed merely as carriers of extant ideas and meanings that arise automatically out of structural arrangements, unanticipated events, or existing ideologies. Rather, movement actors are viewed as signifying agents actively engaged in the production and maintenance of meaning for constituents, antagonists, and bystanders (Snow and Benford 1988). They are deeply embroiled, along with the media, opponents, local governments, and the state, in what Hall (1982) refers to as "the politics of signification." Social movement scholars conceptualize this signifying work or meaning construction by employing the verb 'framing' (Gamson, Fireman, and Rytina 1982; Snow, Rochford, Worden, and Benford 1986; Snow and Benford 1988). This denotes an active, processual phenomenon that implies agency and contention at the level of reality construction. It is active in the sense that something is being done, and processual in the sense of a dynamic, evolving process. It entails agency in the sense that what is evolving is the work of social movement organizations or movement activists. And it is contentious in the sense that it involves the generation of interpretive frames that not only differ from existing ones but may also challenge them. The resultant products of this framing activity are referred to as collective action frames.

Collective action frames serve several important interpretive functions. First they have a punctuating function by underscoring and embellishing the seriousness and injustice of a social problem. What was once considered a misfortune is articulated as unjust, inexcusable, and immoral. Collective action frames also function as modes of attribution including both diagnostic and prognostic attributions. Regarding the diagnostic function, they identify problems and indicate who or what is to blame. Regarding the prognostic function, they offer solutions as well as specify how to achieve those goals. Finally, collective action frames function as signaling and collating devices that decode and slice packages of observed and experienced reality so that each experience does not have to be interpreted anew. Even if diverse and incongruous threads of information, they are woven together in a meaningful, coherent fashion.

Collective action frames vary in the problems and issues addressed, the attributions of blame and causality, their flexibility and rigidity, their interpretive scope and influence, and the extent to which they resonate among intended audiences (Benford and Snow 2000). Regarding the latter, scholars have identified several factors that affect frame resonance, including frame consistency; empirical credibility; the credibility of the frame articulators; centrality of the values, beliefs, and goals articulated to the targets of mobilization; congruency of the movement's framings with the targets' everyday life experiences; and a frame's cultural resonance or narrative fidelity (Benford and Snow 2000; Fisher 1984; Kubal 1998; Snow and Benford 1988). For the sake of simplicity, the relative effectiveness or mobilizing potency of proffered framings can be boiled down to two main factors: the apparent credibility of a frame and its relative salience for its intended audiences.

The scope of the collective action frames associated with most movements is limited to the interests of a particular group or to a set of closely related problems. However, some collective action frames are quite broad in scope, elasticity, and resonance. They function as a kind of master algorithm that colors and constrains the orientations and activities of other movements. Snow and Benford (1992) refer to such generic frames as "master frames," in contrast to more common movement-specific collective action frames which may be derivative from master frames.

Scholars have recently begun to draw on social movement framing theory and constructs to further understand, analyze, and explain the environmental justice movement's dynamics and outcomes.[3] I hope the present chapter not only serves to contribute to that scholarly literature but also stimulates thinking and discussion among activists and other engaged citizens regarding the movement's past, present, and future.

Frame Innovation: From Environmental Racism to Environmental Justice

Today's environmental justice movement was born more than two decades ago from the ideological and institutional remnants of the civil rights movement[4] and, to a lesser extent, from a variety of other contemporary social movements, including the anti-toxics, occupational health and safety, labor, farm workers, public health and safety, indigenous land rights, American Indian, social/economic justice, and welfare rights movements and the traditional environmental movement.[5] As a number of scholars have observed, the EJM's framing strategies were initially innovative.[6] In this section, I focus on the innovativeness of the environmental racism frame and its subsequent evolution into the environmental justice frame.

The Environmental Racism Frame

From its first use in 1982 by the Reverend Benjamin F. Chavis Jr., then director of the United Church of Christ's Commission for Racial Justice, the term "environmental racism" was evocative, provocative, and innovative. It was evocative inasmuch as it evoked feelings and memories of the legacy of intentional racial discrimination, of victimization, of white racism. It was provocative because it directly attributed a pattern of ecological inequalities, including a variety of chronic health problems, environmental hazards, and public health risks disproportionately experienced by people of color, to the policies, practices, and directives of "governmental, legal, economic, political, and military institutions" (Bullard 1993: 17; see also Bullard 1994a, 1999). It was innovative in that, at least for the sake of framing and thus mobilizing support, it discursively linked two of the twentieth century's most vibrant and well-known social movements: the environmental and civil rights movements.

As a collective action frame, environmental racism appeared to be quite resonant, especially among people of color (Essoka and Brulle 2002). It met all of the criteria for frame resonance (Snow and Benford 1988). It was consistent with their everyday life experiences of living in a racist society. It appeared to be empirically credible, as well. All one had to do was to enter practically any "minority" neighborhood to see ample evidence of dumping, noxious facilities, systematic neglect, freeways constructed up against homes, pollution, obnoxious billboards, and the like. And the environmental racism frame had considerable "narrative fidelity." It fit well with the knowledge, folk wisdom, and stories of disadvantaged folks—stories of mysterious illnesses, of chronic diseases such as cancer, of noxious fumes, of air too thick with pollutants to breathe without hacking, of on-the-job injuries, of children injured while playing with discarded items, and so forth.

The environmental racism frame focused explicitly and almost exclusively on diagnostic framing. That is, the frame identified a problem—"any policy, practice, or directive that differentially affects or disadvantages (whether intended or unintended) individuals, groups, or communities based on race or color" (Bullard 1994a: 98)—and attributed blame or causality to "public policies and industry practices" (ibid.). Chavis elaborates:

Environmental racism is racial discrimination in environmental policymaking. It is racial discrimination in the enforcement of regulations and laws. It is racial discrimination in the deliberate targeting of communities of color for toxic waste disposal and the siting of polluting industries. It is racial discrimination in the official sanctioning of the life-threatening presence of poisons and pollutants in communities of color. And it is racial discrimination in the history of excluding people of color from the mainstream environmental groups, decisionmaking boards, commissions, and regulatory bodies. (1993: 3)

Chavis identified racial discrimination in all matters pertaining to the environment as the problem, pointing a finger at government, industry, and mainstream environmental groups as the culprits. But whereas he explicitly and cogently articulated a diagnosis, the prognosis remained unstated and thus had to be inferred.

Obviously, a social movement has poor prospects for longevity in the absence of prognoses or goals. While it has the advantage of not being able to fail, since its goals are unstated, neither could it succeed. Thus, as innovative and resonant as the environmental racism frame was, it was incomplete. Little wonder then that the movement's predominant framing strategies soon changed.[7]

The Evolution of the Environmental Justice Frame

It was a short rhetorical step to move from the specific and radical environmental racism frame to the more general and less radical environmental injustice frame. But this, too, held negative and reactive connotations; and, like environmental racism, environmental injustice only implied a prognosis. However, the simple deletion of the prefix 'in' from the word 'injustice' yielded the more positive- and proactive-sounding term 'environmental justice'. The movement's reframing was complete.

The movement's new frame held many advantages. Cable and Shriver (1995: 434) note that "with so many dimensions to environmental discrimination, the frame of environmental justice was the most accurate and the most inclusive." Indeed, it was so elastic and inclusive that it functioned as a master frame (Agyeman 2002; Essoka and Brulle 2002; Sandweiss 1998; Taylor 2000), a collective action frame that could be readily adapted for use by a variety of movements (Snow and Benford 1992). Moreover, the EJF connotes more positive image and goals. Bunyan Bryant's summary of environmental justice is illustrative:

Environmental justice (EJ) . . . refers to those cultural norms and values, rules, regulations, behaviors, policies, and decisions to support sustainable communities where people can interact with confidence that the environment is safe, nurturing, and productive. Environmental justice is served when people can realize their highest potential. . . . EJ is supported by decent paying safe jobs; quality schools and recreation; decent housing and adequate health care; democratic decisionmaking and personal empowerment; and communities free of violence, drugs, and poverty. These are communities where both cultural and biological diversity are respected and highly revered and where distributive justice prevails." (1995: 6)

The focus on justice represented a revival of the goals of the civil rights movement[8] but also another tactical innovation—something old and something new. Regarding the former, a focus on justice implies a focus on rights (Essoka and Brulle 2002; Melosi 2000). In terms of frame amplification, both justice and rights are highly salient cultural values and thus could be expected to resonate widely. The 1991 First National People of Color Environmental Leadership Summit issued seventeen "Principles of Environmental Justice," several of which focused explicitly on rights. By the early 1990s, EJM activists were pushing rights to center stage at the local level as they mobilized against specific instances of environmental discrimination. In a study of the social construction of the environmental justice frame in the Carver Terrace neighborhood of Texarkana, Texas, for example, African-American activists demanded that residents should have the right to the following:

1. accurate information about situation;
2. a prompt, respectful, and unbiased hearing when contamination claims are made;
3. democratic participation in deciding the future of the contaminated community; and
4. compensation from parties who have inflicted injuries on the victims. (Capek 1993: 8)

These and similar demands for rights would be repeated hundreds of times in hundreds of other places by EJM activists over the ensuing years.

The focus on justice not only signaled a revival of resonant civil rights themes and goals, it also constituted an additional innovation for the movement. Justice framing shifted the victimization focus from the environment to people. In terms of the potential for wider resonance, this was a significant change. Environmental justice was not framed in terms of protecting the spotted owl from the logging industry, wetlands from developers, or a reef from sport fishing. Instead environmental justice was framed in terms of stopping the immediate and ongoing victimization of humans, especially those who were relatively powerless. Thus the EJM could now frame itself as a champion of the underdog.

Consideration of the victims as the underdogs leads back to the diagnosis. Who are the villains under the new framing strategy? Answers to this diagnostic question have implications for prognostic framing and movement strategy, particularly with respect to the selection of targets of change. Some activists "adopted a broader, political economy framework to explain the ways in which institutional arrangements perpetuate American apartheid and shape life chances" (Cable et al. 2002: 32). From this perspective, environmental injustices are perpetuated by global, capitalist systems of production and consumption (Faber 1998). It follows that, if the system is the problem, the system should be changed or replaced. Gottlieb (2001: 45) suggests that the "possibility of breaking free from a bounded environmentalism to become a broader, more socially inclusive movement capable of challenging the very structure and logic of a capitalist social order has become available once again." Yet most EJM activists stop short of calling for revolutionary changes in global or even national political economic structures (Faber 1998), advocating instead reforms in procedural, geographic, and social equity (Bullard 1995). As I will argue in the final section of this chapter, the movement has evinced a reluctance to follow through on the radical implications of its own environmental justice framing by calling for sweeping systemic changes.

The newly constructed environmental justice movement, like a Democratic Party platform, now offered something for nearly everyone with the possible exception of advocates of radical change. The rhetorical spotlight shifted from the problems to the goals and hence became more aspirational, less confrontational (Cable et al. 2002; Cole and Luke 2001; Foreman 1998). Consequently, the new EJF was more aligned with white cultural narrations than its predecessor, "environmental racism," a framing that resonated almost exclusively among people of color. Unwittingly, this shift also hinted at an erosion of the movement's critical, radical edge. Nevertheless, once the environmental racism frame took a back seat to the environmental justice frame, the movement was able to mobilize across a broader spectrum of affected people and thus became more inclusive. Moreover, inasmuch as the new framing resonated more widely, the EJM was able to mobilize additional third-party supporters and conscience constituents, people who could provide additional resources to the now bourgeoning movement.

For both the environmental racism frame and the environmental justice frame, what was most innovative, at least in comparison to other environmental movement framing activities, was not so much what was being articulated or how it was framed as who was doing the framing. Environmental justice movement collective action frames were constructed and articulated by the people most affected by environmental injustice: women and people of color (Di Chiro 1998; Szasz 1994).

Frame Diffusion: From the Grassroots to National and International Venues

In only two decades, the environmental justice movement has spread to virtually every corner of the globe.[9] Its remarkable diffusion across communities and countries, has perhaps been unprecedented in the history of social movements. The EJM's rapid and far-reaching diffusion is, as suggested above, attributable in part to its innovative master frame (Agyeman 2002; Essoka and Brulle 2002; Taylor 2000). As is frequently the case with social movement diffusion, local cultural and subcultural contexts have differentially shaped environmental justice frames in each country and community (Snow and Benford 1999). In the United States, though, the EJF's resonance and diffusion were attributable to "its ability to tap into the discourse and rhetoric of the civil rights movement" (Agyeman et al. 2003; Sandweiss 1998; Taylor 2000).

The EJM has spawned hundreds of organizations,[10] most of which operate at the community level and many of which are organized around specific cases of environmental discrimination. Among the EJM's most significant accomplishments have been the building of coalitions and the establishment of EJ networks and resource centers. Umbrella organizations such as the Environmental Justice Resource Center, the Indigenous Environmental Network, the Center for Health, Environment, and Injustice, the Center for Community Action and Environmental Justice, the African-American Environmental Justice Network, the Asian Pacific Environmental Network, the Farmworkers Network for Economic and Environmental Justice, the Northeast Environmental Justice Network, the Southern Organizing Committee for Economic and Social Justice, the Southwest Network for Environmental and Economic Justice, and the

National Black Environmental Resource Center are ample evidence of the diffusion of the EJM.

The movement has claimed several grassroots victories concerning locally unwanted land uses (LULUs). For example, according to EJM literature distributed at the Second National People of Color Environmental Leadership Summit (held in Washington in October 2002), the Sweet Calley/Cobb Environmental Task Force won a $42.8 million settlement against the Monsanto chemical company in April 2001. The community had to be relocated because of PCB contamination. While there were other apparent EJM victories at the grassroots level, local successes have been relatively rare, a shortcoming on which I will elaborate in the next section.

The EJM has generated and supported scores of research projects demonstrating patterns of environmental discrimination.[11] It has also sponsored several national and international conferences, including the previously mentioned 1991 and 2002 summits. These conferences have served as a venue where EJM activists share stories, experiences, strategies, and tactics (including framing tactics), construct wider movement networks, and seek to set national priorities and agendas.

Agenda setting and getting on the public agenda constitute important achievements of the EJM. Lester et al. (2001: 52) contend that environmental justice has been "legitimized as an issue on the policy agenda." The establishment of the US EPA's Office of Environmental Justice and the National Environmental Justice Advisory Council and President Clinton's Executive Order 12898, "Federal Actions to Address Environmental Justice in Minority Populations and Low Income Populations," have also been cited as evidence of the success of the EJM and its discourse (Agyeman et al. 2003). While national recognition of the EJM's cause by federal agencies is suggestive of the movement's legitimacy and vibrancy, it also hints at potential problems and challenges on the horizon.

Frame Stagnation: From Radicalism to Reformist Tinkering

In view of the widespread diffusion of the environmental justice master frame and the proliferation of local, national, and international environmental justice organizations, it appears that the movement and its discourse are vibrant. Yet there are a number of signs that the movement's framing strategies are yielding diminishing returns. In this section I discuss several factors contributing to the EJF's recent frame stagnation, including an overly defuse conceptualization of environmental justice, the proliferation of environmental justice causes, the subordination of environmentalism to human justice, and the movement's apparently ambivalent stance regarding the radical implications of its claims.

Perhaps the most telling evidence that the environmental justice movement's framings have stagnated comes from the movement itself. Less than ten years after the First National People of Color Environmental Leadership Summit, activists began to plan a second summit to, in their own words, "energize the environmental justice movement," "recognize the significant strides achieved to date," "share information on emerging issues," and "galvanize support."[12] This appears to imply that, at least among the activists at the Environmental Justice Fund who issued the call, there was some sense that the movement was stagnating.

The sense that the movement's framing strategies were not as effective as they first appeared to be has been based in part on apparent contractions in the movement's political opportunity structure and in part on a series of failures in enforcing federal policies forbidding environmental discrimination. By late 2000, it was clear that the newly appointed US president would not be an ally of the EJM. Soon after George W. Bush took office, changes in environmental policies became apparent. For example, by the summer of 2001 the EPA's National Environmental Justice Advisory Council had posted on its web site a notice that it would no longer permit environmental justice groups to submit site-specific issues concerning environmental injustices. This, as with a number of policy changes and appointments by the new administration, signaled a retrenchment from the Clinton years. Monique Harden's (2002) report for the National Black Environmental Justice Network provides further evidence of this retrenchment. The report concludes that the EPA has failed to enforce Title VI of the Civil Rights Act of 1964, the primary strategic focus of the EJM. According to the report, the EPA has consistently ignored complaints by African-Americans and other people of color and has recently dismissed nearly 70 percent of the complaints filed without any clear criteria for doing so. The report also asserts that, of the 129 Title VI complaints filed with the EPA, the agency has not found one case of racially disparate impact. Turner and Wu (2002) suggest that such failures of the EJM to produce significant social change predate the Bush II administration, noting that the 1991 "Principles of Environmental Justice" have not been generally adopted by government agencies.

Some analysts suggest that, while the EJM and its framings resonated among people of color, it "has yet to move beyond this community to encompass a wider political audience" (Essoka and Brulle 2002: 15). A few EJM insiders have recently lamented that the movement's framing efforts are not even working effectively within African-American communities. Damu Smith, then Interim Coordinator of the National Black Environmental and Economic Justice Coordinating Committee, for example, said he was "particularly disturbed by some prominent black business, community, and government leaders who promote the idea that environmental justice blocks economic development for black communities" (paraphrased in Chang and Hwang 2000: 6). Smith concluded that this failure is directly attributable to the EJM's framing strategies when he lamented "We're losing the spin battle, if you will." (ibid.) In view of the EJM activists' recognition that the movement's failures were due in part to frame stagnation, it was not surprising that The Second National People of Color Environmental Leadership Summit (October 2002) included workshops titled "Strategic Media Plan" and "Framing and Message Development." The "hands-on" sessions were run by the SPIN (Strategic Press Information Network) Project, a progressive media consulting organization that specializes in assisting "nonprofit public-interest organizations" with their public relations and framing strategies.

Frame Over-Extension?

As suggested previously, the EJF was broadly conceptualized. The movement's most popular slogan, "where we live, work, and play," epitomizes that breadth (Bullard 1994b; Novotny 2000; Taylor 2000; Turner and Wu 2002). But is it possible to extend a frame so broadly to the point that it loses much of its original mobilizing power? Cable and Shriver (1995: 437) allude to this problem: "Extended breadth across multiple political cleavages is, simultaneously, diluted depth of focus. Mobilization may be enhanced by the extended breadth but inhibited by the diluted focus so that the net effect is problematic." A movement whose framings cover virtually every social problem in the world risks becoming too diffuse. An examination of EJM web sites (table 1) yielded more than 50 distinctive issues the movement is currently seeking to ameliorate. As one critic put it, the environmental justice term is "all-embracing, virtually a bumper sticker attachable to all manner of procedural and policy vehicles and to all community claims for redress" (Foreman 1998: 11). Although, as any sociologist would testify, everything in the social world is linked to everything else, many of the issues represented in table 1 require some elaborate connecting of the dots in order to clarify their relationship to environmental justice. Moreover, how can a single movement keep that many balls in the air? The answer is that it cannot and does not.

It's About Social Justice

While EJM framing has become increasingly defuse in terms of the number of issues it seeks to address, its framings regarding the natural environment have remained narrow. The environmental justice movement is not an ecology movement. It never really was. As a number of scholars and activists

Table 1
Issues mentioned on EJM web sites.

Air pollution	Genocide	Police brutality/abuse
Biopiracy	Globalization	Poverty
Brownfields	Health care	Procedural justice
Consumption	Homelessness	Racial discrimination
Corporate accountability	Housing	Recycling
Corporate liability	Human genetics	Reparations
Corporate welfare	Human rights	Sovereignty
Crime	Immigrant rights	Sustainable agriculture
Cultural disempowerment	Jobs/unemployment	Sustainable development
Decision making	Land use/zoning	Tenants' rights
Deforestation	Lead poisoning	Toxics
Disability rights	Medical research	Transportation
Education	Militarism	War
Energy	Nuclear testing	Waste disposal
Environmental racism	Oil and mineral extraction	Water pollution
Facility siting	Parks and recreation	Wildlife
Food	Pesticides	Worker health and safety
Gender		

have noted, it's about social justice, procedural and distributive.[13] Dobson elaborates:

. . . the environmental justice movement seems, stubbornly, to be much more about human justice rather than about the natural environment—or rather, it is only about the natural environment in as much as it (the natural environment) can be seen in terms of human justice. (1998: 24)

As might be expected, the EJM's collective action frames reflect its ideological focus on human justice. In his comparative analysis of the relative effectiveness of various sectors of the environmental movement, Brulle concludes that

environmental justice is an exclusively anthropocentric discourse. Its concern with nature is limited to examining how ecological degradation affects the human community. . . . Environmental justice cannot provide a basis for the protection of aspects of the natural world that do not affect the well being of the human community. Hence, this discourse cannot inform a cultural practice that could protect biodiversity. (2000: 221)

Part of the problem lies in the fact that "social justice and environmental sustainability are not always compatible objectives" (Dobson 2003: 83). Indeed, as Stevis (2000: 63) points out, "questions of environmental justice could be resolved without solving an environmental problem. Ecological justice, on the other hand, must address both environmental justice and the ecological quality of our practices." Dobson (2003: 91) concurs, citing a specific example: "There is no guarantee that dividing landfill sites more fairly between rich and poor communities will result in an overall decrease in the tonnage of waste consigned to such sites."

Support for these contentions can be gleaned from the "Principles of Environmental Justice." Sixteen of the seventeen principles include a social justice component, eight of them exclusively so (that is, they make no mention of the natural environment whatsoever). Only the final principle is framed exclusively in terms of the environment, and it ironically targets individual behavior rather than corporate, governmental, or military.

Tinkering Away a Radical Cause

From its insurgent beginnings in 1982 in Warren County, North Carolina, when 414 protesters were arrested as they attempted to prevent the passage of trucks loaded with PCB-contaminated soil to a landfill located in a predominantly black community, the environmental justice movement and its framings appeared quite radical (Bullard 1994). But as the movement diffused and the issues grew more defuse, and as it became organized, bureaucratized, and institutionalized, its militant discourse and direct-action tactics gave way to more acceptable, less confrontational, more "collaborative" framings (Pellow 2000) and approaches such as the forging of "good neighbor agreements" (Lewis and Henkels 1998; Pellow 2001).[14]

Yet, even today, the EJM's diagnoses have radical implications (Agyeman et al. 2003). They indict not just individual companies, policies, and agencies; the movement's framings point to a fundamentally flawed political economy. The environmental justice frame constitutes a radical critique of entire social systems—at the local, regional, national, and global levels. As Brulle (2000: 207) so aptly puts it, "the economic system and nation-state are the core structures of society that create ecological problems." This diagnosis implies radical corrective action. "For environmental justice activists," Faber (1998: 13) asserts, "the most immediate mission is to dismantle the mechanisms by which capital and the state disproportionately displace the social and ecological costs of production onto working-class families and oppressed peoples of color."

However, like a reluctant swimmer who sticks her toe in the water only to retreat, the EJM's prognoses almost always fall short of calling for revolutionary social change. Only two of the "Principles of Environmental Justice"—numbers 14 ("Environmental justice opposes the destructive operations of multinational corporations") and 15 ("Environmental justice opposes military occupation, repression and exploitation of lands, people, and cultures, and other life forms")—are radical, and even these stop short of suggesting systemic change, instead implying the need for reforms. Faber concurs, positing that the EJM is limited by its reformist approach in that it fails

to transform the manner in which corporate money and power now dominate the electoral policy-making processes. . . . This is evident in a movement discourse that defines environmental justice in terms of eliminating the *discriminating* or *unequal distribution* of ecological hazards rather than eliminating the root causes of the hazards for all Americans. . . . The struggle for environmental justice must be about the politics of capitalist production per se and the elimination of the ecological threat, not just the "fair" distribution of ecological hazards via better government regulation of inequities in the marketplace. (1998: 14)

Rather than following the logic of its diagnostic framing by advocating sweeping systemic changes, the movement's prognoses remain focused on tinkering with a system constructed from slave labor and predicated on the exploitation of disadvantaged people, whether they reside in the heart of cancer alley in Norco, Louisiana, next to the uranium mines of the Black Hills in the Lakota Territory, by the poisoned Carigara Bay in the central Philippines, or in your community.

It's true that the environmental justice movement seeks equity for exploited people, especially people of color, who have shouldered a disproportionate share of the environmental costs and risks. As innovative and resonant as that strategy has been, by seeking justice, the EJM subscribes to and reproduces the commodification of justice. It does so, in part, by using the tort system to seek redress for past environmental injustices. The outcomes implied by the focus on distributive justice are essentially economic in nature. The EJM seeks to obtain for its constituents environmental benefits equal to those received by others while limiting the costs to their equitable share. Like whites, who have purchased justice for centuries, people of color are seeking to purchase an equal share of that justice.

The Master's House

On the one hand, the problems diagnosed and attributions proffered by the environmental justice movement represent a radical critique of entire social systems at the local, regional, national, and global levels. On the other hand, by framing solutions primarily in terms of "justice" the EJM places its faith in the efficacy of using extant legislative and judicial systems to remedy problems—an ironic commitment to, and reaffirmation of, the systemic status quo. Audre Lorde, a famous black feminist, eloquently outlined the pitfalls of seeking to transform such a corrupt system from within: *"For the master's tools will never dismantle the master's house.* They may allow us temporarily to beat him at his own game, but they will never enable us to bring about genuine change." (1984: 112)

By framing the issues primarily in terms of injustice, and in seeking justice through legislative, judicial, and regulatory systems, the status quo will continue to be reproduced . Lorde's argument is radical, even revolutionary. Yet it fits well with current critical legal theory (Kairys 1998), critical race theory (Delgado and Stefancic 2000), feminist jurisprudence theory

(Smart 1989), and radical criminological theory (Chambliss 1974; Quinney 1974).[15] Those who seek justice within the extant system presume that the law is a neutral arbiter of disputes between adversarial parties; this includes both legislative actions (making laws) and court actions (case law). However, building on Marxist theory, these theorists claim that the law is a site of struggle, which is designed to benefit the elite. Therefore, to seek justice within this system is to tacitly accept the status quo.

The environmental justice movement's power lies in its capacity to disrupt the system rather than to seek to reform it. As Piven and Cloward's (1979) study of poor people's movements reveals, one advantage poor people have over their oppressors is their capacity for mass insurgency. Once a movement accepts a place at the master's table, it is doomed to manipulation, cooptation, and perpetual frustration.

Acknowledgments

An earlier version of this chapter was presented in August 2002 at the annual meeting of the American Sociological Association in Chicago. I am indebted to Bob Brulle, David Pellow, and Michelle Hughes Miller for their suggestions and constructive comments.

Notes

1. This section borrows liberally from Benford and Snow 2000: 613–622.

2. For recent reviews of the literature on social movement framing, see Benford and Snow 2000 and Snow 2004. For critiques of the framing perspective, see Benford 1997; Fisher 1997; Hart 1996; Jasper 1997; Oliver and Johnston 2000; Sherkat 1998; Steinberg 1998.

3. For frame analyses of the EJM, see Cable, Hastings, and Mix 2002; Cable and Shriver 1995; Capek 1993; DeLuca 1999; Edwards 1995; Essoka and Brulle 2002; Kubal 1998; Novotny 2000; Pellow 1999; Sandweiss 1998; Taylor 2000. For related analyses of EJM discourse, narratives, language, and/or talk, see Brulle 2000; Checker 2002; Dobson 2003; Gottlieb 2001; Muir and Veenendall 1996.

4. For analyses of the EJM's origins in the civil rights movement, see Bullard and Wright 1992; Cole and Foster 2001; Di Chiro 1998; Essoka and Brulle 2002; Faber and McCarthy 2003; Gottlieb 1993.

5. For various social movement origins of the EJM, see Cole and Foster 2001; Di Chiro 1998; Dowie 1995; Faber and McCarthy 2003; Lester; Allen, and Hill 2001; Pulido 1996; Szasz 1994.

6. For observations regarding the innovativeness of the environmental justice frame, see Cable and Shriver 1995; Edwards 1995; Essoka and Brulle 2002; Novotny 2000.

7. For analyses and commentaries regarding the EJM's frame changes, see Cable et al. 2002; Cable and Shriver 1995; Edwards 1995; Novotny 2000; Taylor 2000.

8. See, for example, Bullard and Wright 1992; Cole and Luke 2001; Edwards 1995; Taylor 2000.

9. For global and international treatments of the EJM, see Agyeman, Bullard, and Evans 2003; Agyeman 2002; Shiva 1999; Westra and Wenz 1995; Taylor 1995.

10. To my knowledge, a complete census of EJ organizations has not been undertaken. The movement's own estimates vary widely, even when issued by the same source. For example, in one place on the Environmental Justice Resource Center's web site (www.ejrc.cau.edu) it is claimed that the 2000 People of Color Environmental Groups Directory lists over 1,000 groups. Elsewhere on the same site it is reported that the directory lists approximately 400 groups.

11. Since my focus in this chapter was on environmental justice framing, I did not undertake a comprehensive review of the empirical research on environmental injustice. For starters, I recommend the following: Agyeman, Bullard, and Evans 2003; Bullard 1994a; Lester, Allen, and Hill 2001; Robert and Toffolon-Weis 2001.

12. Source: www.ejfund.org.

13. See, for example, Dobson 1998, 2003; Faber 1998; Low and Gleeson 1998; Stevis 2000; Wenz 1988.

14. Good neighbor agreements are arrangements between stakeholders, in this context environmental justice organizations and corporations that provide a "vehicle for a community organization and a corporation to recognize and formalize their roles within a locality and to foster sustainable development" (Lewis and Henkels 1998; Pellow 2001). An alternative to viewing good neighbor agreements as instrumental achievements of the EJM would be to see them as little more than cheap public relations gambits by corporations that may yield a co-opted and quiescent movement.

15. I am grateful to Michelle Hughes Miller for alerting me to Lorde's provocative essays and poetry and for calling my attention to critical legal, critical race, feminist jurisprudence, and radical criminological theories.

4

Mission Impossible? Environmental Justice Activists' Collaborations with Professional Environmentalists and with Academics

Sherry Cable, Tamara Mix, and Donald Hastings

The contemporary environmental movement consists of three component movements that share the goal of shaping the relationship between society and the environment. The professional environmental movement is descended from the conservation organizations established in the late nineteenth century (Andrews 1999) and includes organizations such as the Sierra Club and the National Audubon Society. The anti-toxics movement emerged in the late 1970s as residents across the United States recognized, after Love Canal, that their communities were also contaminated by modern production processes. The environmental justice movement (EJM) began with a 1982 siting controversy in Warren County, North Carolina (Brulle 1996; Bullard 1990; Cable and Shriver 1995; Lee 1992).

The Warren County grievance was adopted in other communities, and EJM protests have broadened to oppose the burden of the costs of modern production processes that political decision makers disproportionately allocate to both minority and working-class communities. In two decades, the EJM has spread throughout the United States as an enduring component of the larger environmental movement. Activists seeking environmental justice from New York to California have scored significant local victories by resisting proposed sitings of potentially harmful facilities and by ameliorating problems associated with existing facilities. Many academics have given credence to activists' complaints by empirically documenting the unequal distribution of exposure to various environmental risks. Professional environmentalists have joined local activists in public pleas for environmental justice that have won bystanders to their view. EJM activities receive considerable media coverage, locally and nationally. The movement is supported by prominent political advocates.

What is the outcome of the EJM after two decades of local victories, widespread media coverage, academic and political elites' support, and sympathetic changes in public opinion? That is, what major structural changes occurred to facilitate a more equitable distribution of the environmental costs of production?

None. No risky facilities are routinely constructed in white, affluent communities. No federal system of corporate compensation pays citizens for the privilege of contaminating their communities. No national policy discussion has emerged to plan the redistribution of the environmental costs and benefits of production. Instead, the organization of production remains entrenched in social institutions whose bureaucratic routines frequently produce racist outcomes, whether intentionally or unintentionally (Feagin and Feagin 1986; Cable and Mix 2003); political processes continue to favor corporate state goals of capital accumulation at the expense of both equality and the environment (Faber 1998); and the courts, those supposedly neutral arbiters of citizen disputes, persist in eliding the complex problem of institutional racism and classism (Cole and Foster 2001).

Why has the EJM failed to generate such structural changes? In this chapter, we adopt a social movements perspective to examine the EJM and offer some recommendations that might increase the likelihood of structural change. We draw on the social movement literature to identify significant movement characteristics that we then employ to distinguish the EJM from the professional environmental movement and the anti-toxics movement. We assess EJM strategies to reveal their relative strengths and weaknesses. We then present the results of our empirical analysis of EJM collaborations with professional environmentalists and with academic researchers. Based on our analysis, we discuss the potential posed by a different type of collaboration with academic researchers for improving the chances of achieving structural change and a more equitable distribution of exposure to environmental risks.

Assessment of EJM Characteristics and Tactics

The three predominant perspectives used by current social movement analysts are resource mobilization, political process, and New Social Movements. Resource mobilization approaches emphasize variables influencing movement emergence (Cable 1984; Cable, Walsh, and Warland 1988; Ferree and Miller 1985; Haines 1984; Halcli 1999; Hirsch 1990; Jasper 1999; Johnson 1999; McCarthy and Zald 1973, 1977; Meyer 1999; Piven and Cloward 1979; Staggenborg 1988; Walsh and Warland 1983). Political process perspectives examine the broad economic, demographic, or political processes that enhance or inhibit the political leverage of the aggrieved (McAdam 1982; McAdam and Paulsen 1993; Morris 1981; Tarrow 1994; Tilly 1978). New Social Movement theories focus on the micromobilization processes related to human agency (Green 1999; Klandermans 1984; Snow et al. 1986; Snow and Benford 1988, 1992; Tarrow 1993; Taylor and Raeburn 1995; Taylor and Whittier 1992).

Contemporary movement scholars aim to increase knowledge of the processes of movement emergence and maintenance, and most studies employ the social movement organization as the unit of analysis. Scholars do not tend to publish pragmatic evaluations of movements that are offered as recommendations to activists for improving their chances of success. In fact, movement analysts seldom address success as a dependent variable and demonstrate little consensus on a conceptual definition of success (see Toffolon-Weiss and Roberts in this volume).

But the literature offers clues for a pragmatic evaluation of movements. The analytical perspectives overlap in treating six significant movement characteristics: grievances, target, goal, constituency, tactics, and funding. "Grievances" refers to activists' perceptions of injustice that motivate them to participate in movements. The "target" is the entity to which activists attribute responsibility for the injustice. The movement's "goal" is its primary, stated intention for social change. The "constituency" consists of the segment of the population that supports the movement goal and stands to benefit from goal achievement, whether or not the individual engages in protest behavior. "Tactics" means the particular protest actions taken by activists to achieve their goal. "Funding" refers to the financial basis for the movement. We use these movement characteristics to distinguish among the professional environmental movement, the anti-toxics movement, and the EJM. We then assess the EJM's primary tactics of litigation and political pressure to identify the most promising one, based on the movement's characteristics.

Distinctions among the Environmental Movements

The Professional Environmental Movement

We designate as professional environmentalists those activists associated with national environmental organizations concerned primarily with conservation issues. The environmental movement that emerged in the mid 1960s combined issues of conservation and environmental quality to produce a youth-centered movement. But as general public concern for the environment increased in the 1970s (Dunlap and Scarce 1991), the movement was mainstreamed and professionalized through the original conservation groups and through new organizations such as the Environmental Defense Fund and the Natural Resources Defense Council (Brulle 1996; Cable and Cable 1995). Ten professional environmental organizations predominate, most with headquarters in Washington and many with semi-autonomous state chapters. (The ten dominant national environmental organizations are the Sierra Club, the National Audubon Society, the Izaak Walton League, the Wilderness Society, the National Wildlife Federation, Defenders of Wildlife, Environmental Defense, Friends of the Earth, the Natural Resources Defense Council, and the Environmental Policy Institute.) The paid employees of these hierarchically structured organizations tend to be white upper-class and middle-class males.

The grievances of the professional environmentalists involve the formulation and enforcement of policies governing the conservation of lands, wildlife, and water resources and the regulation of air and water quality (Andrews 1999; Cable and Cable 1995; Cable and Shriver 1995; Mitchell, Mertig, and Dunlap 1992). The professional environmental movement recently added to its agendum some international environmental issues: ozone depletion, global warming, and ocean dumping. Although several professional organizations advocate environmental justice in their mission statements posted on websites, their selection of issues for campaigns emphasizes conservation.

Professional environmentalists target policy makers and the general public to reach their goals of environmental policy reform and enforcement. The movement's constituency consists of several million members across the United States—overwhelmingly white, highly educated, upper- and middle-class people who contribute membership dues and special donations for specific issue campaigns. Professional environmentalists engage in the tactics of legislative lobbying, environmental research and education programs, electoral actions, land purchases, and occasional litigation. Most of the organizations have multimillion-dollar operating budgets, funded by a combination of membership dues, corporate donations, and grants from nonprofit foundations. Faber and McCarthy (2001) found, for example, that the National Wildlife Federation had a total 1998 income of more than $82 million. The professional environmental movement is strikingly different from the anti-toxics and EJ movements.

The Anti-Toxics Movement

Following Cole and Cole (2001), we designate as anti-toxics activists those residents of contaminated communities who organize local protest movements to oppose threats to public health posed by environmental risks. The anti-toxics movement was forged after the 1978 revelations of contamination at Love Canal, the 1979 partial meltdown of a nuclear reactor at the Three Mile Island nuclear power plant, and continuing discoveries of contaminated communities throughout the United States (Cable and Cable 1995; Cable and Shriver 1995). The movement consists of hundreds of environmental citizen organizations most of whose members are middle-class or working-class whites.

The grievances of anti-toxics activists involve "a new species of trouble" (Erikson 1991) that derives from post-World War II production technologies using synthetic substances that, improperly treated, enter communities and pose potential health risks (Brown 1979; Cable and Shriver 1995; Commoner 1992; Freudenberg and Steinsapir 1992; Schnaiberg 1980; Schnaiberg and Gould 1994). Anti-toxics activists typically target a local corporation and/or government officials at local, state, and national levels. They express far greater mistrust of government and the corporate class than do professional environmentalists (Cable and Cable 1995; Brown and Mikkelsen 1990; Krauss 1989). Corporate failure to design safe production and waste-disposal processes and federal regulatory agencies' failure to protect the public generated many citizens' beliefs that they are victims of a corporate state structure that denies their claims to the right to voice their preferences in decisions that affect the public (Cable and Benson 1993; Cable, Hastings, and Mix 2002; Cable and Shriver 1995; Krauss 1989).

The goals of the anti-toxics movement are to ameliorate contamination and to reduce the threat of adverse health effects. The movement's constituency consists of lower-middle-class and working-class residents of contaminated communities. Their tactics include petitioning, letter writing, public meetings and rallies, participation in electoral campaigns, and occasional litigation and administrative regulatory appeal. The organizations tend to be staffed by volunteers and led by women. Funding comes primarily from the dues of local members and from fund-raising events such as bake sales, raffles, and auctions.

The EJM bears some similarities to the anti-toxics movement but carries significant differences in grievances, goals, and constituency that influence the movement's other characteristics.

The EJM

We consider EJM activists as citizens associated with community-based organizations formed to oppose the disproportionate exposure to environmental risks endured by the working class, the impoverished, and people of color. In the years since the 1982 Warren County struggle, hundreds of similar EJM organizations have formed an organizational analogue to the anti-toxics movement with somewhat different grievances, goals, and constituency.

EJM activists' grievances focus on the disproportionate distribution of environmental risks of all types in workplaces, communities, transportation systems, and recreational facilities. The EJ movement's goal is a more equitable distribution of environmental threats and environmental privileges. The direct targets of EJM protests are corporations and local, state, and federal officials whom residents deem accountable for their influence in racist siting and enforcement decisions. Their indirect target is the corporate state structure that supports the externalization of the environmental costs of production, disproportionately allocates environmental risks to people of color and the poor, and creates racial and class inequalities in communities (Bullard 1990, 1993, 1994; Bullard and Wright 1989; Brown and Mikkelsen 1990; Cole and Foster 2001; Krauss 1989; Lavelle and Coyle 1993; Schnaiberg and Gould 1994).

EJM activists attempt to mobilize large numbers of people to support their efforts to pressure corporate and government officials, legislators, and courts to redistribute environmental risks and benefits. They favor tactics such as demonstrations, petitions, lobbying local elected officials, letter writing, public meetings, citizen-conducted health surveys, educational forums, and occasional litigation. The EJM's constituency is the working-class, impoverished, and minority residents of contaminated communities and communities sited for potentially contaminating facilities.

Most EJM organizations operate on shoestring budgets with highly unpredictable levels of funding. The community-based groups typically charge a small membership fee, but waive it on request. Funding is provided by dues, individual donations, fund raising activities (e.g., bake sales and raffles), and occasional small grants from nonprofit foundations. Research by Faber and McCarthy (2001) documents that organizations in the professional environmental movement obtain significantly more foundation money than do those of the EJM.

The relative poverty of the EJM constituency and its complex goal of environmental equity influence the tactics used by activists and the efficacy with which the tactics are deployed.

Assessment of EJM Tactics: Litigation and Political Pressure

All three components of the contemporary environmental movement—professional environmentalists, anti-toxics activists, and the EJM—employ the tactics of litigation and political pressure in various guises. But the tactics extract greater costs from EJM organizations than from the other components.

Litigation is a disadvantageous strategy for EJM organizations because it requires large amounts of money from people who do not have it, because it is often unsuccessful, because it weakens organizational solidarity, and because even successful litigation does not bring significant rewards.

The primary resource needed for litigation as a tactic is money. Large amounts of money are needed, even if a public-interest lawyer accepts a case with the agreement of taking a proportion of any settlement for payment. Money is needed, for example, for filing documents with a court, for paying court fees, for compensating experts for their time and testimony, and for photocopying evidentiary documents. In the interest of reducing expenses, research for a case is often performed by the activists themselves. Individuals with little or no previous experience undertake such tasks as retrieving and photocopying official documents on land, air, and water resources, collecting ecological samples, researching the potential effects of the environmental risk to public health, and conducting epidemiology studies in search of illness clusters.

Organizational solidarity is often weakened by a litigation strategy because members become less involved in decision making and must draw on increasingly shallow pockets. When attorneys make the decisions, protests and demonstrations typically cease. The major task left to activists is endless fund raising in a community with limited household incomes. As a consequence, the psychological motivation for protest dissipates.

Although litigation by EJM organizations is sometimes successful, success is significantly diluted when the terms of settlements are sealed, as they typically are. As a result, knowledge that might be useful for local movement recruitment, for mobilization in other communities, and for environmental policy formulation is essentially lost.

The most devastating disadvantage of litigation strategies for EJM organizations is that many cases are lost (see Gordon and Harley and Bryant and Hockman in this volume). The losses are due primarily to partisan judges and to difficulties in presenting adequate cases within the constraints imposed by juridical procedures. Three recent reports revealed that anti-environmental rulings are the result of the systematic compromise of the independence and impartiality of the judiciary (Buccino et al. 2001; Georgetown University Law Center 2000; Kendall et al. 2000). The reports document that judges appointed to the federal bench in the past 20 years have radically reinterpreted the US Constitution and Congressional legislation in a conservative, pro-corporate direction that has gutted environmental laws and regulations and weakened citizen safeguards.

Difficulties in presenting adequate cases within the constraints imposed by juridical procedures are presented primarily by two court standards. One standard contradicts the essence of environmental justice claims. EJM activists claim that the burden of environmental risk is disproportionately allocated to working class, poor, and minority communities, yet no statute outlaws discrimination on the basis of class or income. Although laws exist that bar race-based discrimination, such as Title VI of the 1964 Civil Rights Amendment, efforts to employ them in environmental justice cases require new conceptual definitions of natural and cultural resources (Cole 2002).

Another barrier is the contradiction between the court's standards for causality and those of scientists. The judiciary's assumption of "no harm until proven" rests on the legal definition of mechanistic cause: the cause always precedes the effect; the effect does not occur in the absence of the cause, and no other cause explains the effect. In contrast, scientists use a probabilistic inferential model of causality based on multiple causation. The different criteria of causal proof tilt the balance of justice against EJM activists. Consequently, it is inefficient for EJM activists to spend their meager financial resources on litigation (Cable et al. 2002).

How do EJM activists fare with political pressure as a tactic? Political pressure also poses problems for the EJM, but problems that may more easily be remedied than those accompanying litigation tactics.

The primary resources needed for political pressure as a strategy are organizational skills, knowledge of political institutions and routines, and large numbers of voters. Organizational skills for developing adequate structures for decision making and for the resolution of internal conflicts are required to maintain a community-based organization long enough to achieve its goals. Knowledge of political institutions and routines is necessary for understanding the workings of bureaucracies, especially their strengths and vulnerabilities. Large numbers of voters are required, to pressure politicians to the point that they fear being turned out of office if they do not accede in some way to movement demands.

The crucial problem with the EJM's use of political pressure as a strategy is that EJM communities are characteristically deficient in social capital. That is, the resources required for successful political pressure are typically quite scarce in the very communities that suffer disproportionate exposure to environmental risks: working-class, impoverished, and minority communities. Residents of such communities typically have less money, fewer organizational and political skills, and less discretionary time than their more affluent counterparts. Relative to others, they must devote more time, energy, and money to meeting basic survival needs. For many community-based EJM organizations, the available pool of constituents is limited.

How might this deprived population gain greater access to the skills, knowledge, and numbers of people necessary to apply successful political pressure? One such avenue is collaboration with like-minded groups that do have such resources: professional environmentalists and academics.

Collaborations with Professional Environmentalists and with Academics
The second author collected the data for our analysis in three phases, employing archival documents, focus groups, face-to-face interviews, and telephone interviews.

In the first phase, we gained access to archival materials on the "Group of 10" professional environmental organizations via the organizations' web sites to obtain general information on membership, mission, budgets, staff size, and boards of directors and to ascertain their stated positions on environmental justice.

The second phase involved one focus group session with seven participants and ten face-to-face interviews with EJM activists in predominantly African-American organizations in the southeastern United States. The organizations were selected from the 2000 edition of *People of Color Environmental Groups*, compiled and published by the Environmental Justice Resource Center at Clark Atlanta University. This phase served as a pilot study to gain information for the construction of a meaningful interview guide for the third phase.

In the third phase, the second author conducted 20–45-minute telephone interviews with 35 representatives of EJM organizations from across the continental United States. Six of the organizations had Native American constituencies, three had primarily white constituencies, and the majority had African-American or multiracial constituencies, including Latino and immigrant populations. Most of the organizations were located in urban areas.

Collaborations with Professional Environmentalists
More than 100 EJM leaders signed a 1990 letter to the leaders of the "Group of Ten," the most prominent organizations of professional environmentalists. The EJM leaders' letter accused professional environmentalists of racism in their hiring and policy-development processes (Cole and Foster 2001; Shabecoff 1990), claiming that the organizations were "isolated from the poor and minority communities that [the professional environmentalists] said are the chief victims of pollution" (Shabecoff 1990). Thus, collaborations between EJM activists and professional environmentalists are somewhat rare. When such collaborations occurred, the interaction consisted primarily of professional environmentalists' offering technical advice and their limited assistance with EJM direct actions. EJM activists reported mixed experiences in such collaborations. Some reported neutral experi-

ences, and some reported positive experiences, but the majority described their collaborative experiences as negative.

Neutral Collaborations

Some EJM activists reported having only limited interactions with professional environmentalists, which they characterized as neither positive nor negative. Typical of those who described neutral experiences was an activist with a Detroit organization involved in environmental and economic development: "They have helped on some local issues, but our local issues have not been a real focus for any of their activities. We sort of run into their staff at some of the same meetings and hearings, but we don't have a close working relationship."

EJM activists attributed their relative neutrality toward professionals to each group's unfamiliarity with the other. An activist with a community-development organization in Hartford reported: "A lot of work needs to be done to deal with the barrier that exists between our communities. Not necessarily the barriers of class, but just the plain and simple fact that we are strangers."

EJM activists tend to perceive the upper- and middle-class constituencies of professional environmental organizations as far removed from the realities of working-class and lower-class life. Consequently, interaction tends to be infrequent and superficial.

Positive Collaborations

Several EJM activists described positive collaborations with professional environmentalists, citing local Sierra Club chapters in particular. An activist in a working-class Bronx organization opposed to the construction of a medical waste incinerator described the efforts of a Sierra Club chapter to include the local community: "Sierra Club has been one of the groups we have the best relationship with—the local Sierra Club. We have asked to have more representation of people of color, more grassroots people on their board. Matter of fact, they assisted us in many of the demonstrations that we have done."

A Chicago activist also described positive experiences with professional organizations: "The Sierra Club and Lois Gibbs and her organization [the Center for Health, Environment and Justice] were very helpful. Gibbs' organization helped us a lot in terms of grassroots organizing, technical information on ... burning tires and that kind of stuff. The rest of the organizations have different goals. There are very few organizations on a national scope that support local grassroots like this."

Why are some collaborations successful? An Indiana organizer involved in some environmental justice work with a staff of well-educated, middle-class individuals suggested that having a shared background is an important factor in collaborations: "We had common goals, but I'm not sure that is a telling thing. The thing is, we had common backgrounds. I came, actually, from law school and started working here, so I think that had a lot to do with it ... we had similar backgrounds [with] the people who work for Sierra Club and Environmental Defense and that could be helpful."

Collaborations with the Sierra Club and with the Center for Health, Environment and Justice (CHEJ) were likely more successful because each organization differs from the majority of the national professional environmental organizations. The Sierra Club has a participatory structure and is organizationally marked by its federated and fairly autonomous club chapters. Regional chapters are more responsive to local needs than are professional organizations. The CHEJ is a clearing house for connecting local groups and providing technical and organizing information.

Negative Collaborations
Some activists described negative experiences in attempting to forge collaborations with professional environmental organizations. They reported contacting professional environmental organizations and receiving no response. An EJM activist from Columbus, Ohio whose organization formed in response to a chemical spill said "We contacted all those people, but they weren't interested in our community." An activist working on the cleanup of hazardous waste sites in South Tifton, Georgia suggested that professional environmentalists have neither the time for collaboration nor the interest in environmental justice issues: "I don't think they care. That's my earnest opinion. I don't think they care as much, since they are so big and everybody knows them. They have these large organizations. They don't have to get out there and struggle like we do. The larger groups, they don't seem to have time for it. They come in maybe when a lot of publicity was going on and say "We [were] here, we did that." To get their name in the news. No technical or any kind of help."

The majority of the EJM activists who were able to form collaborative relationships with professional environmentalists reported negative experiences. An EJM activist who had previously worked well with a local Sierra Club chapter expressed indignation at his treatment by other professional environmentalists:

The reason why, is that they are condescending a lot of times. Environmental justice is supposed to put a component of equity on the table. We are not just a showpiece. What we have to share is very good knowledge, learned firsthand. We understand what our lives are about. We understand how to articulate that also. But they want you to sit there—like that old cliché about children, to be seen and not heard. We don't want to come and be patted on the head and them say "We know what your problem is, we'll fix it for you." We don't need condescending people. We don't need more racism being poured on us.

A Chattanooga activist felt that professional environmentalists dismissed her ideas and wanted to control the interaction:

I find in dealing with them that they want to dictate. They want to tell you what your problems are, as if they lived there. They can't tell me what my problems are, because they don't know them personally. It is a matter of them either wanting to hear the story or wanting to re-write the story. That's how I see it. I'm the expert in my community. Just like if I go to your community, you're the expert. Treat me with that minimal respect.

Collaborative efforts between EJM activists and professional environmentalists are hindered by their differences in grievances, target, goal, constituency, tasks, and funding. A California activist working on tribal issues derogated the professional organizations for their tameness:

The large grassroots organizations—I shouldn't even call them that anymore—the large environmental corporations are interested in public relations work. [They are] run by . . . it is all attorneys now. They are interested in legislation more than anything else. So their whole focus is on lobbying.

Thus, according to EJM activists' reports of their experiences, the rare collaborations with professional environmentalists were most often unsatisfactory and frequently insulting.

Our interviews with EJM activists revealed that they also cooperate with academics in pursuit of movement goals. Academics pose another collaborator for potentially contributing the necessary resources for using political pressure to instigate structural changes that would facilitate a more equitable distribution of the environmental costs of production. How do EJM activists view their collaborations with academics?

Collaborations with Academics

EJM activists' collaborations with academics involved four types: students' cooperation with EJM groups, university-conducted health studies in environmental justice communities, universities' provision of technical expertise to EJM activists, and traditional research efforts.

Student Cooperation

A small number of EJM activists reported satisfaction in working with college students. Some universities offer programs that bring together community organizations and students who volunteer their time or earn college credit for their participation. Such programs are supported, for example, at St. Lawrence University, the College of William and Mary, Clark Atlanta University, the Tulane University Law Clinic, and the University of Tennessee at Knoxville. An EJM activist in Detroit described the organization's volunteer base of students as follows: "We get people from universities. A lot of times they do it as community service, and a lot of times they come as a class with their instructor for one or two weeks."

An EJM activist in the Southeast reported some of the activities in which they engaged with students from a local historically African-American college: "We are associated with students at Morehouse College and they do our newsletter—they do the printing. They come to most of our weekly, neighborhood meetings. The college donated a computer to one of the community leaders."

Collaborations between EJ groups and college students are rare, most likely owing to the absence of strong connections between universities and non-affluent communities. Such collaborations are likely to decrease even further in the future, as the corporate model of higher education is more widely adopted, liability concerns are more emphasized, and the service mission of universities is further abandoned.

University-Conducted Health Studies

Because of the high rate of health problems in contaminated communities, a few academic institutions have conducted health studies in affected neighborhoods. EJM groups have partnered with academics to identify illness clusters in communities such as New York State's Love Canal neighborhood (Levine 1982), Woburn, Massachusetts (Brown and Mikkelsen 1990), New York City, and Boston (see Brown et al., this volume).

An activist happily discussed the success of his environmental justice group in forming an alliance with a university: "Working with Chicago State University, we established what we call the Urban Environmental Health group, which is headed by myself and the Assistant Dean of Health and Science at the University."

Another activist organizing in the Southeast described the boon of such university involvement: "Through the University of Cincinnati and the National Institute of Environmental Health [Sciences]—we did get funding to do an environmental study of the neighborhood. We've done all of the legwork. Now we are in the process of waiting for the results."

But the majority of EJM activists expressed dismay at the inherent disparities in the relationship between a university and the communities that they study. A Georgia activist whose group attempted to conduct a local health study described the failed attempt: "We didn't complete the health study that was started by [a southern university] because we didn't have no more funds and it takes money to do things. We had a grant with [the university], a combined grant, but they got the money and we got peanuts. I wouldn't say that they didn't give us any. We got $10,000 from the grant [but] they got over $200,000!"

Universities' Provision of Technical Expertise
Academic institutions and researchers occasionally provide technical expertise to EJM organizations. Several activists mentioned Clark Atlanta University Professor Robert Bullard's technical assistance and support for EJM groups. A Connecticut activist described his organization's positive relationship with Bullard:

Dr. Bullard gave us his card, came to town, took on our issue, and made us the subject of his speech that he gave before a gathering of nearly all whites. Charles Lee, one of the founders of the environmental justice movement, made himself available by phone and contributed a lot in helping us understand the options we had available to us—the process and all of that stuff.

But, once again, most activists were dissatisfied with the unequal relationship between themselves and academic institutions:

They'll give these universities—they're really supposed to be historically black colleges and universities, but they are not—the opportunity and the big money to do nothing. But they won't give the communities money to do the real investigation! That's why I have a problem. They've all been here for grant money—[one university in particular]—they're awarded the money and they come looking for us.

But they're working it backwards. They get paid and they don't want to do nothing for us—or leave anything back here for us. They want to take everything and get all the credit. Many people have sold many books off of our miseries and off of our suffering. And we don't get anything.

Traditional Research Efforts

None of our respondents reported interactions with traditional researchers conducting studies in contaminated communities, even though the academic literature is replete with researchers' analyses of environmental injustices in working-class, impoverished, and minority communities (Bailey and Faupel 1992; Brown and Mikkelsen 1990; Bryant and Mohai 1992; Been 1993, 1995; Brulle 1996; Bullard 1983, 1990; Burke 1993; Cable and Degutis 1991; Cole and Foster 2001; Downey 1998; Foster 1998; Hird 1993; Krauss 1989; Szasz and Meuser 2000; Stretesky and Hogan 1998; White 1992; Zimmerman 1993).

Although some of these studies use secondary data analysis, many involve methodologies that likely brought researchers into direct contact with EJM activists. Several EJM activists reached by the second author declined to participate in this study because of their past experiences with traditional researchers. Their typical responses were such remarks as "No! We've been screwed by researchers before!" and "Researchers have messed us over—how do I know you'll come through with your promises?"

Our own experiences in fieldwork plus anecdotal data from informal discussions with other researchers suggest that activists gain little but aggravation from collaborations with traditional researchers. Most researchers prefer to avoid being parasites feeding on a contaminated community and attempt to bring some benefits to the groups they study. But the benefits tend to be limited primarily to the circulation among activists of interview transcripts, early drafts of papers, and the occasional advice on organizing and tactics.

When a novice in the field, the first author once requested permission to study an EJM whose members were deeply dissatisfied with their treatment by previous traditional researchers. She explained to the wary activists her plans for data collection and analysis and for publishing her results. They asked "What do we stand to gain from this study?" Stumped, she finally replied "Nothing at all." After 30 seconds of silence, a group leader successfully urged his counterparts to vote to allow the study because "at least she didn't lie to us—she didn't promise us a goddamn thing!"

Despite the potential of collaboration with academics, EJM activists report the general failure of such connections. Of the four types of interaction, they described that with students as the most satisfactory and expressed appreciation for students' deference to their knowledge and experiences. University-conducted health studies, universities' provision of technical expertise, and traditional research efforts most often impressed EJM activists with the stark inequalities that the interactions revealed and with the academics' reluctance to take any significant actions. A Chicago activist snorted: "I was asked to serve on a panel on environmental justice at a university here in town. But those people have conferences and they just sit around and talk about it! And that's it, baby—you don't get any more help!"

Summary of Collaborative Efforts

We have argued that, despite two decades of activity, the EJM has not generated the major structural changes needed to redistribute more equitably the environmental costs of production. We evaluated the primary EJM tactics of litigation and political pressure and found that political pressure is more successful and more efficient in resource use because of the serious constraints of litigation. The social capital needed for political pressure includes organizational skills for developing adequate decision making and internal conflict resolution structures that facilitate the group's endurance; a substantial knowledge of political institutions for understanding bureaucratic routines, strengths, and vulnerabilities; and large numbers of voters to pressure politicians enough that they accede in some way to movement demands.

We asserted that, since EJ communities typically lack the necessary social capital for successful political pressure, EJM collaborations with professional environmentalists and with academics offered an opportunity for increased access to the necessary resources. Consequently, we obtained EJM activists' reports on their collaborations. But we discovered that activists were generally dissatisfied with them.

EJM collaborations with both professional environmentalists and with academics were most often perceived as negative by activists. Such collaborations fail, according to activists because of race/class divides that lead to ignorance of EJM activists' life experiences and condescending and patronizing attitudes toward them. The common denominator of activists' dissatisfaction with collaborative efforts was the feeling that their voices were not heard and their concerns not seriously addressed. Consequently, EJM collaborative efforts with professional environmentalists and academics have been unsuccessful in expanding the movement's social capital to amplify political pressure for the significant structural changes necessary to facilitate a more equitable distribution of the environmental costs of production.

How, then, can the EJM obtain the necessary social capital for structural change? Professional environmentalists have their own agenda, but what about academics? Are any academics suited by nature and by training to hear the voices that are not commonly heard and to allow the definitions of this silenced population to guide collaborative actions between activists and academics? Theoretically, yes—academics using participatory research methods could provide adequate collaborative partners with the EJM.

Political Pressure via Participatory Research Methods

Collaborations with researchers have been marred by researchers' orientation to EJM activists as objects of study, as relatively passive vessels for receiving the wisdom offered by academics. We recommend that such collaborations may be significantly improved through researchers' use of participatory research methods. In the following sections, we present the rationale for our recommendation by describing participatory methods. We discuss the advantages of participatory methods over traditional research and suggest how such collaborations might enhance resource availability for the EJM.

Participatory Research Methods

Participatory research developed as a response to criticisms that traditional research is inherently conservative and most serves the interests of entrenched economic and political elites, while informants/subjects are relegated to a simple role as the researcher's unit of analysis (Gaventa 1993).

Participatory research is offered as an alternative methodology with an epistemology different from the neo-positivist assumptions underlying experiments, surveys, participant observation, and applied research. Participatory research focuses on local problems and views community residents as knowledgeable change agents. Residents define the nature of the research problem, applying their own knowledge to locate the problem within the context of their daily experiences (Gibbs 1982; DiPerna 1985; Collette 1987; Brown and Mikkelsen 1990). Participatory research reconstructs the asymmetrical and exploitative relationship between traditional researcher and subjects into an equalitarian and cooperative one (Merrifield 1989; Fischer 2000). Participatory research transforms subjects into research partners (Stoecker and Bonacich 1992) and facilitates citizens' learning about the norms and practices of other social groups such as scientists, medical doctors, epidemiologists, lawyers, bureaucrats, and politicians (Freudenberg 1984; Brown and Mikkelsen 1990; Horton and Freire 1990). Citizens feel encouraged to design for themselves a workable solution to the problem they define (Rabe 1992).

Respect for Local Knowledge and Provision of Resources
A number of academic/activists support participatory research as a way for the EJM to build cooperative ties with researchers (Bryant 1995; Bullard and Johnson 2000). Representatives from several disciplines identify the successes of participatory research in addressing a variety of local problems and policy issues in global North and South nations. We argue that participatory research benefits EJM activists through the greater respect granted to activists' knowledge and the improved capacity for providing the necessary resources for a political pressure strategy.

EJM activists' experiences in collaboration with academic institutions indicates their keen awareness of traditional researchers' lack of respect for local knowledge. They reported that their most positive academic collaborations were those with students because students tended to defer to activists' understandings and lived experiences. In contrast, activists reported that their most negative academic collaborations were with researchers who treated them merely as units of analysis. Participatory research maintains the benefits of student collaborations while addressing the deficits of traditional research. The raison d'etre of participatory research methods is to advance the preferences and use the knowledge of research participants in an endeavor which they define.

Our analysis of EJM activists' reports on their collaborative efforts with academic institutions also suggests the enhanced access to resources offered by participatory researchers. The tactic of political pressure requires large numbers of voters and organizational and political skills. The large numbers needed for political pressure are more likely to be mobilized in a participatory research collaboration because community residents observe that, rather than outside "experts," insiders—their own neighbors—are defining the problems and calculating the options. Although both traditional and participatory researchers possess significant organizational and political skills, participatory collaborations are more likely to provide activists' access to those skills.

Recommendations: Do It Like You Mean It
We do not argue that the EJM will rise or fall on the basis of external support—the indigenous networks of black communities, for example, have proved a tremendous strength in the achievement of a wide variety of civil rights. Nor do we argue that traditional researchers have no important role to play in the environmental justice battle—their sincere and continuing efforts to refine research techniques for separating and measuring race and class effects on the distribution of environmental risk can only add to the EJM arsenal. Instead, we argue that EJM collaborations with participatory researchers is a promising, albeit bumpy, road for increasing movement resources to apply greater political pressure and achieve structural changes that will more equitably distribute exposure to environmental risks and eventually reduce these risks for all. But participatory researchers must work harder to assure that their work adequately expresses the voices and serves the needs of the aggrieved.

Participatory researchers have reported problems in their fieldwork, particularly the role conflict sometimes experienced by an individual playing the dual roles of researcher and activist (Cancian 1993; Hall 1992; Park and Pellow 1996; Stoecker 1999). They describe the tension experienced by the researcher over whether to surrender complete control of the research project, to hold a modicum of control as a research facilitator, or to retain significant control as an expert (Couto 1987; Stoecker 1999). Thoughtful researchers offer tips for avoiding some of the pitfalls of participatory research. Fischer (2000) suggests certain task-steps be taken to facilitate cooperation and trust between researchers and activists.

Yet our interviews with EJM activists starkly reveal that the most critical component of an appropriate evaluation of participatory research is missing: we know virtually nothing about activists' views of the value of such research partnerships. Despite Pellow's (1994) questioning whether the patron truly has clothes and whether clients are truly empowered, analysts do not systematically gather activists' evaluations of the researcher's role or explore in detail the effects of differences in education, occupation, income, lifestyle, race/ethnicity, and gender on building effective collaborations. Reading the literature gives one the sense that successful collaborative ties are the somewhat random result of hard work and blind luck.

We assert that collaboration with researchers using participatory methods can be significantly improved by researchers' assiduous solicitation of feedback from their activist partners. Much has been gained from participatory researchers' advice for improved collaboration based on their own reflections on such experiences. Yet more is to be gained from seeking evaluative comments from EJM activists to benefit from their advice based on their reflections on the partnership. Without activists' evaluations, participatory researchers are doomed to repeat the mistakes of traditional researchers. Frequent, respectful, and mutual evaluation is the basis for an accountability that will reinforce productive collaborations.

In the quest for long-term social changes to reduce persistent environmental inequalities, we must all remember to keep our eyes on the prize. EJM groups may not win their first battles. But the greatest hope for significant social change lies in the individual transformations that activists undergo which stiffen their resolve not to be run over again in the future.

5

Who Wins, Who Loses? Understanding Outcomes of Environmental Injustice Struggles

Melissa Toffolon-Weiss and Timmons Roberts

Throughout the 1980s and the 1990s, grassroots environmental justice activists waged contentious battles against industry representatives, government officials, and other development advocates. In some, activists have successfully stopped the siting of nuclear waste facilities or the dumping of toxic waste. In other struggles, industry representatives have won the right to build toxic facilities or maintain landfills. The varied outcomes of these struggles raise the question of what factors contribute to the success or failure of local environmental justice groups.

In this chapter we examine two prominent environmental justice struggles that took place between 1990 and 2000 in Louisiana. The cases are the Louisiana Energy Services uranium enrichment plant siting in Claiborne Parish and the Agriculture Street landfill Superfund site in New Orleans. In both cases, local citizens mobilized and engaged in exhaustive struggles that went on for years.

First we will review the literature as it pertains to the success or failure of a social movement. Then we will provide a brief overview of each case. Finally we will explore the trajectories of these movements to find the common characteristics that contributed to a protest group's success or failure. We realize that comparing a siting case and a contamination case is like comparing apples and oranges. However, we propose that this comparison is useful in an effort to illuminate the differences between types of fruit (or cases). Other researchers have found that siting cases are more easily won by protesters than contamination cases (Gladwin 1987). We want to know why.

The struggles that we explore in this chapter involve grassroots, poor, and people-of-color groups who are fighting against environmental injustice. This is not surprising, since the cultural, political, and economic history of

Louisiana has created a situation in which the populations most affected by the negative effects of development are poor people of color (see Roberts and Toffolon-Weiss 2001). The proposed uranium plant would have had the greatest impact on the poor rural black community closest to the facility, and the Agricultural Street Landfill's potential risk is to the low and middle-income blacks whose homes were built directly atop it.

Why Do Some Local Protests Succeed While Others Don't?

In order to understand how power is gained by a previously powerless group, one must look to theory developed in the study of social movements. Much of social movement scholarship has focused on the emergence and mobilization of protest. However, for the purposes of this study we will focus on a less evolved body of theory that seeks to explain the outcome of social movement struggles (Guigni 1998). In other words, we want to know what made a difference in the successful versus the unsuccessful cases that we examine.

Logically, the first issue to examine when studying the factors that contribute to a successful protest challenge is how to define "success." Social movement scholars have explored extensively how movement outcomes are classified. However, for the purposes of this study we are going to employ a simplified definition of success. A protest will be deemed successful if the protesters achieved the land use that they desired at the onset of the protest. Those protesters who do not achieve such land uses are not successful.

Researchers have identified several variables that affect social movement outcome, such as organizational structure, resource levels, protest tactics, framing of grievances, and political opportunities. Some of these variables are under the control of actors; others describe the structural environment in which the struggle takes place. We will briefly review these concepts.

The structure of a protest group's *organization* is one factor that can affect a social movement's outcome. Tilly (1978) and McAdam (1982) emphasize the importance of a protest group taking advantage of an existing organizational structure. Several social movement researchers (Steedly and Fioley 1979; Mirowsky and Ross 1981, Gamson 1990; Frey et al. 1992) found that groups with unified, centralized, and bureaucratized structures were more successful than groups with more decentralized organizational structures.

A protest group must make many strategic decisions regarding tactics. Many researchers have found that more successful protest organizations use tactics that are disruptive or threaten disruption (Astin et al. 1975; Tilley at al 1975; Mirosky and Ross 1981; Steedly and Foley 1979; McAdam 1983; Gamson 1990; Tarrow 1994). However, several studies of strikes and labor conflicts have found that the use of violence by protesters did not help them meet their goals (Taft and Ross 1969, Snyder and Kelly 1976). After an extensive review of contentious political battles, Giugni (1998) concluded that there was no definitive answer to the benefit or detriment of using disruptive tactics in a struggle.

Several studies have found that the use of a *legal strategy* combined with other strategies, such as demonstrations and lobbying, by protesters (i.e. animal rights, pay equity, Indian rights, and civil rights groups) can lead to a successful outcome. (See McCann 1994; McCann 1998; McAdam 1982; Morris 1984; Silverstein 1996.) McCann theorizes that the use of a legal strategy by a movement organization can compel opponents to make concessions because of the fear of high legal fees and, ultimately, losing control of decision making concerning the issue at hand. He also argues that legal tactics have not been successful for all groups.

A social movement organization must select specific *goals*. Research by Gamson (1990) suggests that single-focus groups tend to be more successful. McAdam (1982) argues that disruptive goals that overtly challenge the existing political and economic structures of society will evoke a strong response and possible repression, while reform goals that seek incremental change may be less threatening, but also, less productive. Gamson (1975), Frey et al. (1992), and Steedly and Foley (1979) argue that groups whose goals required the "displacement" of opponents tend to be less successful than those with "non-displacing" goals.

Another important decision that protesters must make is how to "frame" their grievances. The term "collective action frame" is used to describe the collective beliefs and meanings that are developed by protesters and used to motivate and legitimate their protest (Benford and Snow 2000). Strategic framing of the problem or grievance, of the solution, and of "a call to arms" can serve to attract additional protesters and bring in outside resources and support (Benford and Snow 2000). Walsh et al. (1993) and Gordon and Jasper (1996) found that the strategic framing of protest ideology to appeal to a wide audience may have significantly influenced the positive outcome of grassroots protest against the siting of an incinerator. Similarly, Capek's (1993) analysis of a Texas Superfund site provides evidence that the adoption of an effective environmental justice frame led to the success of grassroots mobilizing for a federal buyout and relocation.

Early social movement researchers stressed that a protest group must have adequate *resources* to mount a successful challenge (McCarthy and Zald 1976; Jenkins and Perrow 1977; Cress and Snow 1996). While the availability of resources is not entirely under the control of protesters, they can develop strategy and tactics to obtain resources from outside supporters. Albrecht et al. (1996) noted that extra-local groups were instrumental in supporting local groups that were protesting radioactive waste facilities by providing strategic, financial, moral, and informational assistance. Kitschelt (1985) noted the importance of resources for the success of antinuclear movements in four countries.

Structural factors, such as political opportunities, directly and indirectly affect the actions, motivation, and aspirations of the actors on both sides in the struggle. The growth coalition and the insurgent groups act within these structural constraints to develop mobilization structures, frames, and strategies to increase their capital and thus their power to affect economic development within their community. Amenta et al. (1999) recognize this link when they argue that the strategies of activists must fit into the current political context in order to be successful. They theorize that the more favorable the political environment the less difficult it will be for the challenger, and that, conversely, a more antagonistic political contest will require more effort on the part of the challenger.

Political opportunities can be created by broad social processes that undermine and create instability in the political structure that serve to elevate a minority group. These occurrences provide an opportunity for insurgent groups to gain political leverage and standing and decrease their susceptibility to repression (McAdam 1982). McCarthy (1996, p. 10) identifies four specific dimensions of political opportunities that researchers have found to provide avenues or obstacles for insurgent groups: the level of openness or closure of the formal political system (e.g., legal and institutional aspects), the level of stability of the elite network that inhabits the political system, the existence of elite allies, and the level of state repression. Amenta et al. (2002)

and other researchers have found that the political opportunity structure can mediate the success or failure of a social movement.

There is an inherent difficulty in developing theoretical concepts for the study of something so complex as a social movement: These theoretical concepts, while often elucidating, can confine your analysis and allow the bigger, more dynamic picture to slip out of sight. Zald (2000, p. 1) states that "definitions, key concepts, and methodological/epistemic commitments provide opportunities and constraints for communities of scholars." A major criticism of classic social movement theory is that researchers tend to look for simplistic causal connections between variables that lead to a movement's success. Most theorists cite the importance of the interaction between variables such as movement strategy and tactics and the larger societal context (political and cultural) (Giugni 1998). An example of this approach is Zald's (2000) call for a refocusing of the study of social movements to center on "ideologically structured action." Zald defines this concept as behavior that is "guided and shaped by ideological concerns." He proposes that this concept can link the frames proposed by protesters with the larger society and expand the focus on social movements from the actual struggle to the way the issue is treated within formal bureaucratic and political channels. This approach links ideological concerns with the action they promote among potential allies and enemies of a movement creating or hindering political opportunities.

In this study, we did not attempt to conduct a rigid comparative analysis and develop a theoretical model for social movement success. The cases do not lend themselves to this task, because siting cases are fundamentally different from contamination cases. However, we do consider the commonalities and differences in the cases in the context of the scholarly literature on movements and draw conclusions about why siting cases appear to be easier for protesters to win than contamination cases.

Two Struggles For Environmental Justice

From 1995 through 2001, we conducted field and archival research on the following cases and the broader context of environmental justice struggles in Louisiana.[1] We interviewed activists, industry representatives, and government officials on each case, and attended numerous meetings, protest events, and hearings as participant observers. We have assembled more than 700 newspaper and magazine accounts of these local toxic struggles, the industries they battle, and the environmental justice movement in general. We have collected hundreds of social movement organizational pamphlets and reports, company materials, and government documents.

The Nation's First Major Environmental Justice Judgment: The LES Uranium Enrichment Facility

On the sunny hot day of June 9, 1989, US Senator J. Bennett Johnston announced at a town picnic in northern Louisiana's Claiborne parish that the area would be the site of a $750 million "uranium enrichment facility," which would be entirely safe and would bring to the area 400 jobs and millions of dollars in tax revenues. The cheerfully named "Claiborne Enrichment Facility" would be run by a group of investors called Louisiana Energy Services. LES was a German-led consortium that included British and Dutch interests and utilities from North Carolina, Minnesota, and Louisiana.

A series of informal gatherings with wealthy residents and owners of local businesses had already taken place. The town council, the industrial development group, the police jury (roughly like county commissioners), and state and national political leaders were all on board for this project. The group they failed to even consider were those who lived closest to the proposed site. Five miles outside of the county seat, Homer, are Forest Grove and Center Springs—small, rural, 100-year-old African-American communities connected by a narrow road upon which the enormous factory was designed to sit. Those residents were neither at the announcement nor invited to the gatherings in the weeks beforehand.

These residents, along with a white real estate agent who had formerly been a manager and a chemical engineer at an aluminum plant, formed a group to protest the proposed land use. They viewed the promised tax revenues as too good to be true, and they felt that their poor communities were being "sold out" for the benefit of local businesspeople and politicians. The protesters shared a fear with most communities in the rest of the country that nuclear energy was not safe. This tiny group, Citizens Against Nuclear Trash—or CANT, "as in you CANT build it here"—eventually secured the legal support of Nathalie Walker of the Sierra Club Legal Defense Fund (now called Earthjustice), Greenpeace, the Nuclear Information Research Service (an established anti-nuclear group), and several other local, national, and international groups. Their coalition, which crossed race and class lines, survived nearly a decade of battle before the matter was finally settled.

Senator Johnston was a popular target among consumer groups in Washington, such as the National Taxpayers Union and Ralph Nader's group, Public Citizen. Both had criticized legislation he sponsored allowing the nuclear industry to write off most of a $9 billion debt to the federal government, which provided them with uranium enrichment services (Associated Press 1989). The consumer groups believed the LES project was little more than a "consumer scam," and that LES had no intention of selling enriched uranium on the open market. Rather, they believed that the companies would merely raise their utility rates to charge the consumers for the investments in LES.

Black churches played a pivotal role in the LES struggle. The activists used the churches as powerful moral pulpits and networking tools. Virtually every CANT meeting was held in one of the black churches. With the skills they learned running the churches' finances, the Forest Grove and Center Spring women ran CANT as a tight ship. A core of twelve families, each of which pledged $100 per month for two years, kept the group alive. Sales of box lunches raised $1,700. The group also received funding from national anti-nuclear foundations.

The protesters took advantage of several statewide and national political opportunities. At that time, Louisiana's Environmental Protection Agency was headed by Paul Templet, an open-minded professor who was sensitive to environmental issues. At Temple's direction, Assistant Secretary Vicki Arroyo wrote to Peter Loyson of the Nuclear Regulatory Commission (NRC) requesting that the commission consider the potential adverse effects of the plant, conduct a cost-benefit analysis of environmental impacts compared to the social and economic benefits, and consider whether any alternative technologies or sites were available and whether greater protections could be added.

Another political opportunity in this case was division within the federal government over the issues the plant was raising. The US EPA's regional administrator, Jane Saginaw, castigated the NRC's impact statement for not considering environmental justice concerns (*News-Star* 1994). Among dozens of specific requests for more information, the EPA administrator required more evaluation of the two other sites besides the proposed tract.[2] The agency was under pressure from the Clinton administration to consider the president's executive order on environmental justice and many speculated that the agency wanted to prevent private companies from competing with its uranium monopoly.

The protesters used several strategies in their fight against the corporate giant. Members testified at congressional hearings. They mobilized dozens of people to attend local and state hearings on the siting and cultivated contacts with national and international groups. They framed their struggle as an environmental racism case by bringing in speakers from the NAACP's national office and the Sierra Club Legal Defense Fund to discuss the siting patterns of dangerous factories. The group's legal representation brought claims involving racist intent and impact of the proposed siting to the NRC, the state environmental agency, and the US EPA. The group also conducted extensive public relations work. Many letters were written to the local newspaper and state and federal agencies explaining the protester's views. They even went as far as sending letters to lenders on Wall Street to warn them of the project's shaky financial foundations (*Minden Press-Herald* 1992).

The battle over Louisiana Energy Services swung back and forth over the next several years. LES faced several setbacks, but it persisted and won some important battles having to do with permits. In 1995, the Louisiana Department of Environmental Quality expressed concern that it might end up with the uranium hexafluoride tailings to clean up by itself if the LES group chose to leave the state, or if it collapsed financially. However, the state agency issued the pollution permits late in 1995. CANT and the Sierra Club Legal Defense Fund appealed the permits and won their reversal in 1996 when the First Circuit Court of Appeals revoked them. Also in 1996, the NRC ruled that LES was financially unstable.

On May 2, 1997, the Nuclear Regulatory Commission released a "partial" ruling on the plant which was "widely viewed as a national precedent in the area of environmental justice" (Shinkle 1998). In the ruling, the NRC cited evidence that "racial considerations had played a part in the site selection process." They also stated explicitly that they were addressing the case in the spirit of President Clinton's Executive Order on Environmental Justice.

After the appeals and the continuing battle over the partial ruling, in early April 1998, the NRC ordered LES to examine the effects of rerouting the road, but stopped short of forcing it to study whether the siting was discriminatory. To many people's surprise, LES finally put out a terse but angry press release on April 22, 1998 (plant opponents immediately noted the appropriateness of its being Earth Day.) It read "LES officials today ended their seven-year quest for a license from the US NRC to build and operate what would have been the nation's first privately owned centrifuge enrichment plant."

The opposition had spent about 1/15 as much money as LES had spent (around $200,000, versus more than $30 million), and had flexed a surprising new type of political muscle by combining the resources of national civil rights and environmental leaders, environmental lawyers, and persistent grassroots organizing.[3] The environmental justice coalition in this case had been successful, it seemed, partly by utilizing what was evolving into a strategic delay tactic, which made the project economically unfeasible by tying up its permits in the courts.

The Politics of Living on a Superfund Site: The Agriculture Street Landfill

The saga of the Agriculture Street Landfill began around 1910 when the City of New Orleans opened the site for operation as the city's municipal waste dump. The dump continued to receive solid waste for 50 years, during which time the waste was incinerated on site and buried in the surrounding area. Nearby residents complained throughout the 1940s and the 1950s of a terrible stench wafting from the facility. Upon closure, the landfill was 17 feet deep and covered 95 acres downriver from New Orleans' famous French Quarter.

The Housing Authority of New Orleans (HANO) and the federal Department of Housing and Urban Development (HUD) first chose Agriculture Street as the site of the Press Park neighborhood, consisting of 167 public housing units. The neighborhood expanded in 1975 when a newly formed group called the Desire Community Housing Corporation (DCHC) submitted plans to construct 67 single-family homes and a senior housing facility. The DCHC completed the construction of these properties, which they named Gordon Plaza, and the Gordon Plaza Elderly

Housing Apartments, using $7 million in federal funds from HUD in 1981 (Daugherty 1998).

Once in their new homes, residents quickly noticed that they were living in a situation that was a far cry from the safe and secure neighborhood they had been promised. Shoddy construction of the houses and landfill debris in the yards foreshadowed impending problems related to living atop a landfill. One resident found the corpse of a cow in her front yard. Another resident found a rusted car door in her garden. Nearly all of the ground surrounding the residents' homes contained broken glass and other debris (Daugherty 1998).

After discovering that the land beneath and surrounding their homes contained dangerous contaminants, some of the most worried residents met with city officials in 1985 to discuss possible relocation of their community. In their struggle for relocation, the residents of Agriculture Street went on to enlist the support of numerous politicians, including New Orleans Mayor Marc Morial, Congressman William Jefferson, and Senators John Breaux and Mary Landrieu. These politicians wrote letters of support and verbally advocated on behalf of relocation of the community. However, residents feel they merely provided lip service to the relocation efforts and have failed to take any decisive action.

The EPA came to inspect the site in May 1986, taking 45 soil samples back to their labs. Some samples had lead concentrations greater than 1,000 parts per million (ppm), and three samples had lead concentrations of more than 4,000 ppm, all far above EPA "safe levels." Soil samples also contained lead, zinc, arsenic, mercury, and cadmium. There were also polynuclear hydrocarbons, potentially dangerous oil products, in almost every sample (EPA 1999).[4]

The EPA, however, initially determined that the site was not dangerous enough to secure Superfund status and the federal monies to relocate the residents and clean up the site that might come with such designation. The neighbors and their advocates continued to fight, with the assistance of a regional environmental justice group—the Gulf Coast Tenants Organization. The organization put pressure on the EPA to reconsider their methods of ranking sites. Congressman William Jefferson brought his office's weight to bear with the help of the Congressional Black Caucus. Then, in 1990, EPA rules changed to include soil contamination in hazard ranking scores, changing the neighborhood's score to 50 out of 100, much greater than the 28.5 needed for Superfund designation (Cooper and Warner 1995).

The Agriculture Street residents were caught in a dilemma that has plagued dozens of Superfund sites around the country: their neighborhood was certified as hazardous enough to get listed, but not hazardous enough to get them relocated. The Superfund program, meanwhile, was embroiled in a politic battle between Democrats and the Reagan and Bush administrations. Many environmentalists feared that the Republican administrations were trying to subvert the program (Szasz 1993).

The Environmental Epidemiology section of the Louisiana State Health Department and the federal Agency for Toxic Substances and Disease Registry (the environmental arm of the Centers for Disease Control) found that the undeveloped area of the site posed a public health hazard, but the residential areas and a nearby school posed "no apparent public health hazard." However, two professors at Xavier University, a historically black Catholic university in New Orleans, contributed to the scientific debate on Agriculture Street (Health Consultation 1997). The director of the Deep South Center for Environmental Justice, Beverly Wright, conducted a door-to-door survey of residents in the mid 1990s and submitted the results to EPA and the community. A white chemistry professor named Howard Mielke did his own tests on lead and other heavy metals in the soils around the Agriculture Street neighborhood and the Moton Elementary school. Mielke found that the site was actually far better than most New Orleans black neighborhoods in soil lead, but these results were largely ignored.

Faced with unsatisfying responses from government officials after a decade of pleas, some residents believed that only lawsuits could achieve relocation. For years the community had difficulty getting public interest lawyers to take up their case, and the private lawyers they found had been interested only in class-action lawsuits against the City of New Orleans, the Orleans Parish School Board, HANO, site developers, and the other parties involved in the construction of Press Park and Gordon Plaza. None of these strategies paid off.[5]

The EPA did not believe that the Agriculture Street site was dangerous enough to warrant relocation, and instead opted to remove two feet of contaminated soil from residents' yards, replacing it with a "geotextile" (a fine porous plastic mesh) barrier and two feet of "clean" soil, at a cost of approximately $20 million. With the two-foot barrier created by the EPA cleanup plan, all trees in the neighborhood were removed and residents were instructed on which trees they could plant. The plans also restricted residents from making additions to their homes and from building in-ground swimming pools.

Despite residents' protests and opposition from the City of New Orleans, the EPA began cleanup of the site in late 1998, starting with the undeveloped portion of the land surrounding the site and the Gordon Plaza Elderly Apartments. When EPA finished cleanup of those areas in March 1999, they sought permission from the local housing authority HANO and the federal agency HUD, which owned 124 of the Press Park public housing units. On March 5, 1999, HANO and HUD granted that permission to the EPA. The EPA began excavation of the Press Park properties on April 29, 1999, and completed work in September. The agency sent "last chance" letters to the owners of the single-family houses in Gordon Plaza, and many accepted the cleanup. In this way, the EPA successfully divided the neighborhood and conquered it piece by piece. Overall, protesters view their struggle as a failure because they have not received what they have wanted all along: relocation.

What Was Important for Success?

In the LES siting case, protest erupted against a proposed siting that had been planned long in advance; however, the most immediate residents, who became the protesters, were never consulted. The protest group was well organized, with leaders who remained focused on a single, non-displacing goal: to prevent the siting. Seeking non-displacing goals is one of the key differences between siting cases and contamination cases. (See also Gladwin 1987.) Courts and administrators may be more reluctant to shut down an already existing facility and displace development and guaranteed tax revenues than to address a proposed siting. In the LES case, the protesters did not have to move an existing industrial operation; instead, they just had to stop or delay the construction of a facility. (For early evidence of this trend, see Gladwin 1987.) And, in fact, governmental authorities did not have to actually reject the proposed sitings—this happened indirectly as they were in the process of deciding what to do. In this successful case, the company, frustrated with the long legal delays, decided to withdraw its proposal.

Framing its struggle as an environmental justice battle served the EJ group well. Because this master frame was popular and came into the public spotlight with President Clinton's 1994 executive order, the protest group was able to attract media attention and support from statewide and national environmental and social justice groups and lawyers.

The timing of this case was very important for another reason: political opportunity. This was a time when the federal government was struggling to create regulations and policy for addressing environmental justice cases. At this time, these agencies were more vulnerable to pressure from the public, media, and lobbying groups. It was the indecision and delay in developing and interpreting policy on the part of the Nuclear Regulatory Agency that ultimately caused the company to withdraw its plans. There was also an opening in the political opportunity structure when the EPA and other federal agencies began to take environmental injustice complaints seriously, which created a division between the federal government and state level political actors—a division that the protesters exploited.

The trajectories of the failed protest struggle was very different from the CANT battle against LES. The Agriculture Street group first sought the help of local and federal officials at the EPA Superfund Program. Similar to the LES siting case, the Agriculture Street protesters did frame their struggle as an environmental justice issue and they received outside support from statewide and national organizations. But this was not enough. One important reason why the Agriculture Street struggle failed was that it did not occur at a time of favorable political opportunities.

The EPA had already established procedures for handling Superfund sites. This was not an issue high on the priority list of the national media or environmental organizations. The protesters resorted to hiring private lawyers to file lawsuits against the owners of the source of the contamination. As stated earlier, this approach is often fraught with problems for the plaintiffs, and in this case, the protesters received little relief from this legal avenue.

In summary, outside resources were not enough and an environmental justice frame was not enough. In the contamination case, these were isolated factors that were not sufficient to lead to a victory for the protesters. One of the main factors that hindered the protesters in this struggle was a political environment that provided few high-level allies and few political opportunities for the protesters. One may argue that contamination cases always face a less politically open environment than siting cases because the corporate actors and industrial operations are more firmly entrenched in the community and supported by allies and policy at all levels of government.

Conclusion

This analysis points to the complexities of environmental justice cases and the significant differences between siting and contamination cases. It was not just one or two characteristics of a protest that decided victory. Rather, in these cases, it was a combination of pursuing a political strategy targeting federal agencies that were in the process of creating policy, "marketing" the struggle to attract outside resources and support, using the media and outside allies to put pressure on the federal agencies, and seeking non-displacing goals. The analysis of these two cases demonstrates that siting cases may be more likely to have the key ingredients that would lead to success as compared to contamination cases. Although the Agriculture Street residents had outside support and adopted an environmental justice frame, their legal strategy, which focused first on the EPA and then on a private toxic tort, was not enough to overcome a political environment that was closed to their demands.

Notes

1. For more detail on these cases and some of our arguments here, see Roberts and Toffolon-Weiss 2001.

2. The full text of the EPA letter was printed in the *Homer Guardian-Journal* on March 3, 1994 under the headline "EPA Responds to Impact Statement for Planned Uranium Enrichment Plant."

3. Earthjustice figures estimated by Nathalie Walker (interview, May 15, 1999); CANT figures estimated by Norton Tompkins (interview, June, 1999).

4. Further testing by the Environmental Protection Agency in 1993 confirmed the 1986 tests indicating excessive levels of toxins such as lead, arsenic, chromium, and calcium. Tests also revealed the presence of "volatile organic compounds, polyaromatic hydrocarbons, metals" and "other dangerous toxins" (Environmental Protection Agency 1999).

5. *Theresa Berry and Phillis Smith v. The City of New Orleans et al.*, 1994.

6

The Environmental Justice Movement: An Activist's Perspective

Carl Anthony

This chapter, adapted from an interview conducted by David Pellow, represents Carl Anthony's personal views and not necessarily those of the Ford Foundation.

My perspective on environmental justice issues differs somewhat from those of most people who have been active in the movement, because I'm older and lived through the 1960s. In the early days I was deeply involved with efforts to link community and environmental design to the civil rights movement. Our focus was on neighborhood environmental issues—the quality of housing, schools, parks, and economic opportunity. We viewed these issues as multidimensional, not single issues. Our efforts bore fruit in movements for community design, advocacy planning, and community development corporations. Regrettably, this early work is not well known or understood within the environmental justice movement.

Throughout the 1960s we worked to bring together the civil rights movement and efforts in community environmental design. That was how I came of age in this movement. As a result, my perspective differs somewhat from the conventional wisdom. Also, because I was trained as an architect, I have a strong bias toward balancing problem identification with solutions.

As an architect, I have been concerned over my entire career with the role of space, place, and environment in the conduct of daily life, and with building political and economic power for the most vulnerable human populations. During the last three decades it has become clear to progressive architecture and urban planning professionals that problems of urban disinvestment, racial polarization, sprawl, the loss of farmland, and wilderness protection are not separate issues but are parts of an interconnected community-building challenge. The long struggle for racial justice is central to meeting this challenge.

It is vital to incorporate a wide range of voices and approaches in addressing these issues. Historically, the civil rights movement started with *Brown v. Board of Education*, then shifted to the Montgomery bus boycott. The next thing you know, there were the sit-ins, then the freedom rides, then Black Power and economic power, and then electoral politics, and so on. All of these different aspects were expressions of the same impulse.

Some of the challenges facing today's environmental justice movement have to do with a lack of historical perspective on issues beyond toxic pollution. During the 1960s, young people of my generation had a similar blind spot. Many of us believed that we could address the full range of civil rights issues by having boycotts and getting rid of separate drinking fountains and securing the right to vote. It took awhile to figure out that people in the 1930s had been working on these issues long before us.

Today's environmental justice movement suffers from a similar lack of historical context. I believe that the popular understanding of environmental justice is based on too narrow a view of "environment" and too narrow a view of "justice." Many environmental justice advocates define the environment as the places "where we live work and play." By that definition, a credible argument could be made that, from an African-American perspective, the environmental justice movement began with struggles against slavery, against the Middle Passage, and against the way people were uprooted from the land, and with attempts—all through the colonial period and all the way up to the Civil War—to escape from slavery and set up new communities. This is the kind of broad thinking about environmental justice that I would like to encourage. But we must go even further.

In 1982, Warren County in North Carolina was the site of what is now considered to be the first major mobilization for environmental justice. This was a significant milestone in the fight against pollution. Yet, in looking at the broader definition of "environment," it becomes apparent that issues of access to and control of resources and land are all part of the same struggle. Native Americans tend to have an especially powerful understanding of this.

Thus a focus on toxic pollution is really a symbol of a much larger conversation that is needed. For people of color, our ancestors' struggles shed light on a great many things that have not been part of the public discourse. To deal with the core issues of environmental justice, we need to take into account the whole sweep of the European expansion and the ways that people and their environments were colonized and dominated. Native Americans have one particular set of histories on that, while African-Americans have a different set. Other people of color also have their own histories in this area. All of these historical perspectives can enrich our current understanding of our collective relationship to the environment.

We have only just begun to explore the relationship between racism and environmental harm.

Paradoxically, African-Americans are not usually associated with land use or rural land management. This is paradoxical because the majority of African-Americans in this country, up until 1950, were basically rural people, yet now we are identified as urban people. For generations, under a regime of forced labor, African-Americans cleared the forests, drained the swamps, and planted and harvested tobacco, rice, sugar, and cotton, for which they received no compensation. Yet this experience of environmental injustice is not visible in standard environmental histories.

Those of us who were around in the early 1960s had little patience with the older generation. We didn't understand the full historical context of our efforts. Still, it was a good thing that young people of the 1960s lost patience—because if we had not, we still would not be able to sit down at a non-segregated counter and get a hamburger, right? At the same time, there was a weakness in our not standing more firmly on the shoulders of those who had gone before, incorporating their wisdom and perspectives. Without a strong sense of continuity going back many generations, vital experiences and insights are lost.

This is the difficulty now facing the environmental justice movement. Its leaders, who are getting on in years, are encountering some of the same challenges experienced by the previous generation's activists. As younger folks come in and engage with the issues, the experience and insight of long-time activists is often discounted.

The challenge of speaking truth to power requires real skill, because it is difficult for many people to accept the truth of what this country is and what is going on. Paradoxically, the people whose work requires that they tell uncomfortable truths may then find themselves shut out—because people cannot handle what they are hearing. That is the interpretation that comes through in *Green of Another Color*, a report on foundation support (or lack thereof) for the environmental justice movement. Thus the most marginalized people often have the most difficulty raising resources—which is, of course, because they are marginalized. The most vulnerable populations are the ones who are the farthest away from power. They suffer the most egregious harms, and they also are not accepted into the heart of cosmopolitan life and philanthropy.

However, I see another element at play here. The ideology that is so fundamental to the environmental justice movement, about the importance of the grassroots and the voices of people who are marginalized, has led to missed opportunities for building bridges to those who are middle class and more established. One of the fundamental challenges of the environmental justice movement is to get people to accept the truth about injustice in ways that do not also make them feel diminished. Although not easy to achieve, there is a way to do this—and some people have consciously worked at it in other fields.

It was no accident that the activists who became prominent in the environmental justice movement were suspicious of and hostile to middle-class people. Many middle-class African-Americans managed to get some benefit from affirmative action in the 1960s and left behind folks who were not able to get access. We need to honor the fact that if the folks who were left behind had not been willing to step up and criticize some people of color— or at least refuse to be trapped by whatever bargains they had made to "get ahead"—we never would have found out about all of these issues.

Having said that, I do think that the class issue here has two sides to it. I question the deeply entrenched yet limited perspective that only people who are grassroots and only people who have never been educated and only people who are suffering have a contribution to make. Of course, many people have achieved personal success and then willingly turned their back and forgotten about folks who live in the inner city and rural areas. The other side, though, is the long history of well-positioned people who have continued to stand up for poor people. Look at W. E. B DuBois, for example. He was Harvard-educated, but he managed to give a powerful voice to these issues. Whether you are talking about Che Guevara, Fidel Castro, Harry Belafonte—the list goes on—you can find a lot of relatively privileged people who have figured out ways to continue advocating for social justice.

One of the worst things in progressive movements is when people working for social justice get to the point of greater visibility and increased capacity to reach out to other constituencies, yet find themselves cut off from their former associates due to resentments about their upward mobility. To put it more plainly: people may face accusations that they have "sold out." At some point you need to be able to move up to have some effectiveness, yet the last thing you want is to be cut off from your base. Lani Guinier has a wonderful chapter about this in her book *The Miner's Canary*.

In short, it is vital to have both an inside game and an outside game. We need strong social movements that are grounded in the real needs of communities, and we need people who have moved into establishment careers and have leverage that can help to strengthen community-based efforts.

One mission of Urban Habitat, the organization I co-founded and directed, has been to build multicultural urban environmental leadership for sustainable communities in the San Francisco Bay Area. Urban Habitat was the earliest environmental justice organization to take on the quest for metropolitan regional equity. The first aspect of this mission was to have people of color understand who they were and whose shoulders they were standing on as they tackled environmental problems in their communities. It was not simply about fixing up a toxic situation, or remediating a particularly egregious environmental challenge. Rather, we helped community leaders gain a sense of continuity with their culture, stretching back over many generations. We spent a great deal of time working with people on such questions, helping them to explore their culture more fully as an integral part of their environmental justice organizing. A second mission of Urban Habitat was to develop among participants a shared understanding of the political, economic, and environmental context of the region where our work was located. Third, we sought to strengthen the leadership skills and capacities within a geographic context larger than individual neighborhoods or workplaces more familiar to them.

I see my current work on metropolitan regional equity and smart growth as an extension of these early efforts within the environmental justice movement. I do not see it as something different. Today, all over the United States, community-based organizations, churches, and labor leaders are joining together to fight for new patterns of metropolitan regional development. They see that the squandering of land through sprawl is connected to the abandonment of the inner cities. The struggle is not only about toxic waste dumps. It's also about just transportation, affordable housing near economic opportunity, decent schools, well-maintained parks, and open space in every neighborhood. The Ford Foundation is supporting these efforts. When I was involved with the first People of Color Environmental Leadership Summit, in 1991, we had some sessions on these issues and people were not yet ready to talk about it. I believe that now, many years later, people are finding this approach more useful.

I was at the Environmental Justice Summit 2 in the fall of 2002. On the one hand, it was extraordinary how many folks from so many walks of life were there. As an effort at mobilization, it was outstanding. On the other hand, some tensions and conflicts arose among activists there. There was so much disorganization, so much chaos—yet the fact of the matter was that all these people came. All these people who had not been part of the original group were there, trying to figure it out and get their two cents in. On the level of the "official" organization, the situation seemed to point to a lot of challenges. Yet the vitality of the dialogue had positive implications for the future.

I see a need for new leadership within the environmental justice movement. I believe that the new generation—the people who have "gotten" the ideas but were not necessarily at all the planning meetings—have an essential role to play. What I hope will happen is that a "coming of age" will occur, with established leaders making a transition to different roles and responsibilities. How a new set of voices comes in, and how they are able to take the strength of what happened and use it and build on it, can lay the groundwork for future success.

In comparing the civil rights and environmental justice movements, I see similar themes. The civil rights movement started in rural areas and in communities that were not at the center of national power. It was in the small towns and in places like Montgomery and Topeka that this energy began to develop. As it matured, it moved more and more to the cities and the city neighborhoods. Toward the end of the 1960s and the early 1970s, it began to influence electoral politics, and people began to get elected.

I see a similar trajectory in the environmental justice movement. Although the movement began mostly in more rural locations, now these issues are having a much greater impact in urban areas. While continuing to work on rural problems, the environmental justice movement has been an important influence on smart growth policies in the cities, something that most people do not realize. The debates currently happening about regional equity would not have been possible if the conversation between social justice and environmental groups had not taken place. In that sense there has been an evolution over time.

Still another dimension is the globalizing of the civil rights struggle. At one point, when I wanted to write a chapter about some of the cities in the South where the sit-ins started, I called folks in Greensborough to find out what happened to the five-and-dime store where people had gone and "sat in." They told me that they were making it into a civil rights museum that would also include exhibits from Tiananmen Square and the Berlin Wall.

It is clear that the civil rights movement had an enormous impact on global events. I think this is true of the environmental justice movement as well. People from all over the world have taken cues from this movement. It is a two-way street: even as people from our communities learn more about these dynamics of globalization and the World Trade Organization and all that, folks from around the world are also looking to communities of color in the United States.

Having said that, I think there are also some particularly important new challenges that were not as visible in the civil rights movement. One of them is multiculturalism and the relationship among different communities of color. How we articulate that and go forward with that is a crucial question. Are we going to have real communication among these different groups that opens up further possibilities to achieve change? Or are we just going to end up at each other's throats?

How far have we come with regard to the movement for environmental justice? I do not think we have come nearly far enough, particularly when we think about the relationship between people of color and the natural world. When I was in South Africa and saw some of the work that the brothers and sisters there are doing around environmental justice, I was surprised to learn that the emphasis was almost exclusively on toxic pollution. I thought: "What about all the natural resources on the whole continent? Why are we not having a conversation about that?"

The entire continent of Africa is being exploited, primarily by foreign corporations and European governments, yet somehow this is not viewed as an environmental justice issue. It seems to me that we have gotten stuck in little boxes, instead of learning and thinking about the broader issues. Can we find a way to shift gears and tap the full potential of thinking about all these things in a totally new way?

My feeling is that the question of the natural world is the work that the emerging generation will take on, and I do believe that there are ways of doing that. The question has always been this: How do you make it real for people who are struggling under the burdens of everyday life and survival, and at the same time occupy the larger moral space that can provide leadership for everybody? The "double consciousness" that DuBois talked about at the turn of the twentieth century, instead of being a liability, can be a real asset. He talked about these two aspects being at war with one another. My feeling is that, as we begin to think of ourselves as global citizens and have some sense that we, as people of color, have to take some responsibility for the outcome of everything, at the same time we can also address the issues of our own neighborhoods and communities.

You do not have to ignore the everyday challenges of people who are trying to pay the rent or who lack food to eat. In fact, that is part of the same conversation. In getting out from under this white-dominated, white-led view, we can come to understand that we're all human and we have an urgent responsibility to take on these larger issues. To achieve healthy and sustainable metropolitan regions would be a huge step in that direction. That is why, at this stage of my life, this is now the focus of my current work.

The quest for environmental justice is to meet the needs of the most vulnerable communities fairly while building a fitting home for humans in the context of all of creation. I like to bear in mind that we are the end product of 4 billion years of life on the planet. As global citizens, we need to think about how we are going to transform this world to make it into a habitable place for not only our progeny but also for other living systems. The environmental justice movement is right on the front lines of this.

II
New Strategies for Achieving Environmental Justice

7

Race and Power: An Introduction to Environmental Justice Energy Activism

Julie Sze

This chapter examines environmental justice energy activism in the United States, which I define as community action by people of color on the issue of energy. What makes this phenomenon specifically "environmental justice" in nature is that it defines activists' engagement with energy issues through the prism of environmental racism. Environmental justice energy activism links local and community-based activism with broad-based energy activism at larger scales—city-wide, regional, national, and global. It also emerges as a result of political discontent with intensifying trends of the expansion of capital with a simultaneous decrease in government intervention and regulation.

Environmental justice energy activism reflects the specific interpretive responses of people of color to the implementation of energy systems that are particularly destructive toward racial minorities in the United States. The burdens of large-scale energy production have destroyed communities in many nations across the world, whether energy is generated by coal (e.g., on the Dine/Navajo land of Black Mesa, Arizona or in various communities throughout Appalachia), oil (e.g., Shell's activities in Nigeria and Texaco's in Ecuador), or hydropower (e.g., dam projects displacing hundreds of thousands of people in Quebec, India, Chile, Brazil, and China). There is a growing awareness of the interconnectedness of global climate change and environmental justice issues at the same time that the fossil fuel lobby is fighting the Kyoto Protocol and other international attempts at regulation.[1] Thus, I am not suggesting the burdens of energy production are unique to people of color. However, I suggest that in the US context race and racism are useful frames for understanding how pollution harms from the energy sector are socially distributed, as well as the larger political meaning of community activism in response to this pollution. These examples of activism are a significant challenge to energy companies' attempts at unilateral decision making on energy issues to promote a pro-business government ideology, most readily embodied in energy deregulation. This type of environmental justice activism represents the cutting edge in movement tactics, linking local, national, and international grassroots concerns about pollution and health to the collaboration between the state and a global corporate structure.

The interests of communities of color are negatively impacted by energy deregulation, which is disingenuously promoted by its corporate advocates and government allies as a race-neutral policy that benefits everyone equally. In their activism on energy issues, communities of color are intervening in larger debates about the need to protect the environment, the public interest, and democracy, in the context of wrenching political and ideological change that is altering the role of the state with respect to the community. After all, deregulation is a largely ideologically driven attempt by proponents to decrease the power of the state in regulating the private sector, and is of direct benefit to corporate interests. I highlight the relationship of racial politics to changing energy systems. In doing so, I show how and why energy policy and environmental justice analyses are linked.

Since the middle of the nineteenth century, energy has been a big business and a corporate enterprise. Coal, oil, and electricity came under the control of large corporations, closely related to the growth of big business and the merger wave at the end of the nineteenth century.[2] The degree to which government regulates industry and the nature of the energy market have been contested by producers, consumers, and regulators since the end of the nineteenth century (Melosi 1985).

While energy has played a critical role throughout American history (particularly for the development of American corporations), it remains central to politics, economics, and the broader culture of consumption. The United States consumes far more energy than any other nation, and leads in per capita consumption. The country's foreign policy is largely driven by its ever-growing energy needs. In 1998, Americans constituted approximately 5 percent of the world's population, but used 25 percent of the world's oil, and released 22 percent of the world's carbon, contributing greatly to global warming (Nye 1998). Insofar as it shapes the foreign policy—and by extension, the military commitments—of the United States, energy policy is a major source of outrage directed at the US.[3]

For these reasons, it is important to examine environmental justice energy activism. Like canaries in mines, specific communities of color face risks due to their particular historical, social, and political situations. But these dangers are more widespread, in this case, from expanding trends of deregulation. I address the larger political implications of environmental justice activism, specifically the retrenching role of the state in moderating or policing the excesses of corporate capitalism. In this case, that contestation is over the diminishing role of the public sphere and state regulation of the for-profit energy sector. This chapter centers on the lives of people of color who are drawn into debates on energy policy because of policies that have a direct and destructive impact on their lives.

I begin by describing how energy is racialized. I show how the politics of energy regulation (and deregulation) and distribution generate racialized consequences. There are at least four areas in which energy development and race are intimately connected: nuclear power, oil refinery pollution, the high-energy society and post-industrialism, and the siting of electricity power plants. At first glance, these examples seem disconnected from one another and from energy development and policy. I argue that they are all related to the larger question of how energy policy affects, and generally hurts, people of color. Contemporary struggles over energy policy have racial dimensions, seen most sharply in the negative pollution costs of energy systems. Discursively and politically, community-based environmental justice energy activism challenges several assumptions. First, it challenges the race-neutral discourse of energy deregulation. This activism also seriously questions the idea that energy is an unalloyed social good that benefits everyone equally. Most important, environmental justice energy activism rejects the notion that energy companies and the government know best in the realm of energy policy. Environmental justice energy activism, like nuclear activism in the 1970s, throws a wrench into an arena that energy companies and the government seek to dominate. Their challenge is of special import in view of the large scale of the problem of energy supply and demand at local, regional, national, and international levels, the changing structure of the industry, and the pollution impacts from energy production.

This chapter looks specifically at a movement campaign in New York City concerned with the siting of new power plants. My case study is a city-wide community-based coalition, Communities United for Responsible Energy (CURE), that was organized in 2001 in response to the siting of power plants in low-income and minority communities in the wake of electricity deregulation in New York City. First, however, we must consider the broader geographic and political economic context in which this single struggle emerged.

Race and Energy Activism

This section provides a brief overview of activism by communities of color on energy issues. Although these examples have been well documented, rarely have they been understood in relationship to one another, or in a larger structural and political frame.

Nuclear Power

Scholars and activists have documented nuclear policy as an example of environmental injustice against Native Americans. Over 60 percent of all known US domestic deposits of uranium are found on Native American lands, with most on the southern edge of the Colorado Plateau (including large sections of Arizona, Colorado, New Mexico, Utah, and Wyoming). Over the decades, these mines have produced over 95 percent of the uranium used in US weapons and nuclear power plants. The nuclear industry has left in its wake thousands of abandoned mines, unprotected and unsecured mine waste, and millions of gallons of waste liquid in largely untreated mill tailing ponds. The long-term burdens are numerous, as evidenced by the polluted bodies of Navajo miners, toxic groundwater, and widespread wildlife contamination. Not surprisingly, nuclear issues have been a focus of Native American environmental justice activism.[4] According to the Indigenous Environmental Network, "the legacy of the nuclear chain, from exploration to the dumping of radioactive waste, has been proven, through documentation, to be genocide and ethnocide and a deadly enemy of Indigenous people."[5] This is because Native American lands are sites where uranium is extracted, nuclear weapons are tested, and spent nuclear fuel is buried.

Oil Refineries

"Cancer Alley," so named by the media and public health advocates, is one of the most heavily industrialized and polluted areas in the United States. It is the area located along the Mississippi River, between Baton Rouge and New Orleans. A series of mostly low-income, African-American communities live within the interstices of more than 100 heavy industrial facilities, primarily petrochemical and plastic industries. Every day, children and adults breathe contaminated air and use water poisoned by millions of pounds of toxic chemicals released annually. Louisiana is "afloat in oil" from offshore drilling in the Gulf of Mexico, and oil companies are major contributors to the "toxic soup" (Roberts and Toffolon-Weiss 2001). The oil refinery problem is not limited to the Southeast. California is the third biggest state for petroleum refining, after Louisiana and Texas. The city of Richmond, California is home to a Chevron/Texaco oil refinery and to scores of petrochemical plants and related facilities, many of which have experienced major accidents over the past 30 years.

From extraction to processing, the burdens of environmental pollution in the oil industry have been distributed unequally. Numerous environmental justice activists and community groups are confronting this extreme pollution.[6]

The High-Energy Society and Post-Industrialism

The third example of a race and energy nexus can be seen in the primary and secondary effects of post-industrialism, specifically manifested through rising levels of computerization. The historian David Nye has documented the "high-energy regime" of the mid-twentieth-century United States, a regime that was dependent on a historical anomaly. Multiple sources of energy were in oversupply. In particular, the overabundance of oil and petroleum enabled the ascendancy of the automobile and of the suburb over the city, facilitated through racially discriminatory public policies. The social effects of the rise of the automobile have been well documented. The movement of homes and jobs from the cities to the suburbs concentrated poor and minority populations in declining inner cities where manufacturing work disappeared (Wilson 1987).

The postwar growth of the suburbs and the rise of energy consumption as a result of changing technologies led to increasing energy demands that the United States could no longer meet. In the middle of the twentieth century, the United States made a gradual transition from an oil-exporting to an oil-importing nation, vastly altering global geopolitics. The 1970s brought the end of the high-energy regime based on electricity, oil, and natural gas. Price hikes and boycotts by the Organization of Oil Exporting Countries stalled the US economy, leading to a sense of impending national crisis.[7]

At the same time, changes in global capitalism resulted in global shifts in production and consumption, driven in part by changing technologies and communications. Computers were one component of the electronic energy regime, which put white-collar "knowledge workers" at the center of the US economy, shifting the majority of workers from blue-collar to service-sector employment. Post-industrialism and increasing computerization are also intimately connected. There are two explicit ways in which the large-scale adoption of computers has produced racial impacts: increased production of computers and rising pressure and demands on electricity grids. Computers, seen in the public eye as a "clean technology," are in fact highly toxic to produce. This distribution of pollution, especially in the production process, is racially stratified.[8] Activist organizations such as the Silicon Valley Toxics Coalition have emerged as industry watchdogs, focusing on these environmental and occupational justice issues.[9]

The steadily increasing demand for electricity, a direct result of increased computer usage, is a primary factor driving the flurry of national and local activity around electric power plant siting and energy deregulation. Thus, a complex set of technological innovations and demands for energy and global economic restructuring in the manufacturing sector intersect with existing racial, gender, and economic inequalities. These trends further ensure that the social and environmental effects of these large-scale changes are most destructive to people of color in the United States and to workers in the global South, particularly women.

Energy Deregulation

The increase in proposals for power plants and the activist campaigns over power plant siting are linked to energy deregulation, which opened up the floodgates of power plant construction. For that reason, it is important to understand the ideological and legislative roots of deregulation.

Deregulation, put simply, is a retrenchment from older forms of state regulation. Its proponents use the language of liberation and the glorification of competition to advance their ideological and political agenda.

By far the largest threats to the utility consensus emerged after the energy crisis of the 1970s. Federal legislation opened the doors to elements of deregulation in the system.[10] It created new classes of participants in the electric utility community and spurred innovation and small-scale technologies outside the realm of the traditional utility system and large-scale utility production facilities.[11] In short, legislation invalidated the philosophical and practical justification for the natural monopoly system by introducing such free-market principles as the creation of a competitive market and pay for performance.

In 1996, California passed the most sweeping state-wide electricity industry restructuring program in the United States. Environmental, consumer-interest, and low-income advocates in California vigorously fought the dissolution of environmental and public-interest protections in the face of deregulation, which was focused on driving prices down without any concern for environmental or social goals. California was supposed to open its electricity markets to competition in April 1998.[12] Because the California deregulation scheme provided billions of dollars to in-state utility companies, competition never materialized. In June 2000, wholesale electricity rates in California begin to rise—as much as 300 percent. By December, the California grid.operator announces the first Stage Three rolling blackout alert, signaling that the state was close to exhausting its electricity reserve capacity. At the same time, wholesale power prices averaged a 3,000 percent increase over 1999 levels (McNamara 2002; Sweeney 2002).

The rush of power plant proposals in the wake of industry-wide deregulation brought to the forefront the relationship among race, pollution, and power plant siting. That was because, in general, proposed power plants were to be sited in communities of color.[13] For example, according to a national report published in 2002 by a broad coalition of civil rights, public health, environmental advocacy and environmental justice organizations, 78 percent of African-Americans live within 30 miles of a power plant, as opposed to 56 percent of the white population (Black Leadership Forum et al. 2002). In addition, African-Americans account for 17 percent of people living within 5 miles of a power plant site, statistically higher than their national average of the population.[14] Proposals for new power plants in California, in particular, had racially concentrated effects in terms of siting decisions.[15] Not surprisingly, power plant siting is a major community organizing issue in California.[16]

New York State Power Politics

In the early 1990s, electricity demand in New York State, driven by population growth and increased computer use, increased approximately 10 percent, at the same time that state spending on energy efficiency and conservation dropped dramatically. Governor George Pataki sought to avoid passing state legislation on the issue (as had occurred in California), going instead through the Public Service Commission (PSC), the state body that regulates utilities.

The PSC's pro-deregulation ideology was clear and explicit. Practically and philosophically, pro-deregulation advocates believed that the market would be a perfect self-regulating system that would render the need for government oversight obsolete. The political and ideological belief was that deregulation and competition would "magically" lead to lower prices that would benefit everyone. Despite this promise, based on a "trickle-down economics" ideology, New York State's energy costs were 70 percent higher than the national average in 2002, higher than when Governor Pataki took office in 1994 (Barrett 2002).

The public relations battles over energy deregulation in New York State and over power plants in 2001 in New York City were clearly shaped by the California energy crisis of 2000. As one community advocate charged, New York State was "using a climate of fear [of the California blackouts] to speed through the process." New York State's deregulation proponents (agencies and companies) argued that communities unhappy with an expedited environmental and siting review process were selfishly and dangerously placing New York City in harm's way, ever closer to possible widespread power blackouts. Proponents of the construction of new power plants in New York City warned ominously that "every day's delay will push New York City one day closer to California" (Johnson 2001). This rationale was used despite the fact that the structure of flawed deregulation was the principal cause of the earlier blackouts in California.

New York City Power Politics

In 2002 there were eight private power plants proposed for New York City, in addition to 10 quasi-public power plants proposed by the New York Power Authority (NYPA). In 2000, the NYPA announced a plan to install ten 44-megawatt natural gas power turbines throughout New York City, at a cost of approximately $510 million.[17] These sites (in the South Bronx, Queens, Williamsburg, Brooklyn, and Staten Island) are in industrial water-front communities where past land-use proposals had catalyzed environmental justice activism.

The shape that deregulation took in New York City was racialized through the siting of power plants, which was concentrated in low-income areas and communities of color. The NYPA plants were sited in communities with a strong history of environmental justice activism and a political and historical framework that interpreted city, state, and corporate initiatives to site noxious facilities to be examples of environmental racism. NYPA's own demographic analysis showed that areas around the sites had higher poverty rates and higher proportions of minorities than city-wide averages, within a half-mile radius.[18] Opposition to the NYPA plan was strong and immediate, mainly based on the local impact of air pollution and exacerbation of asthma rates from these facilities on certain neighborhoods of color.

Communities United for Responsible Energy (CURE) was the city-wide environmental justice and energy coalition that formed in response to the local impacts of energy deregulation. CURE's platform was comparable to that of other clean air and energy advocates, but it foregrounded the language of race and environmental justice by focusing on the racial impacts of air pollution and asthma.[19] For CURE, those most vulnerable—in this case, people of color—were portrayed as exemplifying the public interest and as needing the most protection from corporate greed.[20]

CURE differed from its allies from the mainstream environmental community and consumer interest organizations in how it constructed the "problem" of energy deregulation. CURE organized highly visible public demonstrations and did outreach on the air pollution and asthma problem that highlighted its impact on people of color. For example, CURE organized protests outside the Hunts Point subway stations, where two of the NYPA turbines were to be sited. CURE members carried signs that read "End Environmental Racism," and passed out informational fliers. Other fliers focused squarely on the asthma and air pollution problem, calling for "less wheezing, more breathing" and "less asthma and more justice."

On June 1, 2001, the day the NYPA turbines were to be turned on, CURE organized a protest of about 250 people in front of Governor Pataki's office in Manhattan. The outreach flier for this rally read: "While Manhattan gets one skyline, the rest of NYC gets another. Are power plants Pataki's idea of how to fight asthma?" The visuals are of the World Trade Center (this event took place 3 months before the World Trade Center attack of September 11, 2001), contrasted with two power plant stacks spewing smoke. The two faces are a smiling Pataki and a black youth with an asthma pump in his mouth gasping for air during an asthma attack. This visual contrast between the state's most powerful politician and a child of color with asthma is a literal representation of CURE's essential politics and belief systems, which seek to place the lives and health of children of color at the center of the public's consciousness.

At that rally, a racially diverse mix of community residents from a number of affected communities, accompanied by politicians, marched and spoke out against the Governor's energy policies. A CURE member drove a car with three power plant stacks on the roof to the rally. People wore gas masks, and carried signs that read "South Bronx is choking." These signs reminded viewers and passing pedestrians that air pollution kills surely, even if does so "slower than guns." The rally forced the midtown business crowd, mostly white-collar workers and executives, to see the community's anger over an issue that is literally, politically, and figuratively rendered invisible and marginalized to the periphery of the city's poorest and most vulnerable neighborhoods of working-class persons and people of color. The rally made those in the noonday crowd stop and look at poor people, sick people, and children, and it made them think about where the city's energy comes from and who is hurt in its production and its use.

In the political controversies over the concentration of power plants and their impact on the health of people of color, the social construction of the issue links diverse campaigns. That is, the generalized dissatisfaction with living near an existing or proposed power plant is made racially specific. The power plant issue, rather than being a general environmental, public health, or community concern, becomes a racially charged example of larger problems as identified through the language of environmental racism and the discourse of the environmental justice movement. Energy and power plants become yet another poignant example of how people of color are particularly harmed by large-scale technological and political systems. For people of color living near power plants, deregulation is a concrete policy that hits their neighborhoods particularly hard, with little regard for their health or the environment.

Assessing the Perils and the Promise of Environmental Justice Energy Activism

Communities of color in New York City enjoyed few concrete successes as a result of their activism around energy issues. The pace of power plant construction slowed, but not as a direct result of community activism. By far, the biggest factor was the slowing enthusiasm for energy projects, in part a result of a post-Enron, post-California-energy-crisis disenchantment with deregulation, as well as changing economic circumstances as power companies failed to obtain financing for their projects.

It is difficult to gauge the direct impact of the public demonstrations against energy policies on elected officials and the regulatory process. Environmental justice energy activism has made its greatest impact in the legal arena, which, paradoxically, is partially insulated from this type of community pressure. What is significant about the public displays of community anger is that they are crucial parts of a multi-pronged organizing strategy that mobilizes residents to participate in what is traditionally a closed process. In other words, activists transformed what is normally treated as a technocratic issue controlled by a few experts, into a public concern, a legitimate political subject. The legal history of this campaign exemplifies the limits and successes of using the courts as a means to achieve environmental justice, since lawsuits can be dragged out and appeals can overturn both good and bad decisions.[21] Community groups in New York City sought legal redress in the face of a deeply flawed public review process. In 2001, a coalition of community groups, including several CURE members, represented by New York Lawyers for the Public Interest, sued the NYPA. In the NYLPI case, the judge ruled in favor of the NYPA, concluding there had been no violation of the law (Riccardi 2001). The community groups appealed the ruling even as the turbines were turned on in June 2001 as originally planned. In July 2001, the Brooklyn Appellate Court overturned the decision, ruling that New York State did indeed violate the law. Thus, community groups were vindicated, but that fact did not lead to any practical effect because the ruling did not block operation of the turbines.[22]

Community protests against power plants in New York City did contribute to the sense of instability clouding power plant construction. On a political note, community groups, particularly those representing communities of color, understood that in an ideological climate that favors deregulation over regulation, and the private sector over the public good, concerns of low-income areas and communities of color were guaranteed to be ignored, unless they forced their way into this complex and technocratic policy debate. Environmental justice activists understood that the only chance at improving health and environmental quality at the neighborhood level depended on inserting themselves into ongoing debates on energy issues.

It would be utopian and naive to expect that mere involvement would lead to improvement, especially in a sector whose interests lie in maximizing its profits, and in an ideological context where government acts in active concert with corporations. The social consequence of the power plant activism in New York City was that it mobilized anger and alienation by communities of color from the political process on the most crucial environmental and political issues in our time. Environmental justice activism in New York City, as in other places, has not only shown how the status quo in energy politics involves its share of environmental racism, but also, created a window of opportunity, however small, for improving the energy system in favor of increasing environmental democracy and justice. Examining environmental justice energy activism structurally shows the potential alliances that movement organizations can make if they think critically, both about a large sector, such as energy, and about the changing relationship of the state to corporations, and the impact of that change on local communities of color.

Notes

1. Changing climate impacts fall heaviest on the poor in the United States and the global South. EJ groups are organizing around this issue. The Oakland-based Redefining Progress group held an Environmental Justice and Climate Change Forum on Friday, November 17, 2000, and several hundred grassroots activists participated in the two-day (November 19–20) Climate Justice Summit held in The Hague.

2. During this period, more than 4,000 businesses combined into 257 corporations. By 1904, just 1 percent of American companies controlled 45 percent of manufactured products (Hirsh, 1999).

3. One of the first acts of the George W. Bush administration was to reverse a campaign promise to regulate carbon dioxide emissions from power plants. In 2001 Bush announced his opposition to the 1997 Kyoto treaty on global warming, according to which developed countries were to reduce their emissions of greenhouse gases to 1990 levels by the year 2000.

4. IEN and individual tribal communities are working on these environmental issues. IEN's campaign include the Indigenous Mining Campaign Project and the Native Energy Campaign.

5. www.ienearth.org

6. These include local grassroots groups associated with the Southern Organizing Committee for Economic and Environmental Justice and regional environmental justice research centers such as the Deep South Center for Environmental Justice at Xavier University in New Orleans, the Environmental Justice Resource Center at Clark-Atlanta University in Atlanta, and the West County Toxics Coalition and Asian Pacific Environmental Network in Northern California.

7. One of the proposed solutions to the energy crisis was nuclear power, further fueling the demand for uranium.

8. For an in-depth consideration of the links among race, class, gender, and toxics in the electronics industry, see Pellow and Park 2002.

9. There are also toxic implications for computer disposal, which contributes greatly to toxic dumping and toxic leachate in landfills, both in the United States and globally.

10. Chief among these was new federal legislation, specifically the Public Utility Regulatory Policies Act of 1978 (PURPA). In 1977, President Jimmy Carter urged the nation to respond to energy crisis with the "moral equivalent of war" and sought to advance federal policies that addressed the weaknesses in the energy system as laid bare by the oil crisis.

11. For example, the new technology known as "cogeneration" produced cheap power without the need for massive facilities. It became the most popular source of non-utility power, increasing fourfold from 1979 to 1992.

12. The legislation promised competition and at least 20 percent lower electricity rates by 2002. Under the plan, rates would be frozen at rates roughly 50 percent higher than the national average for up to four years (1998–2002), during which time residential and small business ratepayers were required to pay off the utilities' "stranded assets." Stranded assets are debts from dirty, non-economic power plants, including nuclear. Money was borrowed to lock in these payments—and to finance a "rate reduction" for ratepayers.

13. Whether there is direct targeting of communities of color because of racism or class inequalities is an important topic in environmental justice research. This chapter does not attempt to answer this question, which is outside its scope.

14. This report attempts to contextualize power plant pollution within global climate change. For example, it cites a study of the 15 largest US cities which showed that climate change would lead to more heat-related deaths in the inner city. Due to demographics and social factors, people of color would be more likely to die in a heat wave and to suffer more from heat-related stress and illness. For an illustration of this phenomenon, see Klinenberg 2002.

15. A Latino Issues Forum report titled "Power Against the People" (November 2001) analyzed 18 proposed power plants in California in the wake of the California energy crisis, and revealed that power plants were disproportionately located in Latino and poor communities.

16. In Los Angeles and in San Francisco, major battles over power plants revealed the community's strength within energy-based environmental justice activism (Soller 2001).

17. Turbines are based on a relatively inefficient technology, producing only 1/10 of the energy of a mid-size plant, but they are smaller and relatively cheaper to construct and operate.

18. The city-wide averages were 19 percent below poverty, 29 percent black, and 24 percent Hispanic. At five of the seven sites (excluding Long Island City and Staten Island), the poverty level exceeded the city average. The most extreme cases were in the South Bronx: at the Harlem River Rail Yard site in the South Bronx, 51 percent were in poverty, at Point Morris 44.1 percent. The demographic over-representation was also most dramatic in those locations. The population at Harlem River was 36.9 percent black and 64.7 percent Hispanic, and that at Point Morris was 48.5 percent black and 52.3 percent Hispanic. In Williamsburg, where the poverty rate was 28.7 percent, the population was 7.5 percent black and 57.9 percent Hispanic. In Sunset Park, where the poverty rate was 27 percent, the population was 8.5 percent black and 52.3 percent Hispanic. (NYPA In-City Project Environmental Justice Assessment, January 2001)

19. Many of the ideas being promoted by CURE are basic to energy reform and environmental perspectives, and not necessarily unique to communities of color. These include increasing conservation and efficiency programs and completing an overall energy needs assessment and comprehensive planning process.

20. The concentration of power plants raised the issue of "cumulative impact" of multiple air pollution sources on communities of color, an ideal long promoted by environmental justice and environmental health activism more broadly.

21. On the limits of the law in addressing environmental racism grievances, see Cole and Foster 2001 and the chapters in this volume by Targ, Gordon and Harley, and Bryant.

22. However, the Appellate Division did order an environmental impact study by January 31, 2002, and also directed NYPA to study the plant's output of soot particles as small as 2.5 microns as opposed to the larger PM 10 microns. (The PM 2.5 ruling was later amended.)

8

Food and Justice: The Critical Link to Healthy Communities

Orrin Williams

The possibility of achieving environmental justice is intertwined with policies that are designed and implemented in a manner that both mimics and protects the Earth's ecosystems. While it is true that most "native" or "indigenous" people have historically honored Mother Earth and Father Sky, it is also true that, from the earliest times, we have degraded the ecosystems to which we are intimately interconnected. It is not until recent historical times, however, that human activities have accelerated to the extent of threatening the existence of life on this planet.

From a spiritual and "religious" point of view, we have lost our intimate contact with, and sacred notions of, the natural world. They have been replaced with a notion of "civilization" and "religion" that has disconnected the mind from the body and humans from the natural world. It is the dominant paradigm to worship at the altar of science, technology, and money at the expense of the environment. Though it is impossible to return to the way things used to be, it is possible to incorporate the wisdom of the ancients into our current policies and our future policies and practices.

Though some sustainable policies and practices have been designed and implemented, it is important to note that there are no industrial or economic practices that are entirely environmentally benign. To protect the environment it is logical to modify those human activities (industrial, economic, or otherwise) in a way that minimizes the amount of damage and has the smallest possible ecological "footprint."[1] Current levels of resource allocation are unjust. To reduce the human ecological footprint in ways that are just and sustainable will require a dramatic paradigm shift from the dominant ruling social, political, and economic order. Achieving the goal of environmental (or social or economic) justice will require a monumental shift in the prevailing psychological and spiritual elements of global society.

The current dominant global regime is relentless in its attack on all cultural, spiritual, and psychological patterns that are incompatible with the global homogeneity sought by corporate governments and their handlers: the global corporate elites. International social, psychological, cultural, spiritual, economic, and political actions will have to become grounded in the realization that we are all interconnected and should be viewed in the way the great Vietnamese Zen Buddhist monk Thich Nhat Hahn calls "interbeings." With this knowledge of our interconnectedness, and if we are to achieve any real and lasting justice (environmental or otherwise), we must make a commitment to developing ways of sheltering, feeding, clothing, transporting, educating, recreating, and praying that honor our intimate relationships with one another.

Achieving environmental justice is not enough. The solutions required to overcome global environmental, social, economic, cultural, and psychological problems cannot be accomplished by the movement for justice as it is currently structured. It is not a question of where nuclear waste should be stored; it is a question of stopping the production of additional waste. (See Benford's chapter in this volume.) Justice must be extended to the generations of the next millennia and that can only be done by protecting the natural heritage that we have inherited. The quest for justice is not just a contemporary trend; it is an intergenerational event that does not benefit one group or another but rather applies to all.

The global food system provides us with an opportunity to apply advanced and sophisticated approaches to overcoming injustices. Moving beyond environmental justice means that we must begin to advocate and apply a wide-ranging strategic and tactical approach to problems that render solutions that encompass all areas of human activity while protecting the ecosystems with which we interdependent. Let us end the notion of disproportionate impacts and move toward a goal of no impacts.

The essence of moving to a more sophisticated movement is characterized by becoming oriented toward solutions and solving problems for all communities. Fighting to maintain the moratorium on landfills on Chicago's southeast side or shutting down the municipal incinerator on the west side is only partial justice. It raises the specter that the fight will continue in another community, because we know that injustice follows the path of least resistance. Strategies for managing waste must be developed and implemented that reduce greatly or eliminate the problem so that no community is faced with the burden of handling waste. The solutions must be applied to the global community. That is real justice; justice beyond current applications of environmental justice.

Focusing on Food

Industrial agriculture that is replacing smaller-scale models contributes dramatically to the much larger ecological footprint of the "developed" countries of the global North, including the United States. The large footprint of industrial agriculture can be largely attributed to its reliance on petroleum and petrochemicals for much of its operations. The operations reliant on petroleum-based products include fertilizers, pesticides, herbicides, the operation of agricultural machinery, and transportation.

The importance of food to life itself, as well to the overall health profile of a community, makes it as important an element for vigilance by the activist and academic communities as any other. Air for breathing, water for proper functioning at the cellular level, and food for energy required for all aspects of life demand that their sources be protected and that these resources be available to all in a just and secure manner.

The environmental justice movement can ill afford not to be vigilant about every aspect of the food system. The movement must protect the health of landowners and land workers alike, protect the soil and the waterways, and ensure that farmers and farm workers are paid fair and equitable wages for their work. To fail in this regard would be a monumental disaster and would seriously damage the credibility of the movement. This chapter offers a critical examination of how we feed ourselves and offers some suggestions for solving the environmental and environmental justice problems associated with the dominant model of industrial agriculture.

Food and Justice

Industrial agriculture at all levels of operations produces a negative impact on human and environmental health (Kimbrell 2002). An unhealthy environment places humans at risk for a host of health problems, just as other living beings are at risk when their environment becomes unhealthy. Whether it is a pond, a forest, or an ocean, when an ecosystem is degraded it has a negative impact upon the community of plants and animals occupying it.

Industrial agriculture is a major source of environmental—and, by extension, human—degradation. The proliferation and accumulation of pollutants due to the use of herbicides and pesticides has created numerous events of ground and surface water pollution (Carson 1962; Hynes 1989; Phipps and Crosson 1986; Pimental and Lehman 1993; Pimentel 1992; Soule 1990). Furthermore, the industrial or factory farms for poultry, cattle, and hogs create a monumental environmental threat. Likewise, farmers and farm workers display a variety of symptoms from their exposure to the compounds that produce agricultural inputs such as herbicides and pesticides. The exposure of agricultural sector workers manifests itself in an array of disorders among the workers (Donham 1993; Garry 1996; Hoar 1986; Larson 2001) and in the surrounding rural communities (Gladen 1998; Wing 2000; Thu 1997). The literature is replete with farm workers reporting symptoms from pesticide exposures. The stated concern of the environmental justice movement about protecting people where they live, work, play, learn, and pray is no more compelling anywhere than it is with respect to pesticides in the agricultural (and non-agricultural) setting. Moving beyond environmental justice in this instance means supporting agricultural policies such as organic agricultural techniques in an effort to drastically reduce if not eliminate pesticide use.

Resource depletion such as the loss of topsoil is another negative environmental outcome of the industrial agricultural system. When considered in the context of food production, topsoil ranks near the top (next to water) of the assets we acquire from nature. Loss of agricultural land due to residential or industrial "development" is also a global problem. As many communities expand or sprawl into natural or agricultural lands, they are lost to production for a very long time, if not forever.

The Food Environment and Community Access

The case has been made that food access is an environmental justice issue. Recent research by Kimberly Morland and her associates demonstrates that there is a probable link between higher incidences of various diseases and a distinct lack of access to quality food. The corollary is that there is a link between lower incidences of various disease outcomes in the white community and greater access to quality food and a comparative lower rate of liquor stores (Moreland 2002a). The findings of the research confirmed scientifically what has been known empirically: that there is indeed a dearth of quality food establishments in African-American communities. The study indicates that produce consumption rose by 32 percent for each additional supermarket in the black community, while in the white community the comparable increase was only 11 percent (Moreland 2002b). Fat (a major contributor to obesity, a risk factor for cardiovascular disease) is readily available through the various purveyors of fast and "ethnic" foods found in the community. Grocery stores and supermarkets, on the other hand, can facilitate more healthful food consumption practices. For example, the Morland (2002b) study found that the presence of at least one supermarket in a black neighborhood was associated with a 25 percent increase in the number of residents who limited their fat intake. The shortage of purveyors of quality food within the African-American community is a contributing factor to the overall poor health outcomes in the national black community. Communities have the intellect and the capacity to design and implement the institutional changes required to ensure the kind of nutritional and food environment essential to improved public health incomes leading to healthy communities. These changes are compatible with (rather than inconsistent with) other environmental and ecological improvements that must take place for a whole systems approach to developing healthy and sustainable communities. Local examples of solution-oriented approaches conceived by communities are offered in the next sections.

In the rest of this chapter I present a modest proposal for such a project. I believe that a coalition of groups, organizations and institutions will be necessary to achieve the desired results: a just, equitable and secure food system that has broad implications locally, regionally, nationally, and globally.

The Disappearing Black Farmer as a Human Metaphor for All Limited Resource Production Farmers

People of African descent have experienced a loss of land that makes them essentially a "landless" people. According to a June 1985 *Ebony* article titled "The Disappearing Black Farmer," between 1920 and 1978 the number of black farmers declined from 926,000 to 57,000. During that same period, land ownership among black farmers declined from 15 million to

4.5 million acres. In 1997 there were only 18,451 black farmers in the United States (compared to 1,882,652 white farmers), indicating a continuing precipitous decline. Of all black farms, 93 percent were in 15 southern states, and, significantly, the states with the weakest tradition of slavery and plantation agriculture (Florida, Texas, and Oklahoma) experienced the smallest declines between 1982 and 1997. Texas, the state with the largest number of black farmers, experienced an increase in this population, making it the only state not to experience a decline. Black farms totaled approximately 2,080,112 acres in 1997 (Wood and Gilbert 2002).

The problems that have plagued black farmers, such as the lack of access to capital and the indifference and downright complicity in the loss of land by governmental agencies, remain in place (EWG 2004). Others have a more recent experience of displacement, such as immigrants from Mexico and Central America who have been removed from the land by industrial and corporate agricultural conglomerates putting at risk ancient indigenous agricultural systems. Many of these immigrants may now be found hard at work in some restaurant kitchen or dirty factory job, knowledge withering on the vine.

Now we are all part of the labor pool, competing with each other for our souls in metropolitan areas across the United States in clusters of under and unemployment wanting desperately to be found "qualified"` and bestowed the gift of a job. What we need is life giving and affirming institutions; the environmental, social, and economic justice movement's call for jobs is not enough. Rather, healthy communities where people are free from toxic exposures through their food, air, water, or the land is what the struggle is truly all about.

The plight of black farmers underscores the plight of all farmers, regardless of race, with limited resources. It requires infrastructure investment and acquisition for farmers to bring their production crops to market. The infrastructure required is also an issue for those urban communities that require greater access to food and food security in their quest for healthy and livable communities.

Sustainable and Just Food Systems: A Proposed Model

An ecologically responsible agricultural system will be at its core both urban and rural and, to the greatest extent possible, organic. The scale of the individual agricultural operations of such a system should be small to medium-size and should have a regional and local market focus. While industrial agriculturalists who farm organically do not use pesticides, they essentially function the same as conventional agribusinesses by squeezing out the smaller players. For example, Horizon, a Colorado company, controls 70 percent of the "organic" dairy market. They over process milk (ultra pasteurized) supplied from cows that, although fed organic grains, are locked in lots without being allowed to roam freely in pasture. The fact that "organic" food has been co-opted to such a large degree is not surprising when you realize that the organic niche is the fastest growing food sector, worth billions of dollars. The big boys see a cash cow, not a principled way of life that protects the ecosystem or the humans who work in the fields.

Small and medium-size farmers who have formed the backbone of an organic alternative to industrial agriculture deserve the support of local and regional markets that consciously buy their products and help to ensure their survival. Elements of the proposed system of sustainable agriculture would, for example, foster the reestablishment and proliferation of family farms. New farm families would be developed from several sources, including immigrant farmers, agricultural students from regional or special programs established to develop new farmers, and urban dwellers who may be compelled to return to a more rural lifestyle. This element of the proposal would incorporate a program that would function as the equivalent of a domestic agricultural Peace Corps (Ag Corp or perhaps Food Corp) where farmers and farm workers would be trained and then assigned to various regions of the country to establish farms (urban and rural), primarily for the production of food crops.

The Politics of Health and Nutrition

The role of several institutional entities in the design and implementation of sustainable food systems is critical. The most important institutions include the following.

Foundations

These institutions are needed to provide seed funding for various elements of food system projects such as land acquisition (urban and rural), training programs, infrastructure, equipment, seeds, research protocols, etc.

Foundations will need to change their funding approach by supporting development programs based upon research and entrepreneurship rather than social service and charity.

Universities

On-campus and off-campus facilities would be designed to assist in developing various aspects of a just and ecologically oriented agricultural system. It should be noted that many of the major land grant institutions might not be part of the institutional framework because of conflicts with the work done for the biotech and conventional agricultural system. Many of these institutions are beginning to develop an interest in more suitable forms of agriculture, which is cause for optimism. Smaller public and private institutions may form the backbone of this element of the project. Universities perform an important research function, particularly in regard to developing research protocols and providing technical assistance on various elements of an emerging urban agricultural system.

Government

At all levels of government (municipal, county, state, and federal) there must be some assistance for the development of the system outlined above. If government can provide assistance to corporations and other special interest groups, it can surely provide assistance for community food programs. Equity in this realm necessitates communities receiving a return on the revenue that they have produced to support community-based (local and regional) initiatives such as farms (urban and rural), grocery stores, and other food related businesses. The Bethel New Life (BNL) organization in Chicago offers an example of how government can work with communities to create progressive commercial operations in communities. (See the chapter by Lee in this volume.) BNL is receiving substantial funding of $4.5 million dollars from a combination of local, state, and federal sources for a 23,000-square-foot "smart, green" building that will house a child and infant daycare center, employment services, and five storefronts. Assistance can be provided in the form of tax incentives, grants, infrastructure construction and improvements, and other forms of technical support. The right to food choices must also be reiterated; corporations must not be able to dictate what we eat and who has fair and equitable access to the health and life giving properties of high quality food. Brownfield redevelopment in urban centers is one example of how the government can provide assistance for urban communities by providing space for large-scale operations and providing funding for cleanup of contaminated sites. Brownfield sites could be utilized after cleanup for greenhouse and hydroponic projects. Greenhouse projects located near landfills could utilize potential energy sources, such as methane that is otherwise burned off, to heat massive greenhouse structures that could, for example, be a place to produce seed starts for agricultural and ornamental plants.

Nongovernmental Organizations (NGOs)

NGOs and/or nonprofit organizations are pivotal in the organization of a widespread food ecosystem that will provide food security and vastly improve the prospects for healthy communities. Organizations that focus on various issues will be required to become partners in a coalition of institutions and organizations to facilitate meaningful social and policy changes. Organizations such as the American Farmland Trust would be utilized to save farmlands from "developers" and other proponents of sprawl.

Farm cooperatives and consumer outlets such as food cooperatives, natural foods groceries, and even larger chain grocers are important elements in the process of developing an ecologically and human oriented food ecosystem. Farm cooperatives could work directly with food cooperatives, natural foods grocers, and distributors to provide a range of food items that coop members and conscientious consumer's desire. All of this could be linked by community-based distribution and warehouse operations that serve the network of community-based grocery stores and food coops. A wonderful example of the potential for these kinds of relationships to develop can be found in Virginia. In a project created to assist tobacco farmers to convert to other crops, the nonprofit organization Appalachian Sustainable Development formed a group of farmers that grow a variety of organic produce. The organization markets their products under the label Appalachian Harvest in a local grocery chain named Food City. The project sells products to stores and restaurants in Virginia, in North Carolina, in Washington, and as far away as Philadelphia (Halweil 2003).

In Massachusetts, a nonprofit organization called Red Tomato provides opportunities for small farmers to market their produce to stores in the Northeast. With assistance from Oxfam, Red Tomato supported African-American farmers from the Federation of Southern Cooperatives, encouraging them to add seedless watermelons to their product line. These smaller farmers, usually left out of the markets monopolized by large agribusiness, were able to make a profit and serve satisfied consumers.

Nonprofit organizations with the mission of providing management and organizational technical assistance would be utilized for assisting a variety of organizations to enhance their capacity to do the work. Coalition and capacity building are critical to ensuring the security and safety of our food supply. Alternative systems require interlinked strategies and commitments just like mainstream institutions. Activists and advocacy organizations must begin to forge serious policy and institutional development strategies if the movement for justice is to be effective.

Financial and Investment Institutions

A sustainable financial plan must be developed and financial institutions must be involved to provide the capital assistance required to purchase land, to manufacture and purchase equipment, to design and build farm buildings, and to develop transportation and distribution centers. It is imperative that we find or formulate the expertise required to create community development credit unions and development banks, which will provide the financial backing for family farms, community-based natural foods grocery stores, and other components of sustainable food systems. Then we have to buy and invest in locally grown produce, bread baked in local bakeries and in small community-based grocery stores. We cannot design nor proliferate the urban agricultural systems that will be heavily dependent upon greenhouses, hydroponics and land purchases without a capital investment strategy. The activist/advocacy community often loathes the thought of seeking support from business leaders. This distaste is not unwarranted, but the movement must begin to understand and operate from a position that a business culture can be created that is indeed palatable and just. Our future and the future of the other sentient beings with which we share the planet depend upon a shift in our financial behavior. There can be no environmental justice without economic or social justice.

Discussion

Food and farming offer a unifying point for a movement that is multicultural, anti-racist, and anti-sexist and that embraces all aspects of the environmental justice movement. Few other projects can advocate worker protection, land and water conservation, pollution prevention, public health, and urban-rural connections the way food and farming can. All of these elements that form the core concerns of the environmental justice movement crystallize around food and farming, making it an area of human activity that all advocates and activists working on behalf of environmental, social, and economic justice should readily support.

Critical first steps have been taken in the struggle to create healthy and sustainable communities and secure local food environments. Food is the frontline element in our overall health outcomes. The envisioned agricultural program will improve the economic and community development profile, create new employment opportunities, and improve the public health conditions in both urban and rural communities. As Shuman (2000) pointed out, "small scale systems to grow, process and market food are becoming not only cost-effective—in both rural and urban areas—but also essential to preserve the genetic integrity of the world's edible plants."

A decidedly more local and regional agricultural system has major implications for a range of goals, such as the reduction of various pollution sources, positive public health benefits for those employed in the agricultural sector, increased employment opportunities for urban communities suffering from higher than average rates of unemployment, and an increase in food security due to risk reduction that would be caused by interruptions in the food chain.

That is what is meant by "beyond environmental justice." As an activist for environmental, social, and economic justice and as well as a socially engaged Buddhist practitioner, I am bound to advocate on behalf of all things sentient and non-sentient. As stewards of the land and justice we are also bound to protect all sentient beings and the environment.

In the next section I present a case study of a food system collaborative that is trying to put these ideas to work.

Local Case Study: The Chicago Food System Collaborative

The Chicago Food System Collaborative (CFSC) is an emerging model that is combining many of the elements discussed above. The CFSC is a community and university partnership whose stated goal is "to improve the quality, accessibility and safety of food choices for Chicago residents."

CFSC was created via meetings and discussions that arose out of the Chicago Community Food Security Roundtable (CCFSR). The collaborative framework was formulated through a consortium of Chicago-area universities, the Policy Research Action Group (PRAG). PRAG was founded in 1989 as a noble attempt to ameliorate what historically were difficult and frequently one-sided university and community research collaborations. (See chapters in this volume by Bryant and Hockman and by Cable et al.) Under the auspices of PRAG, universities, churches, farmers, and non-governmental organizations have come together around this effort.

Out of the meetings and discussions surrounding of the CCFSR, the Collaborative was created with three primary goals:

1. The development of a system to provide access to fresh, organic foods supplied by local farmers. The approach is a strategy to support a local farmers market, support urban agriculture and develop a local grocery store with a focus on natural, minimally processed foods.

2. The initiation of a public policy discussion that could support the development of sustainable projects and build consensus among stakeholders in the food policy arena.

3. The creation of a food security research agenda designed to enhance short-term community food choices and develop long-term strategies for food safety and security.

The mixed-income African-American community of Austin on the West Side of Chicago was chosen as the first neighborhood for the CFSC project. In addition to the farmers market and the development of the grocery store, the CFSC is conducting several research projects utilizing survey methods and the development of maps utilizing Geographic Information Systems (GIS). Another fascinating aspect of the project is the School-Based Nutrition Program (SBNP). The SBNP will address the growing public concern with obesity in general but in school-age children in particular, assess the quality of the dietary intake of school-age participants, and evaluate the effect of a multi-tiered school-based nutrition program in reducing the impact of poor or marginal dietary quality. The program was initiated in one public and one parochial school in the Austin community.

Data are beginning to emerge about various aspects of the food environment of the Austin community. For example, community members recruited by the Westside Health Authority teamed up with students from Loyola and Chicago State universities (all three are PRAG partner organizations) to visit every store in Austin and the bordering suburban and largely white community of Oak Park, Illinois to begin an intensive study of food availability. The teams visited a total of 134 stores in the two communities, gathering data on the availability and price of food from a list of 102 basic food items (Block 2004).

One of the findings from the research was that a major difference exists between the food environment of Oak Park (a suburban community) and Austin, even though Oak Park sits on the western border of Chicago and is adjacent to Austin. Austin has many more outlets selling food than Oak Park, with 95 of the 134. Of the 95 stores, 50 were small "mom and pop" stores and 19 were liquor stores that also sold food items. Austin's food environment included only one chain grocer, two chain discount grocers, and three independent grocers. The researchers looked at how the stores in the two communities differed in terms of price and availability of produce. The data revealed that the chain grocer in Austin carried almost every item on the list of 102 basic food products. By contrast, the discount chains and small stores were missing a vast number of products from the list and the discount grocers did not carry culturally significant (in the African-American community) items such as greens. The most striking finding is that produce determined to be of poor quality was found only in the Austin food environment and organic food was virtually unavailable.

Overall prices were lower in Austin, however the variables that perhaps explain that difference are the availability of food from discount outlets and lower prices for meat and produce in the independent groceries and small stores, in contrast to the prices in the chain groceries. The quality of goods in the Austin food environment are unquestionably inferior when compared to the Oak Park food environment. This is with great probability one feature in the leakage of dollars spent on food by Austin residents in nearby communities such as Oak Park.

Having demonstrated a real need for quality food in the African-American community of Austin, I enlisted as the organizer and manager of the Austin Farmers Market for the CFSC. In addition to providing produce and meats direct to consumers, we also broker arrangements that allow farmers to sell products to local stores and restaurants. This role provides me with interesting insight into many of the impediments faced by small, limited resource producers in getting their products to market. The impediments include inadequate labor to assist in harvesting and packing for market, the lack of refrigerated transport, the need for assistance to pay for fees and insurance, and the need for housing for those farmers wishing to sell at multiple markets.

It is clear that a huge paradigm and policy shift will be needed to make healthy food available to low-income communities of color and to support small farmers in their efforts to sustain their livelihoods. The Chicago Community Food Security Roundtable (CCFSR) is an important first step that manifests many of the aforementioned elements, including universities, governmental agencies, non-governmental agencies, and foundations, in an effort to create an emerging environmentally, socially, and economically just food environment for underserved communities. Much work is still ahead in developing healthy communities with sound food environments, but with collective participation and effort many beneficial changes lie ahead. As evidence is gathered regarding what is needed to ensure vibrant communities that are ecologically and economically sustainable, from field to table, the future looks bright for all.[2]

Notes

1. The ecological footprint is a tool used for calculating the amount of ecological resources required to support a human in a particular society. The ecological footprint of a person in the United States measured in hectares is 9.72. The global average is 2.03 hectares.

2. Maps and printed materials regarding the Chicago Food System Collaborative are available through Maureen Hellwig of the Policy and Research Action Group at Loyola University.

9

Autonomy, Equity, and Environmental Justice

Devon G. Peña

Sharing the Fate of Others?

The discourses of environmental justice (EJ), which rose to prominence in the late 1980s, transformed much of ecological thinking and politics in North America and other parts the world (Gottlieb 1993; Taylor 2000; Peña 2003a). EJ discourses challenged environmental thinkers to reconsider the meaning of basic concepts like nature, environment, ecosystem, wilderness, and biodiversity; they forced many to consider the role of race, ethnicity, national origin, class, gender, and culture in the framing of environmental history, environmental ethics, and ecological politics (Cronon 1996; see also Milton 1996). EJ discourses recentered the problematic of ecological politics in the constellation of cultural differences that construct variant epistemologies of nature (i.e., as natural resource, commodity, wilderness, ecosystem, and homeland). Recall Rama Guha's (1989) notion that the wilderness of the nature-appreciating eco-tourist from the First World is the homeland of the displaced native in the Third World. The local is denied access to the means of right livelihood, the collective resources of the land, and the memories of place that sustain her identity, and all because of unjust acts of brutal enclosure for the sake of "economic development" or "wilderness preservation." (See also Peña 1992.)

Many EJ theorists analyze ecological problems by relying on a social justice critique of environmental racism, which is defined as procedural, organizational, and geographic inequities expressed in persistent patterns of institutionalized discrimination in environmental policy making and decision making. The chief culprit behind discriminatory and disparate impacts is the state as embodied in the norms, values, administrative practices, and institutional structures of a socio-political system that emerged from and perpetuates unequal power relations on the basis of racial and other socially constructed differences. Some have criticized this stance for obscuring the effects of the economic system as a factor that limits the prospects for ecological democracy as mediated through the state (Foster 1994, 1998). This view draws attention to the limits of liberal reform-oriented social movements. Such limits result because social movements accommodate their demands within the existing regulatory regime (Levidow 1992: 117–18; Peña 1997: 306–8; Faber 1998: 1–17). Yet EJ discourses have also produced critiques of capitalism. "The refusal to separate the struggle for the environment from issues of social justice has made the environmental justice movement sharply critical of the history and logic of capitalism." (Foster 1994: 138)

EJ theory is also criticized for using simplistic and commonsensical concepts of racism. Researchers often fail to account for nuances in the socio-spatial structuring of racial and class privileges. Laura Pulido (2000) suggests that white "spatial privilege" extends beyond the usual list of disproportionate risks and impacts associated with "toxic racism," the unwanted and harmful land uses that are imposed on communities of color everywhere. White spatial privilege is also structured through a wide range of complex processes that may include changing legal frameworks of property law, which transform patterns of land tenure and access to "natural resources." One example of racialized restructuring of spatial power unfolded during the 1890s at the time of the establishment of the federal forest and national park systems (Peña and Martínez 1998; Martínez 2002). The law rationalized private and public enclosure of the common lands of people of Mexican origin after the Supreme Court, in the infamous *US v. Sandoval* decision, rejected the communitary forms of property of the post-conquest Southwest. The consequences of these unjust enclosures reverberate through the present in the form of an intense Chicano land rights movement that has come to play a major role in environmental justice politics across the region (Ebright 1994; Pulido 1996; Peña 1998; Hicks and Peña 2003).

The structuring of white spatial privilege may also involve distinct land and water use politics articulated by the economic interests of a new "post-industrial" economy that is based on "amenity industries." The new economy is presumed "sustainable" because it allegedly involves "non-extractive" activities. Instead of the old destructive industries of mining, logging, and commercial ranching, the new economy is built on service industries that cater to a growing mass of "aficionados" of cultural and natural diversity as objects of amusement, consumption, and appreciation. The rise of "nature-culture amenity industries" brought about significant changes in rural and urban communities by inducing economic and political displacements associated with the growing markets for second homes, outdoor recreation, tourism, and urban "renewal." Of course, all this is directly tied to the rise of a global economy based on ski resorts, dude ranches, art galleries, museums, and the "generalized elsewhere" associated with "gentrification." This involves the construction of "privileged spaces" for the consumption of "exotic" locales, cultures, and nature as "spectacles" (Rodriguez 1987, 1989, 1994; Peña 1992, 1998, 2003a,c). These examples clearly extend and modify the conventional concept of environmental racism by departing from the main tropes of "toxic racism" to embrace the study of "exoticist" strategies that restructure racial privilege through the socio-spatial organization of places. (See also Soja 1997.)

In this way, EJ discourses are expanding beyond the more limited scope of earlier research and a focus on the racialized politics of environmental risk assessment. More recent work involves case studies of communities struggling for equitable access to and participation in the co-management of the environmental conditions in place (Pulido 1996, 1998; Peña and Martínez 1998: 168–72; Bullard, Johnson, and Torres 2000; Mutz, Bryner, and Kenney 2002; Hicks and Peña 2003). Other scholars (e.g., Boyce and Shelly 2003) have focused on EJ struggles that rely on community-based "asset-building strategies" to mobilize environmental assets (natural capital) or increase their control by communities of color. Some researchers have documented the agroecological landscape-shaping practices of "keystone" communities, the sustainable local cultures that generate a wide range of ecosystem and economic base services (Peña 1999, 2003b; Hicks and Peña 2003). These studies focus attention on the forms of ecosystem management that are "autochthonous"—that is, locally generated or emerging from place. Agroecologists and ethnoecologists, in particular, are revaluing the environmental wealth and ecological services produced by the livelihood practices, land ethics, and social organization of place-based communities (Peña and Martinez 1998; Peña 1999; Peña 2003b; Hicks and Peña 2003).

Despite these divergent and highly interdisciplinary theoretical developments, the "equity paradigm" continues to function as the "master frame" in EJ discourses. In their recent book *Just Sustainabilities*, Julian Agyeman, Robert Bullard, and Bob Evans reiterate this commitment to a focus on the equity-environment link:

> Our usage of the term 'justice' is a direct consequence of our concern to understand 'environmental justice', and we need to emphasize that our principal focus here is upon questions of equity and equality, as opposed to social justice. This is not to underplay the importance of debates around justice, but simply to recognize the inextricable equity-environment link. (2003: 324)

Agyeman and his colleagues explicitly state their intent to not systematically interrogate the underlying political ethics of EJ (ibid.: 3). However, it is my contention that the "foundational" ethics of EJ discourses must not be left unexamined. The ethics articulated by the EJ equity paradigm involve a faintly acknowledged "meta-frame" that derives from the liberal paradigm of justice. Critical interrogation of the political values and ideological presuppositions underlying liberal social justice ethics will help clarify how these normative structures inform and limit the nature of theoretical thought in EJ discourses. This critique has significant strategic implications for future best practice frontiers and organizational forms in the environmental justice movement (EJM).

In fairness to *Just Sustainabilities*, it includes a chapter by Andrew Dobson (2003) that initiates a deeper examination of the compatibility of social justice and environmental sustainability ethics. Dobson has "come to the reluctant conclusion that social justice and environmental sustainability are not always compatible objectives" (ibid.: 83). This chapter follows a different path because I am not convinced of the merits of a project seeking to reconcile environmental sustainability and distributive social justice ethics because such a theoretical program may be inherently ethnocentric in assuming rational individuals can play equally in determining the definition and the distribution of needs. My concern is more focused on exploring the distinction between equity and autonomy.

Ernest Partridge explains the liberal concept of justice by noting that "in a Rawlsian society, justice requires that to some degree, each member of society 'shares the fate' of the others, while, at the same time, the freedom, dignity and autonomy of each individual is scrupulously respected" (1996: 4). This notion that we "share the fate" of others is evident in EJ discourses. It is clearly illustrated by movement advocacy of ethical and strategic positions that, for the sake of justice, demand that environmental risks and benefits be equitably distributed. These ideals of distributive justice (qua shared fate) are also evident in the oft-repeated claim that ecological sustainability is only possible if accompanied by social justice (qua racial equality) in the policy-making and decision-making processes of environmental governance and regulation (Agyeman, Bullard, and Evans 2003: 324–29). (For a challenge to this claim, see the chapter by Cheryl Margoluis in the present volume.)

The Principles of Environmental Justice (PEJ) insist that the problem of shared fate is ultimately not about equality (of opportunity or result). Instead, the deeper problem involves the elaboration of pathways to "just sustainabilities" (Agyeman, Bullard, and Evans 2003).[1] It is not consistent with EJ ethics that we settle for an uncertain shared fate, if all that means is that ultimately everyone gets an equal part of the same rotten carcinogenic pie (Peña 1998). This apparent incommensurability of liberal and environmental justice values compels further reflection on the limits and contradictions of equity-based theories of EJ and exploration of the prospects for a theoretical project focused on autonomy instead of equity.

Why autonomy? A focus on autonomy presents a far wider range of issues and problems for EJ theory and politics. The problematic of autonomy relates questions of justice and sustainability back to the contested realm of discursive politics.[2] To be sure, contested discourses unfold in the context of dominant politico-administrative and legal regimes, but the extended repertoire of institutional practices of subaltern groups often involves the assertion of communitary rights whenever bounded communities successfully negotiate and legitimize their claims to organize their space according to the lexicon of the local culture and its norms of self-governance in place (Spiertz 1998).

The Rawlsian paradigm conceptualizes autonomy a priori as a universal value because it is the preferred "natural" state for the existence of the "individual rational self" as sole political actor and subject of the fundamental right to exercise freedoms (Rawls 1971, 1993). But political liberalism misconstrues the narrowly constructed utilitarian interests of a historically situated, socially constituted, and singularly egotistic class of social actors to be the universal norm for the free association of individuals in civil society. It mistakenly constrains "rightful agency" by placing limits on the distribution of rights and freedoms since these are exclusively allocated to abstract individuals rather than specifically located groups or communities. The logic of this rationalist system of "neutral" and "objective" positive law privileges individual utilitarian rights as the singularly significant precondition for the attainment of a state of justice.[3]

Rawlsian ethics privilege a specific class of propertied interests to impose a restrictive definition of autonomy as a state enjoyed exclusively by abstract individuals. Through logical development, this has meant that the legal order is a "skewed Rawlsian" universe because the most fundamental form of individual freedom and autonomy is ultimately reduced to that which has inscribed power over space under the right to own private property free of interference by the state and other free individuals. Significantly, this serves as an ideological rationale for the most practicable elaboration of the power to exploit the natural and social conditions that sustain what Marx called our "species being." (See the discussion of Marx and Harvey below.) It also partly accounts for liberalism's failure to effectively rationalize or "governmentalize" the "second contradiction of capitalism" (cf. O'Connor 1991). The globalization of neoliberal models is an expression of this tendency to privilege private property rights over other forms of social and environmental wealth including those controlled by Third World and other "marginal" or "subaltern" communities (Pulido 1996: 3–56; 191–211; cf. Martínez-Alier 1999 and Guha 2000).

The concept of autonomy should not be reduced to the anthropocentric iterations of liberal individualist-rationalist discourse. There are alternative epistemologies (systems of local knowledge) with their own perspectives on autonomy, which they derive from autochthonous sources. These alternative epistemologies have been widely documented and are especially evident in the work of anthropologically grounded legal pluralists (e.g., Spiertz 1998) and environmental anthropologists (e.g., Berkes and Folke 2000; Peña 2005). Some of this research shows that existing legitimate forms of customary law and practice are based on a prior commitment of individual rights holders to a system of mutual reliance interests which the individual cannot simply reject, ignore, or unilaterally modify (Hicks and Peña 2003; Peña 2003d). This means that agency has, in an often dialectically interlaced manner, individual and collective iterations. The commitment of local stakeholders to mutual reliance interests embedded in a network of shared ownership rights to common pool resources (CPRs) is one significant example of the "communitary" (as opposed to individualist) basis of autonomy (Esteva and Prakash 1999; Guha 2000; Hicks and Peña 2003).

Gustavo Esteva (1997) relates the story of an intervention by a Yaqui elder at the third meeting in 1995 of the National Plural Indigenous Assembly for Autonomy (ANIPA), a grassroots organization that is part of a nationwide movement in Mexico for indigenous autonomy that emerged in the aftermath of the Zapatista uprising. The Yaqui elder called for respect of the indigenous worldview and the values it places not on individual rights and freedom but on the self-determination of right livelihoods by indigenous communities in place. Zapatista concepts of local autonomy made their appearance in the global discourse on "democracy" in 1994 with the "First Declaration from the Lacandon Jungle," wherein the indigenous rebels renounced the nation-state without falling into the myth of globalization:

By rooting themselves in their local spaces and weaving webs of solidarity with others like them,[4] [the Zapatistas] are effectively applying the necessary antidote for the "Global Project," local autonomy. . . . *Their claims are no longer concentrated in demanding that the state meet their needs. Instead, their quests for liberation are defined by exercising their freedoms.* . . . People are giving to autonomy the specific meaning appropriate for their localized contexts and concerns. (Esteva and Prakash 1999: 41–42; emphasis added)

An underlying problem with equity-based EJ theory is a deep yet largely unquestioned commitment to the "master's tools." EJ equity theory uncritically engages the politics of regulation without interrogating how the state seeks to restrict agency by imposing a presumably neutral technical rationality on political ecological discourse and risk assessment.[5] Politically, this has meant that social movements ultimately limit their strategies to pressuring the state to administer justice by promoting equality and equity. But this effort occurs in a legal and politico-administrative "universe" that privileges interests derived from the norms of the individualist-rationalist project.

In contrast, the theory of autonomy is grounded in the actual struggles, discursive practices, and knowledge systems of grassroots communities of resistance. These struggles and practices most often revolve around communitary asset-building strategies that promote collective use of a community's social, cultural, financial, and ecological capital. Civic associations, kinship groups, and informal exchange networks, common pool resource management councils, mutual aid and self-help institutions, and the myriad forms of cooperative labor are the autochthonous resources generated and mobilized (outside the market and state) by the "submerged networks" of everyday life in their struggle for autonomy.[6] Local knowledge, including "traditional environmental knowledge" (TEK), is an important resource for the exercise of such communitary freedoms (cf. Hunn 1999). The self-organization of autochthonous ecosystem management practices and institutions is thus an effective antidote to an anemic strategy that meekly accepts the limits imposed on social movements by states and other bureaucratic structures committed to the language games of imposed modernity, market-steered values, and an anti-ecological rationality.

Local knowledge and other communitary assets are constantly mobilized by communities engaged in struggles to restore and protect local spaces in rural and urban places and sustain right livelihoods against the intrusive vagaries of the globalizing market and its "meta-state" of the World Trade Organization (WTO).[7] As Subcomandante Marcos has written: "We live now with the firm hope of finding the long peace in open spaces." This chapter presents a critical reading of the concept of autonomy in EJ theoretical discourses and initiates discussion of an alternative approach that deconstructs contrasting paradigms of "participatory environmental management."[8]

The relevance of theories of autonomy to the EJM is evident in the growing strategic significance of community asset-building strategies that guide the work of many movement organizations and networks. EJ organizing campaigns have increasingly embraced community asset-building strategies in their search for a just sustainability. Examples include campaigns for sustainable agriculture and local food security through the establishment of farm-worker-owned and self-managed producer cooperatives, urban community gardens, and community-supported agriculture (CSA) projects that link low-income inner city people of color, and especially the elderly and youth, to farmers and farm workers of color and other progressive allies.

Another example is the acequia, an institution of the Upper Rio Grande. The acequia is a gravity-driven, snow-melt dependent, earthen-work irrigation ditch. Collectively maintained and democratically managed, it is used by traditional (mainly Chicano) farmers in Colorado, New Mexico, and other parts of the Southwest. The acequia has been celebrated as a sustainable irrigation technology appropriate to conditions in arid and semi-arid life zones. It is also widely celebrated as one of the oldest institutions of local self-government (the irrigation municipality); Jose Rivera calls the acequia a "water democracy," a reference to the "one farmer, one vote" rule underlying the management of water use and irrigation practices in these civic associations (Rivera 1998; Peña 1998; Hicks and Peña 2003). The persistence of the acequia as a sustainable technology and as an institution of local self-government is thus a tribute the power of local place-based cultures as sources of autonomy. This means autonomy is not just a lofty goal for the future; it may very well be part of our cultural heritage. Remembering and restoring the heritage of local self-governance may well become an important objective of the EJM.

Theorizing the "Open Spaces" of Autonomy

The theorizing of autonomy in EJ discourses has remained largely limited to discussions of concepts of Native American "sovereignty" and what is vaguely termed "self-determination" for people of color. (See, e.g., Rechtschaffen and Gauna 2002: 421–60.) In a significant synthesis of the EJ paradigm, Dorceta Taylor (2000) explicitly conceptualizes autonomy as a "component value" that is directly derivative from the Principles of Environmental Justice. Taylor frames this theoretical project by listing autonomy as a subset issue in a "very complex ideological package or coherent body of thought." Autonomy is listed as the third in a set of six issues that she outlines as what I take to be the main "submerged frames" of the PEJ (ibid.: 540). Taylor's outline seems to present autonomy as a concept grounded in a pluriverse of culturally diverse communities and identifies the need to respect each other's belief systems about the natural world as the key to the successful assertion of autonomy and self-determination.

Taylor proposes that autonomy is "a major component of environmental justice" and this principally involves "recognizing treaties and the legal relations between native peoples and the US government" (ibid.: 542). A related theme is "self-determination," which "refers to the rights of people

of color to determine their own political, economic, and cultural futures."
For Taylor this involves "reflection and healing." The PEJ "respect . . . cultural diversity" and appreciate "a variety of belief systems that relate to the
natural world." In the absence of mutual respect "some cultures and peoples are deemed superior and others inferior" and this often "leads to asymmetrical power relations and to the domination, destruction, and/or
elimination of inferior cultures by dominant ones" (ibid.). This is an important contribution, but Taylor does not ground these principles in spatial
and historical contexts. Taylor's discussion of autonomy is problematic in
several ways:

1. It presents historically vague and romanticized notions of sovereignty,
self-determination and autonomy.

2. It conflates causes for effects by assuming that ideology produces power;
i.e., asymmetrical power relations are by-products of the imposition of
dominant ideologies of cultural superiority and inferiority.

3. It overlooks how autonomy is conditioned by the degree to which independent groups in civil society can organize economic activities (production and consumption) on the basis of customary law, access to CPRs, and
workers' control of the labor process.

4. It reproduces the liberal language games of universal individual rights
and freedoms in framing the concept of "environmental self-determination" and fails to recognize place-based forms of communitary autonomy
for the assertion of mutual reliance interests instead of individual utilitarian interests.

5. It assumes that mutual respect for cultural differences in beliefs about
nature is a sufficient basis for "environmental self-determination'—i.e., a
genuinely multicultural environmental ethics will lead to autonomy in the
environmental management of places.

Re point 1: General declarations in support of "native sovereignty" and
"self-determination" are not very helpful because these concepts have multiple, shifting, and contradictory meanings. We must situate these concepts
in their historical and spatial context. In the United States, the legally extant
concept of sovereignty was largely a creation and extension of Western colo-
nialist discourses. Sovereignty was "invented" in the hostile encounter with
native civilizations, which required some accounting for the indigenous rep-

resentatives that could serve as legitimate actors endowed with the authority to negotiate treaties and other agreements in time of war and other conflicts. Article 1, Section 8 of the US Constitution clearly defines Native American sovereignty in this narrowly construed and self-serving manner (Pevar 1992). However, early federal case law established that native sovereignty involves much more than the ability for "tribal nations" to negotiate and sign treaties. For example, the 1831 *Worcester v. Georgia* ruling upheld the constitutionality of the "government-to-government" relationship between American Indian tribal nations and the US government. The courts also ruled that, by law, Indian nations are "distinct, independent political communities possessing and exercising the power of self-government" (Waller and Yellow Bird n.d.: 6, citing the *Worcester v. Georgia* decision).

The most significant authority associated with Native sovereignty is the principle of local self-governance. Waller and Yellow Bird (ibid.) observe that "Sovereign Indigenous Nations have inherent powers of self-government. They have the right to make, pass, and enforce laws." Waller and Yellow Bird suggest that this power is uniquely reserved to Native Americans, implying that other subjugated and colonized communities do not enjoy this type of legal (law-making) authority. However, there are many different types of communities and civic associations in the United States, not all of them Native American, that have attained or continue to maintain variant forms of political authority for vigorous local self-governance. While the forms of Native American sovereignty are unique, the extension of principles of autonomy through diverse institutional forms of self-determination applies rather broadly to many different kinds of communities and civic associations. Examples include irrigation municipalities (like the aforementioned acequias), traditional use area councils and land use planning councils, community gardens, community-supported agriculture, artisan and producer cooperatives, and mutual aid societies.[9]

It is difficult enough that dominant groups perpetuate and impose racialized identities on "subjugated natives" to justify the extension and hegemony of the individualist-rationalist project. More difficult dilemmas are posed when our own voices reproduce racialized and essentialist identity constructs. Kimberly TallBear (2001: 3-4) offers a brilliant analysis of this complex problem and articulates a clear vision of the implications this has for the theory of autonomy, which she defines as a form of "self-determined political and cultural development":

While tribal governance today measures degrees of blood, the work of some of our foremost activists, writers, and scholars uses another mechanism to racialise tribal peoples. Tribal identity is often characterized in . . . simplistic, traditionalist rhetoric. . . . Indian authenticity is often depicted as rooted in vague spiritual connections to nature.

In other words, activist discourse itself can embrace racialized beliefs about authenticity. This is evident in the criticism of elected tribal governments in the United States for not being "traditional" enough. John Gledhill (2000: 14) notes that "the modern politics of ethnicity frequently takes the form of the invention and reification of 'tradition.'"

TallBear (2001: 4) notes how traditionalists often assume that tribal governments "do not legitimately possess governing authority." They characterize tribal governments as suffering from "widespread corruption" and guilty "of selling out to . . . an American capitalist dream . . . completely neglecting tribal cultural practices, and . . . not caring for the land." However, TallBear states that many tribal governments find it difficult to rise to the challenge of "applying cultural values and philosophies to contemporary governance, economic development, and institution building."

The political institutions imposed on native communities are problematic because historical events disrupted the efficacy and continued evolution of self-governance. Few communities can rise to the level of organizing knowledge and political and legal resources to restore the governance structures that existed prior to 1934. It is easy to demand respect for traditional governance. It is more difficult, given the sustained deleterious impacts of the 1934 Indian Reorganization Act, to restore and support the continued evolution of cultural and political institutions grounded in autochthonous customary law and practice.

Exactly what EJ discourses mean by appealing to sovereignty and self-determination is not at all clear then. TallBear notes that these concepts are not very useful if they remain a clever set of slogans and dead letters articulated by organic intellectuals while they drift from one conference on globalization to the next. This may seem like a cruel judgment, but the question of autonomy demands a more exacting view of what it means to be free in a "made" place.

Re point 2: Asymmetrical power relations are not effects of the imposition of dominant ideologies of cultural superiority and inferiority. The opposite proposition seems more plausible: Ideologies, whatever their guises and aims, are simply expressions and by-products of established and shifting unequal power relations, even when these function to extend, reproduce, and rationalize the forms of domination and resistance, which is to say oppressive and emancipatory discourses (Rosaldo 1989; Eagleton 1991). While dominant racializing ideologies are a fundamental expression of unequal power, essentialist constructs are also evident in the resistance discourses of "alterity." (An example is Bonfil Batalla 1996; cf. Gledhill 2000.) The imposition of ideologies that rationalize hierarchical racial differences (and thus "superior" and "inferior" cultures) is a function of power and not the other way around.

One reason that autonomous models of social movement mobilization must be more thoroughly evaluated is because they may provide alternative frameworks for the engagement of communities of resistance with the ideological and political economic forces that structure these power relations. In practice, local autonomy means that communitary interests have sufficient authoritative force to override asymmetrical power structures whenever and wherever place-based imperatives and norms hold sway. A critical aspect of this highly contested process involves "legitimation games" and this simply means that communities have to struggle with attaining ecological legitimacy in order to act "lawfully" to assert autochthonous norms and customary practices in organizing environmental management practices in place (Pulido 1996; Peña 1998).

Re point 3: Uneven patterns of "development" are a consequence of inequitable power structures that encapsulate the organization of economic activities across space. This "objective condition" of the existing capitalist socio-spatial organization of "species-being" presents both daunting challenges and ambiguous opportunities for the pursuit of localized autonomy. If the "spaces of hope" outlined by David Harvey (2000) have any relevance to these matters it is mainly because of how they illustrate the point that the most fundamental problem of power is ultimately related to struggles over the definition and control of the natural and social conditions under which individuals and communities organize production and consumption. Unabashedly drawing on Marx, Harvey proposes that we again recognize and revalue the old historical or dialectical materialist idea that "the role of transformative activity—human labour—is fundamental to our species being" (1999: 134), and this has profound consequences for the quality of human-environment relations.[10] Harvey is suggesting that anthropogenesis is an inescapable quality of our species being, but he also seems to be suggesting a sensible strategy to overcome rampant "culture-nature dualism," especially when compared to the alternative posed by the liberal individualist-rationalist dream of freedom as the right to advance the exploitation of the natural and social conditions of our species-being under the rule of law of the commodity-form.

Autonomy may be conditioned by the degree to which communities can organize production and consumption within the framework of place-specific norms of self-governance. In other words, for autonomists the fundamental problem of power is not so much about challenging racialized ideological constructs that privilege one culture over others. It is instead about the ability of local cultures to assert control over their own space (and places) by exercising freedoms to organize production and consumption in sustainable and equitable patterns that derive from self-generated ecologically and culturally appropriate norms. I believe this requires serious and concerted study of legal pluralism by EJ theorists, especially in the context of discourses on "participatory environmental management." It is not enough to celebrate respect for diverse cultural belief systems about nature. The theory of autonomy encourages us to pursue strategies to account for the criteria we might use to evaluate and privilege the claims articulated by place-bound cultures and communities. (See the discussion of item 5 below.)

Re point 4: Taylor proposes that EJ ethics seek recognition of the right to "environmental self-determination of all people." This includes the idea that people have a right to be free from "human experimentation and ecological destruction." They have rights to clean air, land, water, and food. EJ also affirms workplace rights—"the right to work in a clean and safe environment" (2000: 541). Taylor further clarifies the concept of environmental self-determination by adding it to a list of existing human rights (i.e., the individual freedoms outlined in the Bill of Rights). This elaboration celebrates individual rights and freedoms, albeit within a framework that recognizes cultural diversity. In the end, Taylor relies on individual "measures" of autonomy such as rights to "simple lifestyles" and "job satisfaction" as indicators of environmental self-determination (ibid.: 543).

This formulation overlooks the major structural barriers to the attainment of environmental self-determination, not the least of which is the dynamic flux in the degree to which communities are able to negotiate with legal regimes to create spaces where they can organize social and economic activities in a manner consistent with autochthonous norms and values (Spiertz 1998; Peña 2003d). Inevitably, this process involves highly contested legitimation games between dominant and subaltern discourses. The result is a dynamic (shifting) set of politico-legal administrative regimes in place. The myriad encounters between place-bounded communities and the intrusive social forces of the globalizing meta-state and market are illustrative of such dynamic and ambiguous relations of power. Self-determination needs to be reconceptualized with an eye toward specifying the hundreds and thousands of strategies that local communities use to assert control over the socio-spatial organization of economic activities and their inevitable (but not necessarily harmful) anthropogenic effects.

The PEJ may actually embrace worker control over the processes that affect environmental quality in the workplace and surrounding locales (Peña 1997). It is simply not enough to demand a right to clean and safe workplaces or job satisfaction, if the power structures of capitalist managerial authority in the labor process are actually left unchallenged. The theory of autonomy requires more than an allusion to the language of rights and freedoms, even if these involve the pursuit of worthy practices like "simple lifestyles" or workplace organizations that nurture "job satisfaction." Autonomy means that the social actors have created a social field of interrelationships in which the power to control the conditions of production and reproduction is diffused (or horizontally distributed) and self-generated by the participants-in-place. This means power is not so much a "thing" to be possessed or some object to be equally distributed. Instead, it is largely a discursive and relational process through which multiple and shifting subjectivities are created, negotiated, and restructured (Foucault 1977; Braun and Castree 1998).

Re point 5: Is mutual respect for cultural differences in beliefs about nature a sufficient basis for the articulation of environmental self-determination, as Taylor suggests? Respect and celebration of diverse cultural belief systems about the natural world present a comfortable relativist position. But how can we respect that which remains largely unknown or is often subject to "systematically distorted communication"? Autonomy-based EJ theory can propose a clearer set of organizational principles and criteria to guide the evaluation of legitimation processes in eco-ethical discourses. An important aspect of this is the previously mentioned role of local knowledge, and especially TEK. Taylor's inadvertent adherence to unacknowledged Rawlsian political ethics privileges universal individual rights and freedoms and limits the ability for EJ theory to clarify the legitimacy of communitary rights and knowledge claims. The theory of autonomy proposes that we focus on place-specific forms of communitary control of environmental governance that derive from the persistence of local customary law and practice.

Legal pluralism provides a framework to accomplish this degree of localized specificity by proposing a set of ethnographic and ethnohistorical methods and materials for the comparative study of the social significance of the law in culturally diverse societies (Griffiths 1986; Merry 1988; VanderLinden 1989). Legal pluralism challenges the idea that the only meaningful framework for the study of law is that which pertains to the formal sphere of institutional or "lawyer's law" (Spiertz 1998: 8–10). According to legal pluralists, "besides the norms of state agencies and legal science, versions of religious [and other customary] law, or traditions and various forms of self-regulation may also be part of the local legal universe" (ibid.: 10). Legal pluralists insist on starting with peoples' daily lived experience so we can observe how various sets of normative systems become intertwined in the local processes of social ordering (ibid.: 11; see also Benda-Beckmann 1995). This allows us to locate and analyze "people's daily experience regarding their normative environment, with all its ambiguity, variation, and contradiction" (Spiertz 1998: 12).

EJ and Collaborative Environmental Management

A good place to start this type of discussion is championed by some political ecologists and environmental anthropologists. This involves critiques of divergent models of "participatory environmental management." Michael Redclift early on proposed that we deconstruct two important variants: One is the model of top-down "environmental managerialism" (EM) and a second is a "bottom-up" model for place-based "collaborative environmental management" (CEM). (See Redclift 1987, especially chapter 7.) These are outlined in table 1, which summarizes the organizational principles and value orientations for the comparison of variant strategies of participatory management. EM is the dominant form, and it privileges the expert knowledge of development planners and environmental scientists. In contrast, CEM privileges local knowledge or TEK. A fundamental difference between these two is in the definition of the governance structure of co-participation: The EM model limits local participation to "needs identification" in project scoping and design; it also privileges implementation of project objectives by planning experts. The CEM model privileges local mobilizing around "self-identified needs" (self-valorization) and is based on organizational collaboration with external allies in project scoping, design, and implementation.

These differences are more than a simple matter of semantics and pose serious questions that go to the core assumptions of liberal approaches to environmental planning and management. In the conventional managerialist paradigm, environmental planners impose land use planning techniques on environmental users to define their space; the same applies in the imposition of expert control over environmental risk analysis. The planners engage in technology appraisal to define the production (or mitigation) system for the targeted users. The planners assume the a priori legitimacy of structural policies to define for users their market and state links (Redclift 1987: 158).

In the grassroots collaborative paradigm, environmental users define the geographical and cultural boundaries of place to establish the parameters of land-use (and related) planning processes. Indigenous knowledge and patterns of ecological adaptation define the process of technology appraisal, and CEM rejects externally imposed and technically inappropriate methods. An underlying assumption of CEM is that household livelihood requirements define the basic structural policies; again, market-steered and state-defined imperatives assumed by hierarchical managerialism are rigorously rejected. The heart of the matter is that an increasing number of local communities are challenging the privileges accorded expert planners and their assumptions. They are elaborating—often in collaboration with the NGO sector—thousands of autonomous (non-state-sponsored) projects to mobilize resources to implement their own initiatives in restoration ecology, cultural resource and heritage landscape management, community-based

Table 1
Organizational principles in environmental planning and management (extrapolated from figure 7.2 of Redclift 1987).

	Environmental managerialism	Collaborative environmental management
Source of knowledge	Experts; development planners	Local communities; indigenous people
Knowledge discourse	Science (ecosystem management)	Ethnoscience (ethnoecology)
Institutional context of decision making	State agencies, NGOs, planning groups	Local CBOs, family units, clan, tribe
Problem definition	Etic-driven	Emic-driven
Structure of participation	Local participation in needs identification and project design; implementation by experts	Local mobilizing around self-identified needs and priorities; collaboration with external allies in local implementation
Problem characterization	Internal problems; cultural, social, or economic deficiencies	External forces impinging on internal dynamics (colonialism, modernization)
Economic resources	External (imported); aid programs	Internal; local natural, social, and cultural assets
Relationship to market	Open; global and national market linkages (allows for commodification, patenting)	Closed or limited; local and regional market linkages (restricts biopiracy and patenting)
Technological inputs	External (transfers from developed nations)	Internal; local technical assets; perhaps some smaller-scale appropriate technology transfers (need to recognize South-North technology transfers)
Legal framework	Global development regimes; multilateral institutions; UNCED paradigm	Sovereignty of local institutions and autonomy of local customary codes and practices (political ecology paradigm)
Property regime	Private and public domains; common heritage of humanity (e.g. MAB reserves)	Locally owned and self-managed common pool regimes (homeland commons)

Table 1
(continued)

	Environmental managerialism	Collaborative environmental management
Principal objectives	Biodiversity conservation; environmental protection; reducing impact of poverty on ecosystem degradation	Conservation of material basis of local livelihoods; reducing inequities related to colonialist and modernist domination of access to natural conditions of production
Access	Open, public access	Closed or limited public access

economic development, and other similar grassroots-oriented programs (see, e.g., Ghai and Vivian 1992; Peet and Watts 1996; Bryant and Bailey 1997; Peña 1997; Burger et al. 2001). To move beyond clichés and slogans, EJ discourses must develop a similar set of evaluative criteria to ascertain the legitimacy of claims and counter-claims with respect to the organizational values that frame localized (rural or urban) environmental management discourses and planning processes and their outcomes.

It may be tempting to argue that EJ discourses are bifurcating into two distinct political philosophies, one focused on equity and the other on autonomy. We can differentiate between the critique of environmental racism (in the equity discourse) and the search for what I will call "autonomous sustainabilities" (in the emergent autonomy discourse). However, there are bountiful examples that illustrate how place-based communities often struggle to address both concerns: Through equity-based struggles, they address threats posed to their communal welfare by the disparate impacts of ecological degradation; by searching for local autonomy, they seek to sustain the powers of self-governance under customary law and to use TEK as a framework for ecological restoration and ecosystem management in their locale.

These kinds of place-based practices and environmental rationalities constitute a form of "autonomous sustainability," because they shift our emphasis from the reactive strategies of an equity-based struggle against the disparate impacts of environmental racism toward a focus on autonomy-based struggles for the sustenance of right livelihoods through self-governance of environmental management in local places. The future prospects for "environmental self-determination," I believe, lie in the direction of the exploration of autonomy, not in a continued and one-dimensional allegiance to the "heroic" but ill-fated struggle against toxic racism and its rampant inequalities of place and power. I plan to explore the concept of autonomy further, elaborate how autonomous sustainabilities are self-organized in other places, and outline strategies for more effective challenges to neoliberal logic in the political ecology of production and consumption in this era of globalized spaces.[11]

Notes

1. Refer to Principles of Environmental Justice 6, 7, 8, and 14. Principle 14 poses a deeper critique in calling for opposing the "destructive operations of multinational corporations." For critical studies on the sustainable development discourse, see Redclift 1987; *Ecologist* 1993; Escobar 1994; Peet and Watts 1996; Bryant and Bailey 1997.

2. My use of the concept of "discursive politics" refers to contested encounters between political actors articulating variant ideologies in struggles over "legitimation" of divergent worldviews.

3. Of course, it may be too much to claim such an impact of Rawlsian social justice ethics on the actual existing political, normative, and legal order.

4. This idea that the Zapatistas articulated a local struggle by weaving global webs of solidarity with "others like them" has been widely noted (Castells 1997; Nash 2001, and Peña 2003c), but I am also interested in the proliferation of autonomous communities in all the indigenous regions of Mexico and the southwestern US.

5. Here I will not address the relevant debate between Habermas and Rawls over the related issue of individual abstract norms versus community specific norms, but the distinction is one I make in agreement with Habermas; see Habermas 1996.

6. For more on the theory of collective identity in social movements and the role of submerged networks of everyday life, see Melucci 1989.

7. We might conceptualize the World Trade Organization as a type of "meta-state," or at any rate as a supra-national bureaucratic formation that exists to impose discipline, command, and control structures that serve the self-regulation ends of corporate global reach across a pluriverse of nation-states. See Sassen 1998; Hoogvelt 1997.

8. In a related work (Peña 2003d), I initiate the study of the "open spaces" of autonomy through an examination of the history and ecological politics of the acequia communities in south central Colorado's Rio Culebra watershed.

9. On Hispano "irrigation municipalities" as an example of autonomous self-management of a local watershed environment, see Hicks and Peña 2003 and Peña 2003d.

10. Harvey draws on Marx's elaborate "philosophical" conceptualization of the principles of political economy in the "Paris manuscripts" of 1844. See Marx 1964.

11. Latour (1998: 236, 237n2) notes the significant development in France of the 1992 water law and its requirement that "catchment of sensible rivers [is] to be represented in 'Commissions locales de l'eau,' which are a very original experiment in the French context since they aim in part to make politically visible the river's health and sustainable well-being."

10

Environmental Justice and the Legal System

Holly D. Gordon and Keith I. Harley

Advocates seeking environmental justice come in all shapes and sizes and include grassroots organizers, health care workers, government employees, and single mothers as well as attorneys. How significantly these groups of people have changed the American legal system can be evaluated using several criteria. First, are there viable legal theories with which to address allegations of environmental discrimination? Second, are environmental legal services available to the residents of affected communities? Third, are the US Environmental Protection Agency and its state counterparts developing meaningful strategies to address environmental justice concerns?

Attempts to remedy allegations of environmental discrimination using theories arising under civil rights and environmental laws are ongoing and vigorous but have been largely unsuccessful. At the same time, environmental legal services are more available to affected communities, with attorneys applying public participation and citizen enforcement tools traditionally used in the mainstream environmental movement. Although some states have developed environmental justice initiatives, a lack of uniformity exists because of the US EPA's delay in issuing final guidance defining state responsibilities under Title VI of the Civil Rights Act of 1964.[1]

Does the Legal System Provide Meaningful Remedies for Environmental Discrimination under Either Civil Rights or Environmental Laws?

Environmental justice activists have pursued several legal avenues in attempting to remedy potential or existing environmental discrimination. The basis for most of these legal remedies begins with Title VI but has evolved to include other federal statutes, traditional environmental statutes, and potential new state laws. Title VI prohibits all programs and activities that receive federal funds, including the US EPA's state partners, from discriminating on the basis of race, color, or national origin.[2] Under the US EPA's regulations, recipients of EPA financial assistance are required to implement their programs and activities in a non-discriminatory manner.[3] Applicants for this assistance must also certify compliance with Title VI in order to be eligible for assistance.[4] As a practical matter, this requires the US EPA to enforce a standard provision in its grant agreements with its state-funded partners, in which states agree that they comply with all federal statutes relating to non-discrimination, including Title VI of the Civil Rights Act of 1964 .[5]

On February 11, 1994, against this backdrop, President Bill Clinton signed Executive Order 12898, "Federal Actions To Address Environmental Justice in Minority Populations and Low-Income Populations."[6] This order does not create a new legal remedy.[7] As an internal management tool of the Executive Branch, it directs federal agencies to design procedures that make achieving environmental justice part of their basic mission.[8] President Clinton explained that federal agencies have the responsibility to promote "nondiscrimination in federal programs substantially affecting human health and the environment."[9] Accordingly, agencies must take steps to address disproportionately high and adverse human health or environmental effects of their programs, policies, and activities on minority and low-income populations and federally recognized Indian tribes.[10]

In a memorandum issued contemporaneously with Executive Order 12898, the president "underscored certain provisions of existing law that can help ensure that all communities and persons across the nation live in a safe and healthful environment."[11] The memorandum emphasizes that Title VI of the Civil Rights Act of 1964 provides an opportunity for federal agencies to address environmental hazards in communities of color. This purpose is accomplished by ensuring compliance with the existing non-discrimination provisions in federal contracts with state agencies.

Advocates have attempted to use these non-discrimination provisions to remedy environmental injustice by suing in federal court or by filing an administrative action with the US EPA. In addition to these largely thwarted attempts, advocates are likely to turn to other legal methods to seek environmental justice, such as uncharted state law remedies and/or provisions of existing environmental statutes.

Private Legal Actions

Perhaps the most commonly recognized method to remedy discrimination is to file a lawsuit in federal court. For years, communities supported by the best and brightest environmental legal advocates have pursued private legal actions based on Title VI of the Civil Rights Act of 1964 and section 1983 of the United States Code. Despite their efforts to diversify the methods for advancing the environmental justice movement, traditional civil rights theories have generally not accommodated environmental discrimination claims.

A private legal action under Title VI to remedy environmental injustice generally consists of individuals or communities suing to enjoin state environmental agencies from issuing a permit that would allow a polluting facility to operate. Arising from evidence that polluting facilities are more frequently sited in communities with disproportionately high minority populations, private legal actions based on Title VI seem to offer a promising option for the environmental justice movement. Efforts to advance these legal claims, however, have encountered significant obstacles. Because of the knotty legal issues involved and the presence of strong industry groups, many such actions have turned into protracted struggles that have drained energy and resources. The growing presence of conservative judges has ultimately tipped the balance against the use of private legal actions for environmental justice claims.

A prime example of these legal battles arose recently when a community group in South Camden, New Jersey sued under Title VI alleging that the New Jersey Department of Environmental Protection (NJDEP) had wrongfully issued an operating permit to a cement processing facility.[12] The potential environmental injustice was abundantly clear: 91 percent of Camden's residents are persons of color; the facility would emit particulate matter, mercury, lead, manganese, nitrogen oxides, carbon monoxide, sulfur oxides, and volatile organic compounds; large trucks causing noise, vibrations, and increased traffic would come in and out of the community thousands of times per year; a disproportionately high rate of asthma already exists among community residents; and numerous other industrial facilities already exist in this neighborhood.[13] The question in this type of Title VI direct legal action, however, is not simply whether communities of color will be affected by adverse environmental impacts, but whether Title VI affords these individuals and communities the ability to obtain a remedy via this type of lawsuit in the first place.

The language of Title VI clearly allows for private persons to sue and obtain a remedy in federal court based on intentional discrimination.[14] However, in the environmental context, only a very limited set of circumstances would enable private persons to prove that the burdens of adverse environmental impacts occurred intentionally. In reality, most communities of color suffering from adverse environmental effects may be capable of proving disparate impact, but not intentional discrimination. In other words, communities can often prove that the siting and operation of a particular industrial facility will *result* in a significantly disproportionate amount of adverse environmental impacts in that community of color; however, proving that an industrial facility was placed in a particular community to intentionally *cause* discrimination is very difficult.

Unfortunately, the language of Title VI that was drafted by Congress does not explicitly denounce discrimination arising from disparate impact. The language only requires agencies receiving federal funds to implement regulations that effectively achieve the objectives of Title VI.[15] As a result of this directive, many federal agencies, including the US EPA, choose to implement regulations prohibiting discrimination based on disparate impact.[16] Since the ban on disparate impact discrimination comes from a federal agency rather than from Congress, courts have struggled to determine whether they can appropriately offer remedies to persons making claims of environmental injustice based on disparate impact as opposed to intentional discrimination.

In April 2001, environmental justice advocates appeared to have achieved a breakthrough when a lower federal court issued a decision in the *Camden* case to enjoin the cement processing facility from operating because it would likely result in disparate impact discrimination.[17] But the victory was short lived. Just five days after the favorable ruling in *Camden*, the Supreme Court handed down its decision in *Sandoval*, a non-environmental Title VI case.[18] In just one sweeping decision, the Supreme Court forever changed the legal landscape for the environmental justice movement by holding that private persons, such as the Camden community group, cannot bring an action to obtain a remedy under Title VI based on discrimination arising from disparate impact.[19] In a 5–4 decision, the

Supreme Court ruled that plaintiffs like the Camden residents would be held to a much more difficult standard, requiring them to plead and prove intentional discrimination.[20]

As a result of the *Sandoval* decision, the injunctive relief issued in *Camden* was effectively eliminated.[21] But the Camden community group and its legal advocates would not be dissuaded. Just weeks after the injunction was vacated, they alleged claims under §1983 in an attempt to revive the injunction against the facility.[22]

To succeed in a §1983 claim, adversely affected persons, such as the Camden community group, must sue a person, such as the Commissioner of the NJDEP, for violating a federal right, such as those found within Title VI.[23] As a threshold matter, courts differ as to whether regulations drafted by a federal agency, as opposed to statutes drafted by Congress, provide an appropriate basis for asserting a violation of a federal right under §1983.[24] Although Judge Stephen Orlofsky issued a second injunction based on the §1983 claim,[25] a majority of appellate court judges quickly vacated the injunction, finding that it was inappropriate to bar discrimination based on disparate impact under §1983 when the language prohibiting disparate impact does not appear explicitly in Title VI.[26]

After experiencing momentary success, the Camden community group ultimately failed in their efforts to use a private legal action alleging disparate impact discrimination to prevent the cement processing facility from operating. Although the Camden community group experienced some success when Judge Orlofsky agreed to hear claims alleging intentional discrimination in the siting of the facility,[27] the facility is still operating and polluting the community more than three years after the initial legal action. And the legal battle to enjoin the facility from operating continues.

Based on the Supreme Court's decision in *Sandoval*, persons seeking to remedy environmental injustice in a private legal action based on Title VI must prove intentional discrimination.[28] The likelihood of success for an environmental justice §1983 claim based on disparate impact discrimination is still unclear, but the situation is not promising. A majority of courts that have addressed this threshold issue came down against this type of legal claim.[29] Since the Supreme Court refused to review the *Camden* decision,[30] the door is still slightly ajar for disparate impact claims under §1983. However, even if the threshold issue is overcome, a §1983 action based on allegations of environmental injustice must overcome additional significant legal hurdles to succeed. In addition, as long as the Supreme Court retains a conservative majority regarding these issues, success at the federal level will likely be limited.

Despite these failures, the struggle to gain legal footing for adversely affected communities seeking to bring private legal actions has resulted in renewed vigor to continue pressing other avenues for addressing environmental injustice. Civil rights and environmental justice advocates have the opportunity to use new state law, rather than established federal law, as a means to achieving success in the courts. (See the chapter by Targ in this volume.) *Sandoval* and *Camden* are based on Title VI and §1983, both federal statutes. Since the Supreme Court closed the door to a Title VI private right of action based on disparate impact discrimination, Illinois and some other states are proposing state level legislation to close the gap left open by the *Sandoval* decision.[31]

Administrative Complaints Alleging Violations of Title VI

In 1993, in order to fulfill its responsibility to ensure non-discrimination in federally funded state programs, the US EPA's Office of Civil Rights began accepting complaints that federally funded programs discriminate on the grounds of race, color, or national origin, thus violating Title VI.

On first glance, the administrative complaint process appears to have several advantages over the alternative of filing a private legal action in federal district court, especially after *Sandoval*. In the context of environmental issues, an administrative complaint permits any person who believes he or she has been discriminated against by an organization or agency receiving US EPA financial assistance to file a complaint with the US EPA's Office of Civil Rights.[32] Perhaps most important, the US EPA's implementing regulations require only evidence of discriminatory effects, not of intentions.[33] Because states receive federal funding to administer federal environmental laws, states are subject to this Title VI analysis. The risk to a state is significant: If a claim is meritorious and the violation is not corrected, federal funding can be withdrawn.[34]

Activists seized the opportunity to remedy discrimination by state environmental agencies by filing administrative complaints with the US EPA's Office of Civil Rights. A recent survey prepared by the Office of Civil Rights indicates that 147 complaints against 30 states have been filed since 1993.[35] The vast majority of complaints seek redress for the discriminatory aspects of state permitting decisions; others complain of unfair public participation practices and inequitable enforcement of environmental laws.[36] Most complaints emerge from state decisions to issue permits to industrial facilities that will be new sources of pollutants, including landfills, power plants, chemical plants, transfer stations, incinerators, and hazardous waste treatment and disposal facilities.[37] In several cases, the complainants are represented by public-interest attorneys, including attorneys from the Sugar Law Center in Michigan, the Public Interest Law Center of Philadelphia, the Sierra Club, the California Rural Legal Assistance Foundation, and several local law clinics and private attorneys.[38]

After 10 years of receiving, evaluating, and investigating complaints, the US EPA has never made a formal finding that a federally funded entity has violated Title VI, nor has the US EPA imposed a sanction of any kind against any entity. The US EPA's administration of the complaint process suggests it will never make a formal finding of a Title VI violation, but that it will use this process from time to time to coerce federally funded entities into choosing to implement reforms.

There are several reasons for the US EPA's failure to identify a single act of discrimination in the administration of environmental programs by any federally funded entity. First, the EPA has not decided what constitutes environmental discrimination that violates Title VI. President Clinton's broad mandate to apply Title VI to environmental protection generated an ongoing debate among members of the public, regulated entities, state agencies, and the US EPA staff about what constitutes discrimination and how to recognize that discrimination. The evolution of the US EPA's deliberations is on display in two documents: Interim Guidance for Investigating Title VI Administrative Complaints Challenging Permits (issued in 1998 by the EPA) and Draft Revised Guidance for Investigating Title VI Administrative Complaints Challenging Permits (65 Fed. Reg. 39650, 2000). These documents offer some insight into the factors the US EPA investigators will weigh in evaluating allegations of discrimination; however, the most important factors are unapologetically portrayed in both documents as highly subjective. More important, the documents are "interim" and "draft"—that is, not binding or even reliable.

Another reason the US EPA has not identified discrimination despite 147 written complaints to the contrary is that in virtually every case it has resolved complaints without having to issue final, formal decisions. Of the 115 cases closed as of May 28, 2004, only 28 were even accepted for investigation.[39] Most other complaints were rejected at a preliminary stage because they did not meet procedural requirements.[40] Of the 28 complaints accepted for investigation, only 15 were resolved on their merits.[41] In each of these 15 cases, the complaints were dismissed, usually because of a failure to find a "significant impact," and the files were closed.[42]

Perhaps the most important reason for the US EPA's failure to identify discrimination is that the agency depends on its state partners and the traditional permitting system to achieve the environmental goals mandated by federal law. A state agency's logic is that if it issues a permit that meets the requirements originating in federal law to protect human health and the environment, how can this have any adverse effect on any community, regardless of its racial composition? According to this logic, without an adverse impact—a defined harm –the issue of disproportionate burdens is not even broached.

This, then, is the paradox: How can a legally adequate permit containing terms and conditions to protect human health and the environment also create significant harm? Increasingly, the challenge for the US EPA will be to develop a consistent method to identify omissions in permitting processes, extrinsic evidence of harmful effects that permits are not designed to remedy, and the cumulative burdens borne by communities of color because of newly permitted facilities in combination with existing sources. In other words, even if every facility that affects a community of color has a legally adequate permit, the cumulative burden of these facilities nonetheless could create significant harm.

Using Existing Environmental Laws to Address Discrimination

In December, 2000, the US EPA's General Counsel, Gary Guzy, issued an internal memo analyzing whether existing environmental statutes provided a basis for addressing environmental justice concerns.[43] Guzy concluded that provisions of the Clean Air Act, of the Clean Water Act, of the Resource Conservation and Recovery Act, and of several other federal statutes could be interpreted to accommodate environmental justice concerns in permitting processes. However, Guzy acknowledged that his interpretation of these provisions was untested, not developed through implementing regulations, and largely without precedent in permit writing. Nonetheless, his "blue sky" survey of federal environmental laws offers another avenue for environmental justice activists and attorneys to explore.

In his memo, Guzy noted a few examples in which environmental justice concerns were acknowledged as legitimate in permitting. In a series of administrative decisions, the US EPA's Environmental Appeals Board has addressed environmental justice in permitting some categories of sources.

Some permitting decisions must be appealed to the US EPA's EAB before judicial review can be sought. On several occasions, petitioners have challenged permits before the EAB because of the way permitting agencies handled environmental justice concerns. In reviewing these kinds of environmental justice appeals, the EAB has decided that a permitting agency may include environmental justice considerations in its permitting decisions for hazardous waste facilities[44] and for new, major sources of air pollution that could degrade regional air quality.[45] Moreover, in at least one case the EAB remanded a permit to construct a new source of air pollution for further review because a local permitting authority failed to provide an environmental justice analysis in response to public comments.[46] At the same time, the EAB has indicated that social and economic impacts alone are not an adequate basis for denying a permit.[47] Nonetheless, because of the EAB's central role in many permit appeals and its willingness to consider environmental justice concerns, Guzy's analysis suggests this may offer a fruitful opportunity for activists to explore.

Are Legal Services Available to Environmental Justice Activists?

Another measure of whether the legal system is evolving to address environmental injustice has nothing to do with new legal theories and everything to do with legal services. Are increasing numbers of attorneys working with and for residents of affected communities of color? This question is especially important for two reasons. First, when the environmental justice movement first emerged there were very few attorneys available to serve environmental justice activists. Is this being remedied, thus making the legal system more accessible? Second, this question is important because of existing mechanisms in environmental laws allowing for public participation in rule making, permitting, and enforcement.

Environmental law provides rich opportunities for public participation. The US EPA cannot develop the administrative rules to implement broad statutory mandates without providing opportunities for public comment and, in some cases, judicial challenge. Legal and regulatory requirements are applied to individual sources through a permitting process that typically offers public notice, written comment opportunities, a public hearing, and third-party appeals. Citizens are integral to enforcing statutory, regulatory, and permit requirements, not only as informal complainants, but also through statutory provisions that authorize citizens to file enforcement actions in federal district court. Many federal statutes include petitioning processes through which members of the public can prompt US EPA attention to community concerns. All these opportunities exist in addition to state and local processes that include public participation.

In many cases, capitalization on these opportunities is significantly enhanced if community members have access to attorneys. In essence, in order to achieve the strategies of an environmental justice constituency, these attorneys use many of the same legal tools traditionally employed by mainstream environmental organizations. But do such attorneys exist?

Over the last decade and a half, the number of attorneys representing individuals and community groups facing environmental injustice has increased exponentially. These attorneys include volunteers, solo practitioners, employees of small and large environmental organizations, and employees of law school clinics.

The environmental justice movement has moderately reoriented the structure of a few of the traditional environmental organizations. And although some of the "Big 10" environmental groups (for example, the Sierra Club and Environmental Defense) have stepped up their efforts to address environmental injustice,[48] the true surge in legal representation has resulted from local organizations and from law school environmental clinics.

Since environmental injustice often occurs in pockets of low-income and minority communities, smaller local and state environmental organizations, such as Communities for a Better Environment, are better equipped to provide vital support to combat discrimination. For example, CBE is "an environmental health and justice non-profit organization . . . with a unique three-part strategy [that] provides grassroots activism, environmental research and legal assistance within underserved urban communities."[49] Providing this type of local activism has proven to be more difficult for larger, national organizations, because combating environmental discrimination requires immersion in the community and gaining the trust of local residents.

In addition, the number of law school environmental clinics has more than doubled since 1990. There are now 29 such clinics across the country. Law school clinics vary somewhat in function, but most, if not all, have one important feature in common: providing representation to underprivileged and minority persons facing adverse environmental effects.[50] At this point, a majority of the clinics are staffed by a handful of attorneys and law student volunteers, with minimal support staff. However, the growing trend is to provide students and those needing representation with an interdisciplinary clinic that combines the skills of attorneys, law students, engineers, and engineering students to bring about a more comprehensive method for providing environmental representation.[51] In addition, by actively engaging law students and providing them with real-life experiences, these clinics serve the important function of ensuring a continuous supply of energetic and well-trained environmental lawyers.

Another source of attorneys for environmental justice activists is legal aid organizations, many of which operate in the midst of the most impacted communities. Beginning in the 1980s, several not-for-profit clinics, such as the California Rural Legal Assistance Foundation[52] and the Chicago Legal Clinic,[53] added attorneys to focus on the environmental problems affecting their low-income clients. In many cases, there was a natural overlap between the civil cases these organizations routinely handled and environmental cases. For example, it is difficult to advocate for safe, habitable housing without encountering the problems of lead poisoning, indiscriminate use of pest-control chemicals, and unsafe drinking water, all of which are subject to regulation under environmental laws. In a similar way, advocates for migrant worker communities quickly identified the improper use of agricultural pesticides in the workplace as directly affecting the health and safety of their clients.

Today, most legal aid organizations do not have environmental attorneys on staff. Just as the movement was growing, the federal Legal Services

Corporation imposed strict limits on federally funded legal aid groups restricting their ability to provide complete representation to their clients in many environmental (and other) cases. Nonetheless, a recent survey of environmental legal services groups identified more than three dozen organizations operating in 29 states, in the District of Columbia, and in Puerto Rico.[54] Some of these groups date back to the mid 1960s and only later added environmental services; others came into being concurrently with the rise of the environmental justice movement with a mission to serve this constituency.[55]

Are Federal and State Agencies Developing Proactive Strategies to Address Environmental Justice Concerns?

A third measure of whether the environmental justice movement is changing the legal system focuses on the federal, state, and local agencies that are engaged in activities affecting the environment. Are these units of government developing and implementing policies and procedures to incorporate environmental justice considerations into their decisions?

Federal Agencies

In order to comply with President Clinton's executive order, many federal agencies developed environmental justice strategies in the mid 1990s. Some of these agencies are obvious because of their direct involvement in environmental affairs, including the US EPA, the Council on Environmental Quality, the Department of the Interior, and the Department of Justice.[56] However, the Departments of Agriculture, Defense, Energy, Health and Human Services, Labor, and Transportation also developed environmental justice strategies. Though these strategies may appear to be relics of a previous administration, and are not legally enforceable, they continue to provide a basis for environmental justice considerations to be incorporated into federal decisions, especially if members of the public insist. For example, the Council on Environmental Quality developed a sequential method for evaluating environmental justice concerns throughout the process of preparing environmental assessments and, especially, environmental impact statements.[57] In other cases, agencies used environmental justice strategies as a means of focusing resources to address recurring problems in affected communities. For instance, the Department of Housing and Urban Development asserted that it would "champion" the principles of environmental justice by focusing its resources on lead poisoning, on the development of empowerment zones, on the remediation of brownfield sites, and on the problems of the *colonias* (low-income communities within about 150 miles of the Mexican border).[58]

The US EPA's Interim Guidance to States

Later in the 1990s, the US EPA, in consultation with stakeholders, including the National Environmental Justice Advisory Committee, began developing guidelines for state environmental justice programs. Primarily because many states were fundamentally opposed to the introduction of civil rights into the administration of environmental law, the process for developing these guidelines was torturous. The federal government was sending contradictory messages to these states. On one hand, the US EPA was delegating federal environmental protection programs to states to implement. This delegation only occurred if states agreed to conduct permitting activities in strict compliance with the legal and technical standards contained in federal laws and regulations. On the other hand, under its new policy on Title VI, the US EPA was suggesting that states could be penalized if a legally adequate permit created a disproportionate impact on a community of color. States also complained that the US EPA was vague in defining what constitutes discrimination in the environmental context and naive in its belief that a permit could untangle the complex land use, housing, public health, and economic conditions that create disproportionate exposure to pollutants.

In June 2000, against this backdrop, the US EPA released the Draft Title VI Guidance for EPA Assistance Recipients Administering Environmental Permitting Programs (commonly referred to as "the Draft Recipient Guidance").[59] The Draft Recipient Guidance is an attempt by the US EPA to explain to states what ongoing program elements should exist in order to comply with Title VI. The US EPA also describes alternative approaches to incorporate environmental justice into permitting. The agency characterizes an environmentally just permit as the culmination of a fair process that provides a full and complete opportunity for public participation. In addition, an environmentally just permit will develop meaningful responses to community concerns, often in the form of risk-reduction measures that go beyond what strict legal compliance dictates.

State Responses

Initially, few states voluntarily established environmental justice programs. Today, several states are making at least some effort in this direction.[60] In the absence of final US EPA guidance on recipient responsibilities, states are developing these initiatives without reference to any uniform national standards. Consequently, state programs are uneven and there is little incentive for states that have not developed environmental justice programs to do so.

There are several reasons why some states have developed environmental justice programs. First, as was noted above, the US EPA will use Title VI Complaints filed by citizens to coerce states to develop programs to comply with Title VI. Second, for some states environmental justice is a useful tool for coalescing resources to address intransigent environmental problems. In Massachusetts, for example, environmental justice and brownfields redevelopment share an office. For other states, including California, environmental justice programs are a legislative or administrative response to a constituency that insisted the state develop an environmental justice initiative. Third, despite its controversial beginnings, the Draft Recipient Guidance helps demystify what the US EPA expects of its state partners as recipients of federal funds under Title VI. At the same time, the states are granted significant flexibility in tailoring their own programs. Finally, the Draft Recipient Guidance offers states an incentive. If a state establishes a program with the elements described in the Draft Recipient Guidance and administers its permitting activities consistently with this program, the US EPA is unlikely to investigate a Title VI Complaint emerging from that state.

Conclusion

Environmental justice advocates have sought to transform the legal system by convincing courts and administrative agencies to apply traditional civil rights theories to remedy environmental racism. This strategy clashed with courts that were shrinking, not expanding, the scope of civil rights laws. Further obstacles included the US EPA's inability to define critical elements necessary to establish a violation of Title VI of the Civil Rights Act of 1964 and the reluctance of states to permit the introduction of unfamiliar considerations in their administration of environmental laws. Consequently, after more than 20 years and hundreds of court and administrative complaints, there is no environmental version of *Brown v. Board of Education*.

Despite failing to achieve a defining legal precedent, environmental justice advocates nonetheless succeeded by every other measure. They created a network of legal service providers that are applying traditional citizen participation and enforcement strategies to transform endangered poor and minority communities. They also persuaded traditional environmental organizations to change their agendas and reallocate their resources to respond to communities that are disenfranchised from promises of equal environmental quality. Perhaps most important, by articulating the predicaments of environmentally endangered communities in formal complaints, they stimulated the US EPA and its state counterparts to change the way they do the business of environmental protection.

Ideally, the measures now being implemented on a state-by-state basis will help defuse the tensions that boiled over into lawsuits and administrative complaints. This can only occur if states develop proactive, programmatic strategies to remedy intransigent environmental problems in poor and minority communities, and if they develop new approaches to permitting capable of generating meaningful public participation, hazard characterization, and risk reduction. These changes can occur only if the US EPA develops clear and consistently administered guidelines defining its own and state responsibilities under Title VI and other authorities. It is not clear that these changes will come to pass. What is unmistakably clear is that environmental justice advocates—organizers, health care workers, government workers, mothers, attorneys—will not relent in their pursuit of environmental justice.

Notes

1. 42 U.S.C. §2000d et seq. (2003).
2. 42 U.S.C. §2000d.
3. 40 C.F.R. 7.35 (2003).
4. Office of Management and Budget, Standard Form 4248, prescribed by OMB A102.

5. Ibid.

6. 59 Fed. Reg. 7629 (February 16, 1994).

7. Janet Reno, Department of Justice Guidance Concerning Environmental Justice (January 9, 1995), p. 2.

8. Ibid.

9. Ibid.

10. Ibid.

11. Ibid.

12. *South Camden Citizens in Action v. N.J. Dept. of Env. Prot.*, 145 F. Supp. 2d 446, 452 (D.N.J. April 19, 2001) ("Camden I").

13. Ibid. at 450–451.

14. 42 U.S.C. §2000d (2003).

15. See 42 U.S.C. §2000d-1 (2003).

16. See 40 C.F.R. 7.35(b) (c) (2003)

17. *Camden* I, 145 F. Supp. 2d at 502.

18. *Alexandar v. Sandoval*, 532 U.S. 275 (2001). In *Sandoval*, the State of Alabama amended its constitution to declare English the official language of the state. Ibid. at 278–279. As a result, the state administers drivers' license examinations only in English. Ibid. A non-English-speaking Alabama resident brought an action claiming disparate impact discrimination based on national origin in violation of Title VI. Ibid. at 280. Title VI is initially triggered because the Alabama agency that administers the tests receives federal funding from the Departments of Justice and Transportation. Ibid. at 278. The DOJ Title VI implementing regulations prohibits disparate impact discrimination based on national origin. Ibid. at 281. The Supreme Court dismissed the lawsuit holding that Title VI does not create a private right of action for federal agency implementing regulations. Ibid. at 293.

19. Ibid. at 293.

20. Ibid.; *South Camden Citizens in Action v. N.J. Dept. of Env. Prot.*, 145 F. Supp. 2d 505, 509 (D.N.J. May 10, 2001) ("Camden II").

21. *Camden* II, 145 F. Supp. 2d at 509–510.

22. Ibid. at 511.

23. See 42 U.S.C. §1983 (2003).

24. See *Loschiavo v. City of Dearborn*, 33 F.3d 548, 551 (6th Cir. 1994); *Samuels v. Dist. of Columbia*, 770 F.2d 184, 196 (D.C. Cir. 1985) (both holding that a regulation may create an enforceable right under §1983) and *Harris v. James*, 127 F.3d 993, 1009–1010 (11th Cir. 1997) (holding that a regulation, on its own, may *not* create an enforceable right under §1983).

25. *Camden* II, 145 F. Supp. 2d at 548.

26. *South Camden Citizens in Action v. N.J. Dept. of Env. Prot.*, 274 F.3d 771, 790 (3rd Cir. 2001) ("Camden III").

27. *South Camden Citizens in Action v. N.J. Dept. of Env. Prot.*, 254 F. Supp. 2d 486, 499 (D.N.J. April 16, 2003) ("Camden IV").

28. See *Sandoval*, 532 U.S. at 280.

29. See Camden III, 274 F.3d at 790; *Save Our Valley v. Sound Transit*, 335 F.3d 932, 935–936 (9th Cir. 2003); *Harris v. James*, 127 F.3d at 1009–1010; *Smith v. Kirk*, 821 F.2d 980, 984 (4th Cir. 1987) (all holding that a regulation, on its own, may not create an enforceable right under §1983).

30. *South Camden Citizens in Action v. N.J. Dept. of Env. Prot.*, 536 U.S. 939 (2002).

31. Illinois Civil Rights Act of 2003, 740 Ill. Comp. Stat. 23/1 et seq. (Public Act 93-0425, effective January 1, 2004).

32. 40 C.F.R. 7.120.

33. 40 C.F.R. 7.35.

34. 40 C.F.R. 7.130 et seq.

35. Status Summary Table of EPA Title VI Administrative Complaints, U.S. EPA Office of Civil Rights, May 28, 2004.

36. Ibid.

37. Ibid.

38. Ibid.

39. Status Summary Table of EPA Title VI Administrative Complaints, U.S. EPA Office of Civil Rights, May 28, 2004.

40. Ibid.

41. Ibid.

42. Ibid.

43. Gary S. Guzy, General Counsel, Office of General Counsel, U.S. EPA, EPA Statutory and Regulatory Authorities Under Which Environmental Justice Issues May Be Addressed in Permitting (December 1, 2000).

44. *Chemical Waste Management, Inc.*, 6 E.A.D. 66, 1995 WL 395962.

45. *Ecoelectrica*, 7 E.A.D. 56, 1997 WL 160751; *Puerto Rico Electric Power Authority*, 6 E.A.D. 253, 1995 WL 794466.

46. *Knauf Fiber Glass*, 8 E.A.D. PSD Appeals. 98-3–98-20, 1999 WL 64235.

47. Chemical Waste Management, Inc., 6 E.A.D. 66, 73.

48. Sources: www.sierraclub.org and www.environmentaldefense.org (both visited May 28, 2004).

49. Source: www.cbecal.org (visited May 28, 2004).

50. For example, the mission of Chicago-Kent College of Law's Environmental Law Clinic is "to enable people who are confronting urban environmental problems to have equal access to environmental justice. The Clinic offers environmental law students the opportunity to learn by serving people who, but for the Clinic, would be unrepresented in environmental matters that directly affect the health, safety and

welfare of their families and communities. The Clinic does not impose an environmental agenda or ideology on its clients, but rather provides legal education, advocacy and volunteer services in response to community-directed concerns." Source: www.kentlaw.edu (visited May 28, 2004).

51. See e.g. www.wulaw.wustl.edu.

52. Source: www.crlaf.org (visited May 28, 2004).

53. Source: www.clclaw.org (visited May 28, 2004).

54. Robert D. Bullard, *People of Color Environmental Groups* (Charles Stewart Mott Foundation, 2000), 173.

55. Ibid.

56. Source: www.epa.gov (visited May 28, 2004). These strategies may be freely obtained from the National Center for Environmental Publications and Information, P.O. Box 42419, Cincinnati, Ohio 45202.

57. Environmental Justice Guidance under the National Environmental Policy Act, Council on Environmental Quality (December, 1997) (www.whitehouse.gov).

58. Environmental Justice Strategy, Department of Housing and Urban Development, Publication No. 200-D-95.905 (1995).

59. Draft Title VI Guidance for EPA Assistance Recipients Administering Environmental Permitting Programs, 65 Fed. Reg. 39650 (2000).

60. Hillary Gross, Hannah Shafsry, and Kara Brown, Environmental Justice: A Review of State Responses, 2000 (www.uchastings.edu).

11

The States' Comprehensive Approach to Environmental Justice

Nicholas Targ

More than 30 US states have statutes, policies, orders, or other agreements (hereinafter "authorities") that explicitly address the issue of environmental justice.[1] For the most part, states developed and promulgated these authorities between 1999 and 2004, demonstrating a new level of maturation for the environmental justice movement. At the same time, tremendous diversity exists in the approaches that states have adopted, suggesting that the issue is still gaining political acceptance and that states pursue environmental justice authorities for a multitude of reasons.

Frequently, states adopt environmental justice authorities in reaction to a specific catalyzing event or policy decision on a closely affiliated matter (e.g., brownfields, "smart growth," transportation, public health). Consequently, many authorities have tended to be limited in scope. For example, a number of states have enacted environmental justice permitting authorities in response to citizen actions or petitions (i.e., Title VI of the Civil Rights Act).[2] A growing number of states, such as California and Maryland, however, have adopted broadly encompassing authorities in the absence of a particular catalyzing event. In these cases, the spur to action typically has come from the urging of constituents or community-based organizations, or from a government decision maker's sensitivity to the issue based on direct, personal experience and/or a basic notion of fairness. Broader in scope, these "comprehensive approach" authorities are discussed, herein, as a promising development.

The first section of this chapter provides an overview of the comprehensive approach—its attributes and an overview of the benefits and drawbacks associated with the approach. The next section takes a more detailed look at California's comprehensive approach legislation. This section reviews the statute's legislative history, examining why and how competing interests found common ground in the broad and somewhat open-ended strategy. It also analyzes the constituent elements that typify the comprehensive approach. The third section uses this analysis to review the policies of the other states that have adopted the comprehensive approach. The chapter concludes with the observation that the flexibility offered by the comprehensive approach is at once a virtue and potentially a liability, noting that the approach's lack of a sharply delineated "environmental justice test" necessitates strong political leadership and accountability from government decision makers in order to help ensure success.

The Comprehensive Approach

The comprehensive approach broadly integrates environmental justice into the work of a state government, rather than focusing on a specific facet (e.g., permitting, siting, brownfields, enforcement) that may raise issues associated with environmental justice. Hence, comprehensive approach authorities respond to the multi-dimensional aspect of most environmental justice issues and to the general applicability of the issue to activities, programs, and policies undertaken by a state. The approach allows states to address a matter using the full range of policy and legal tools available to them. In the words of one decision maker: "If an environmental justice issue comes in the door as a permitting matter and is later identified as an enforcement issue, we are not boxed in. We can address the problem using the right tool."[3]

This flexibility responds to two additional issues. First, the approach's flexibility accommodates the still evolving understanding of the appropriate use and value of environmental justice. Second, and perhaps ultimately more important, the approach's breadth of scope and its emphasis on intergovernmental coordination promote targeting, leveraging of resources, and programmatic initiatives that cut across multiple agency portfolios and the "stovepipes" within particular agencies.

Comprehensive approach authorities also have some potential drawbacks. Because comprehensive approach authorities frequently lack specificity and enforceable regulatory standards, owing to broad scope, they may be difficult to implement and evaluate. Therefore, to be successful, sustained, strong leadership from senior government officials and specific accountability measures may be critical for successful implementation of comprehensive approach authorities.

Attributes of the Comprehensive Approach

Uniformly, comprehensive approach authorities include a broad directive to address the issue of environmental justice in all programs, policies, or activities, in addition to having one or more of the following elements.

capacity-building: provisions that enhance the ability of agency staff and members of the public to identify, address, and participate effectively in decisions with environmental justice implications

integration: focused mandates directing the development of environmental justice strategic plans that integrate environmental justice into the state's work

accountability: provisions that promote "benchmarking" and facilitate mid-course corrections

coordination: provisions creating government and non-government entities that promote coordination, transparency, and connection to affected stakeholders (e.g., environmental justice coordinators or offices, advisory councils, state workgroups).

Entities can be designed to assist agency staff and/or stakeholders in a number of ways—for example, providing advice and recommendations, promoting consistency in implementation of the environmental justice directive, or helping to work effectively across political jurisdictions or stakeholder groups. Advisory councils can also, formally or informally, check progress and evaluate implementation of the comprehensive approach. Each of these elements can help a state coordinate and undertake activities that reduce, prevent, or mitigate the full range of interrelated environmental, public health, economic and social concerns that collectively define environmental justice issues.

Inventory of States Adopting a Comprehensive Approach

As of 2004, six states have adopted comprehensive approaches to environmental justice through statute,[4] strategic plan,[5] policy,[6] administrative order,[7] or some combination of the four. Though other states have enacted laws or promulgated policies that explicitly address specific issues of environmental justice, such as those associated with the siting or permitting process, to date only California has enacted comprehensive environmental justice legislation. California, however, may soon be joined by other states; New York, Hawaii, and Connecticut have comprehensive environmental justice bills pending.[8] In view of California's highly industrialized economy, relatively high percentage population of people of color, direct experiences of several elected representatives with environmental justice, and environmentally progressive legislature, that state's early leadership in the area of environmental justice is understandable, and perhaps, almost predictable.

Benefits of the Comprehensive Approach

States adopting a comprehensive approach, whether through legislation or other authority, do so for a variety of reasons. Typically, states recognize value in coordinating agency efforts to address the multifaceted and interlocking issues of environmental justice; addressing the different aspects of environmental justice (corrective, distributive, procedural, and social justice) government wide, through a single set of directives; leveraging the advice and recommendations gathered from advisory councils; establishing an administrative structure with sufficient latitude so as to permit those agencies with the greatest jurisdictional competence and expertise to develop and implement strategies that are tailored to certain needs and that meet bureaucratic imperatives; and, importantly, creating a process that will aid in compliance with Title VI of the Civil Rights Act of 1964.[9] Moreover, the comprehensive approach has the virtue of adaptability. Rather than offering a fixed adjudicative test, the comprehensive approach promotes new collaborative and community-led initiatives that can be tailored to address the specific issues facing residents.

Potential Drawbacks of the Comprehensive Approach

Comprehensive environmental justice authorities are often broadly worded, creating two distinct but related types of potential drawbacks: lack of clear standards and accountability and (2) lack of specific legal authority.

First, by adopting a general policy framework rather than a specific regulatory standard or adjudicative test, comprehensive approach authorities can be difficult to implement and can produce results that are not easily quantified. Unlike Title VI of the Civil Rights Act of 1964, which allows individuals to bring (or petition the federal government to bring) actions against recipients of federal assistance (i.e. states and municipalities), comprehensive authorities typically lack a direct right of appeal to the adjudicative branch of government. They also tend to lack clear-cut standards of conduct to which individuals, industry, and government must conform. Instead, comprehensive approach authorities, especially when implemented by policy rather than statute, rely on the executive branch to establish policy, to implement requirements, and, when taking a specific action (e.g., reviewing a permit application), to adjudge whether those requirements have been met. This amalgamation of traditionally separate government powers (e.g. legislative, executive, and judicial), combined with a lack of direct right of appeal, can create a bureaucratic incentive for a state to establish open-ended or discretionary environmental justice requirements. Should this happen, decisions may be somewhat less predictable, objectives and outcomes harder to quantify, and potentially portions of the authority unimplemented.[10] In contrast, adjudication-based approaches rely on an adversarial model and on separation of government functions to check compliance.

Second, lack of specificity in the authority's provisions can lead to questions of legal affect and of availability of legal authority to address environmental justice issues in the decision-making process.[11] Because the comprehensive approach authorities frequently carry no new grant of legal authority, civil servants and members of the regulated and legal communities may question how and on what legal basis issues of environmental justice may be considered. Concerns with legal authority and effect can create confusion within the regulated community. Lack of specific legal authority requires increased political leadership in order for the comprehensive approach to succeed.

Development of California's Comprehensive Environmental Justice Statute

California's environmental justice statute, as amended, includes the five elements that typify the comprehensive approach. The California legislature enacted the core of the state's environmental justice statute in two consecutive legislative sessions in 1999.[12] The first round of legislation established the general comprehensive approach. Subsequent amendments added provisions that address issues of accountability and implementation, supporting the underlying approach. Both the specific language of the legislation and its legislative history help explain its purpose, the pressures that can result in adoption of a comprehensive approach, and administrative mechanisms that a state can adopt to overcome implementation challenges that can attend the comprehensive approach.

A Compromise and an Approach: California's Environmental Justice Act

The bill that ultimately came to serve as the basis for California's comprehensive statute, SB 115, was passed after no fewer than five attempts to enact environmental justice legislation. Still, SB 115 was amended six times in one legislative session before Governor Gray Davis signed it into law.

California Senator Hilda Solis,[13] who now represents her district in the US House of Representatives, introduced SB 115 one year after Gray Davis succeeded Governor Pete Wilson. Solis's interest in environmental justice comes from direct personal experience and the needs of her constituents. In a recent edition of the American Bar Association's *Human Rights Magazine*, Solis wrote the following:

> Many of us who are active in the environmental justice movement were victims of environmental injustice early in our lives. My own experience growing up in the San Gabriel Valley, a part of the California district I now represent, undoubtedly forged my interest in environmental justice. Made up primarily of hard-working immigrants from Mexico and Asia, the area suffers from poor air quality due to freeways and gravel pits, industrial toxic waste in the water supply, and few public parks. The health of the community has been compromised—incidences of asthma, cancer, and other environmentally related diseases exceed common norms. . . . My political efforts have attempted to redress these injustices.

The Solis bill was modeled on SB 1113, which the California legislature passed, but Governor Wilson vetoed, a year earlier in October 1997. In its initial form, and through the first two amendments, SB 115 addressed environmental justice issues primarily through a planning-based approach, requiring the State Office of Planning and Research, to amend the state's environmental planning statute, the California Environmental Quality Act (CEQA). The bill, in this early form, would have required an environmental justice analysis as part of the existing environmental planning and review process. Environmental justice, thus, would have been considered on a case-by-case basis, as projects came along.

However, the bill also would have included broader provisions, requiring research, and the policy finding that people of "all races, cultures and incomes must be treated fairly with respect to the development, adoption, implementation, and enforcement of environmental statutes, ordinances, regulations, and policy options."[14] Thus, the statute as originally conceived was fairly specific regarding approach and implementation.

SB 115 was amended several more times before September 9, 1999, when it was amended for a sixth and final time. These amendments further supported the comprehensive provisions, creating specific responsibilities within the Cal EPA, providing increased clarity as to implementation obligations and yet stronger coordination. While the governor's Office of Planning and Research retained overall responsibility for coordinating the state's environmental justice program, the new amendments specifically modified Cal EPA's mission to address the issue of environmental justice. In addition, the amendments also gave Cal EPA specific responsibilities with respect to addressing disproportionate impacts, enforcement, research, data collection, and public participation. The amendments further obliged Cal EPA, which has jurisdiction over six sub-agencies, to foster consistency in implementation by developing model environmental justice mission statements for the sub-agencies by January 1, 2001.

On the day after these amendments, September 10, 1999, the Assembly passed the bill and the Senate ratified it. On October 6, Governor Davis signed the Environmental Justice Act of 1999 into law.

As enacted, the act gives broad directives to both the Office of Research and Planning and Cal EPA to coordinate the statewide implementation of the statute. Moreover, the statute also directs Cal EPA, specifically, to integrate environmental justice into its mission and those of its sub-agencies, underscoring the act's breadth. For all its breadth, however, the act lacks specificity with respect to goals, objectives, strategy, measurable outcomes, and implementation, leaving tremendous discretion and political leadership to the state's executive branch.

Further Amendments to California's Environmental Justice Statute: Shoring Up the State's Comprehensive Approach

Three subsequent statutes, enacted in 2000, increase the clarity of goals and tasks to be accomplished and strengthen the institutional capabilities of the entities directed to implement the Environmental Justice Act.[15] The first of these statutes, a provision of the state's annual appropriations bill, created and funded the position and duties of the Office of Assistant Secretary for

Environmental Justice within the California Environmental Protection Agency (Cal EPA). The legislation directs the Assistant Secretary for Environmental Justice to coordinate activities of Cal EPA, including development of the strategic plan, and to provide education regarding environmental justice. Perhaps more important, the funding provision elevated the stature and visibility of the program, increased the potential for leadership from the state government, and helped ensure the stability of the state's fledgling environmental justice program.

As enacted, the appropriations language requires the Assistant Secretary to review the activities undertaken by each of the Cal EPA sub-agencies and "identify shortcomings," conduct public education around the issue of environmental justice, and ensure that environmental justice considerations are addressed in the CEQA review process.

The second statute to follow the Environmental Justice Act was introduced by Senator Martha Escutia as SB 89. The bill provides for the establishment of an Environmental Justice Working Group, comprising the directors of Cal EPA's sub-agencies, the Director of the Office of Research and Planning, and an associated multi-stakeholder Advisory Group. The Advisor Group and the Working Group have a mandate to assist Cal EPA "in developing an agency wide strategy for identifying any gaps in existing programs policies, or activities that may impede the achievement of environmental justice."[16]

The Advisory Group also holds the promise (1) of linking the state-led effort to the work of environmentally burdened communities and other stakeholder groups (e.g., business and industry, tribal communities, and tribal/local government) and (2) of functioning informally as an accountability mechanism. Though the Advisory Group is not established as an oversight body, the involvement of a motivated panel of respected individuals representing diverse interests and the deference afforded a statutorily authorized advisory group give it independence and legitimacy.

Thus, the legislation following enactment of the Environmental Justice Act provides for increased coordination, greater specificity in tasks to be accomplished, clarity in the effect of the directive, a degree more accountability, and leadership through the establishment and funding of the Office of Assistant Secretary of Environmental Justice. Each of these modifications supports the implementation of the Environmental Justice Act and its comprehensive approach, and helps compensate for the comprehensive approach's lack of specificity.

Elements of California's Comprehensive Approach

Since the passage of the second round of environmental justice statutes, California's comprehensive approach consists broadly of the following elements, each of which addresses the open-ended nature of the comprehensive approach:

Ensure fair treatment in programs, policies, and activities, and enforcement of health and environmental laws and greater public participation in the decision-making process.

Improve research and data collection by identifying different patterns of consumption of natural resources through use of demographics and consultation with the Working Group and Advisory Group and by initiating environmental justice education.

Develop a mission statement; and an agency-wide strategy.

Establish an Office of Director of Environmental Justice in Office of Governor to provide coordination across agencies, an Assistant Secretary of Environmental Justice to provide leadership and coordination within the decentralized Cal EPA, a Cal-EPA-wide Working Group, and a Multi-Stakeholder Advisory Council.

Establish a time line for a Cal EPA model mission statement.

As of this writing, it is too soon to ascertain whether the accountability mechanisms established in California's comprehensive approach will be sufficient to ensure consistent, full implementation throughout the state. Indeed, the state's comprehensive approach may face special challenges in view of California's current severe fiscal condition and changes in political leadership.

The Experience of States with Non-Legislative Comprehensive Approaches

The other states adopting a comprehensive approach to environmental justice have done so through administrative means rather than statute. Moreover, they tend not to have as well-articulated directives or as fully developed administrative coordinating structures as California's comprehensive approach authority. Nonetheless, they uniformly include the same basic constituent elements as found in California's legislation.

Aside from their varying phases of development and different administrative forms of issuance, several of these state comprehensive approaches have striking and innovative features that either further support the comprehensive approach or address its deficiencies. These features are likely to be adopted by other state environmental justice programs in the future. A cursory analysis reveals the following.

Capacity Building (Education and Research)

Most states have recognized that providing training and environmental justice oriented tools (e.g., geographic information systems and other information based tools) to staff, community members, and other stakeholders is necessary both to enhance public participation and to provide a common understanding of how environmental justice issues can be identified and addressed. Education is necessary to foster cultural change with agencies, helping agency staff understand the importance of distributional issues and working across program areas. In several states, including Massachusetts, cross-stakeholder training (e.g., training involving community, industry, and government) has proved especially effective in establishing a common understanding of the issue of environmental justice and creating a basis for working together.

Translation services, and development of fact sheets and other materials in "plain language" are also common features of state environmental justice capacity building elements. Similarly, to enhance communities' ability to participate in the decision-making process, some states (such as Indiana) have developed grant and technical assistance programs for local communities.

Integration

Most states have included the integration elements identified in California's strategic plan. For example, Tennessee's approach, like California's, includes three major components: "Achieving an integrated system for meaningful community involvement and participation through networks . . . and other organizations. . . . Integration of environmental justice through a major ongoing initiative to reengineer the Department's environmental regulatory programs . . . [and] developing and strengthening partnerships." In addition to broad integration provisions, Massachusetts has an unusually detailed plan for integration. Among other things, the policy describes how environmental justice issues will be integrated into the Massachusetts Environmental Policy Act.

A split, however, exists in the process by which states develop their strategic plans. The California legislation directs Cal EPA and its constituent agencies, along with the advice of the Advisory Council, to develop the strategic plan. Other states, such as Tennessee, appoint multi-stakeholder advisory committees to develop their strategic planning documents. Important in this split is the amount of direction that a state gives to the strategy-developing body (i.e., agency or external advice-rendering stakeholder group). In states that leave the development of the plan to an external stakeholder group, significant direction is given. In states assigning development to the state entity that will later implement the plan, more latitude is given.

The split is understandable insofar as agencies have shown a reluctance to give independent, external advisory bodies decision-making authority. Interestingly, in terms of ensuring thorough integration of environmental justice throughout a state's program, it may be that the accountability and liaison functions of an advisory group are as important as the degree of control over the initial policy development.

Coordination
Since the second round of environmental justice legislation, California has, perhaps, the most complete level of coordination of any state with a comprehensive approach.[17] California coordinates with the US Council on Environmental Quality in the Executive Office of the President, with the US EPA, with state agencies, with each of the component parts of Cal EPA, and with a variety of stakeholders through the Advisory Council. More typically, however, states include both internal and stakeholder advisory groups and establish a single point of contact for environmental justice issues.

Accountability
Although recent amendments (including those discussed above) help ensure greater accountability, California's legislation lacks clear criteria for measuring progress. The state statute mandates timetables only for development

of model mission statements, and it provides for periodic reports to the state legislature on implementation of the strategic plan. Although the appointments of the high-level policy maker, the Assistant Secretary for Environmental Justice, and external advisory committee increase the chances for successful leadership and transparency, the lack of specificity in the statute will require these entities to exhibit an unusual level of independence and leadership to thoroughly integrate environmental justice and to improve environmental quality systematically in burdened communities.

Tennessee's plan helps ensure accountability by establishing no fewer than 14 performance measures by which the state will annually review progress and achieve accountability. Moreover, the findings of these evaluations will be made publicly available and will serve as the basis for modifications of the plan. However, without a high-level titular director of the environmental justice program and a defined funding source, it is unclear who holds the ultimate responsibility for the successful implementation of the initiative and how they will obtain resources to fulfill their mandate. Thus, establishing performance measures without assigning specific responsibility for the program to a high-level state employee may not be enough to ensure success.

Conclusion

Comprehensive approaches to environmental justice allow states to address a broad spectrum of environmental justice issues and to coordinate approaches across agency jurisdictions. As a first step toward institutionalizing environmental justice, the comprehensive approach allows a state the flexibility to weave regulatory and programmatic environmental justice activities into its day-to-day activities. The comprehensive approach also creates an institutional framework upon which additional legislative or policy initiatives (e.g., enforcement, land use planning, facility activities) may be overlaid. Because of the comprehensive approach's broad scope of effect and lack of precisely defined requirements, it may be difficult to implement. To avoid this potential difficulty, states adopting a comprehensive approach should provide clear direction, establish strong leadership and coordination within the agencies and other bodies affected, form an external body of stakeholders that both provides recommendations and performs an oversight function, and provide for well-defined goals and evaluation. With these elements, the opportunity for tailored integration and coordination, which is the comprehensive approach's appeal, may have the greatest chance of making a tangible difference to people facing environmental justice issues.

Notes

1. *Environmental Justice for All: A Fifty-State Survey of Legislation, Policies, and Initiatives*, ed. Steven Bonorris (American Bar Association, 2004).

2. On March 3, 2003, after several divisive, high-profile environmental justice disputes associated with permitting decisions, Illinois issued its Interim Environmental Justice Policy. An interesting and central feature of the policy is the establishment of an investigation process to respond to allegations of environmental injustice. Similarly, in Arkansas, Representative Irma Hunter sponsored the first state Environmental Justice Act (Ark. Code Ann. 8-6-1501), reportedly in "react[ion] to national and local evidence that areas populated predominantly by poor, minority residents drew the highest concentration of pollution-producing industry" (David F. Kern, "'Project Delta' to help Poor, Minorities Escape Pollution," *Arkansas Democrat-Gazette*, November 7, 1994).

3. Interview with Andrew Sawyer, Director of Environmental Justice, Maryland Department of Environment, March 2004.

4. As of this writing, California is the only state to have enacted comprehensive environmental justice legislation. See Cal Pub. Resources Code Sections 72000–72004 (West 2001).

5. Three states have issued either draft or final strategic environmental justice plans. See, e.g., "Draft Environmental Justice Strategic Plan," Indiana Department of Environmental Management (May 2001); "Draft Strategic Work Plan Fiscal Years 2001 and 2003," Rhode Island Department of Environmental Management (June 2001); "Environmental Justice Strategic Plan," Tennessee Department of Environment and Conservation.

6. Source: "Environmental Justice Policy of the Executive Office of Environmental Affairs," www.state.ma.us (October 9, 2002).

7. New Jersey, through a series of three administrative orders, established a comprehensive approach to the issue of environmental justice.

8. See, e.g., New York Assembly Bill 1468, introduced by Hon. Vivian Cook (D 32nd Dist.) on January 21, 2003; Hawaii Senate Bill 1593, introduced by Hon. Colleen Hanabusa (D, Waianae) on January 23, 2003; HR 6360 introduced by Joint Committee on Public Health on January 29, 2003.

9. Interviews with Andrew Sawyer, Director of Environmental Justice, Maryland Department of Environment (March 2004); Veronica Eady, Director, Environmental Justice, Massachusetts Department of Environmental Quality (March 2003); Romel

Pascual, Assistant Secretary for Environmental Justice, California Department of Environmental Quality (March 2003).

10. Models for Change: Efforts by Four States to Address Environmental Justice, "Lessons Learned, Leadership and Accountability," National Academy of Public Administration (June 2002): 1, 119–127

11. The National Academy of Public Administration, for example, recommended that "California's boards, offices, and departments should use the findings from Cal/EPA's examination of existing state legal authorities to advise their staff about the legal options available to address environmental justice." Ibid. at 114.

12. Exec. Order No. 12,898, Federal Actions to Address Environmental Justice in Minority Populations and Low-Income Populations, 30 Weekly Comp. Pres. Doc. 279, 280 (February 11, 1994).

13. Solis, like a number of other state representatives who have introduced environmental justice bills, was raised in an environmentally burdened community of color and represents residents in what has been described as an "environmental justice community."

14. SB 115 (1999–00 legislative session), introduced version, cited in Ellen M. Peter, "Implementing Environmental Justice: The New Agenda for California State Agencies," 31 Golden Gate U.L. Rev. 529, 551, note 105 and accompanying text.

15. The third of these provisions, which requires consideration of environmental justice in the permitting of power plants, was enacted entirely outside of the comprehensive approach framework, and is not further discussed. See 2000 Cal. Stat. Ch. 329 § 5. The state legislature has enacted other environmental justice or environmental justice related statutes, more recently, however like the power plants legislation these statutes do not affect the core comprehensive approach initially adopted.

16. See Cal. Pub. Res. Code §§ 72002, 72003 (West Supp. 2001).

17. However, some states, such as Indiana and Rhode Island, have identified additional, specific state entities with which to coordinate, building on existing efforts related to environmental justice.

12

The Health Politics of Asthma: Environmental Justice and Collective Illness Experience

Phil Brown, Brian Mayer, Stephen Zavestoski, Theo Luebke, Joshua Mandelbaum, and Sabrina McCormick

Asthma rates have risen so much in the United States that medical and public health professionals invariably speak of asthma as a new epidemic. The number of individuals with asthma in the United States grew 73.9 percent between 1980 and 1996, with an estimated 14.6 million people reporting suffering from asthma in 1996 (Mannino et al. 2002). This is widely believed to be a real increase, not an artifact of diagnosis (Woolcock and Peat 1997; Sears 1997; Goodman et al. 1998; Mannino et al. 2002). In the same period hospitalizations for asthma rose 20 percent, and by 1995 there were 1.8 million emergency room visits a year. The estimated cost to society from asthma is greater than $11 billion a year (Pew Environmental Health Commission 2000). As the number of cases has increased, medical and public health professionals and institutions have expanded their treatment and prevention efforts, environmental and community activists have made asthma a major part of their agenda, and media coverage has grown.

In the midst of this attention, there is significant disagreement over the role of environmental factors in causing or triggering asthma. The widely accepted belief in psychogenic causes for asthma has shifted in the last two decades to a focus on environmental conditions, including indoor ones such as animal dander, cockroach infestation, tobacco smoke, mold, and other allergens; and outdoor ones, particularly $PM_{2.5}$ (particles under 2.5 μm in diameter, which penetrate deep into the lungs and are linked to asthma and other chronic respiratory symptoms, especially among children and the elderly). Some environmental groups and community activists have made asthma central to their work, and in several areas, have entered into coalitions with academic research centers, health providers, public health professionals, and even local and state governmental public health agencies.

Despite grassroots efforts to highlight environmental factors in asthma, this remains a contentious debate; these disputes are important because they substantially influence public health prevention and government regulation.

We argue that asthma has become for many people a "politicized illness experience" whereby community-based environmental justice organizations show people with asthma how to make direct links between their experience of asthma and the social determinants of their health. Medical sociologists study the illness experience in many ways. They have studied the personal experience of illness and symptoms (Conrad 1987). Others have examined how individuals adapt to their illnesses in order to function in everyday life (Charmaz 1991). Beyond the experience of symptoms and subsequent adaptation, sociologists have also studied how illness shapes personal identity (Bury 1982). Finally, sociologists have studied how individuals search for a cause of their illness and subsequently how they attribute responsibility for the illness (Williams 1984).

In the case of asthma, we are interested in studying not how the illness shapes the individual experience, but rather how community-based organizations forge a collective identity from the experience of asthma. Collective identity links social and physical realities and tends to be a function of shared grievances that might result from discrimination, structural dislocation, shared values, or other social constructions. Through the process of collective framing, these organizations transform the personal experience of illness into a collective identity that is focused on discovering and eliminating the social causes of asthma. This collective framing leads to the politicized illness experience. While our concept of the politicized illness experience is new, it fits well with existing studies by medical sociologists and medical anthropologists on community-based approaches to environmental hazards and catastrophes (Erikson 1976; Balshem 1993) and to collective approaches to illness experience, as with breast cancer (Kasper and Ferguson 2000).

Our approach integrates several important areas of medical and environmental sociology—illness experience, environmental justice, and lay discovery of environmental health effects—in order to explore two community environmental justice organizations working to reframe the etiology of asthma. We begin by pointing out why asthma is significant for health and social policy. Then we examine the social discovery of asthma and its environmental correlates, the political and economic conflicts surrounding asthma research and regulation, and the transformation of the dominant view of the triggers of asthma. Building on those bases, we explore how activist groups have used the issues raised in terms of asthma and the environment to build a collective "politicized illness experience," in which people with asthma make direct links between their experience of asthma and the social determinants of their health.

This linkage of environmental justice and "politicized illness experience" has a strong national impact, since so many EJ groups have pursued asthma as a core concern, and because even asthma programs that do not focus on air pollution take a strong EJ position on the disproportionate impacts of asthma due to poor housing conditions. This linkage can apply to other diseases in which environmental justice activists are concerned with. For example, there has been recent attention by environmental justice activists to lupus, various cancers, and diabetes. Hence, this linkage also offers the potential to build stronger bridges between environmental justice activism and environmental health activism.

Methods and Data

We focus on two community environmental justice organizations, Alternatives for Community and Environment (ACE) in Boston's Roxbury neighborhood and West Harlem Environmental Action (WE ACT) in New York City, both of which organize around environmental factors in asthma and respiratory health as part of a broader program. We chose these two organizations because they are well-known environmental justice groups that have put significant emphasis into asthma education and organizing, and that maintain connections with academic researchers who study air pollution. We also provide data from our interviews with members of academic-community partnerships that are funded by one or more federal agencies.

Our methods include content analysis of government documents and scientific literature in medical, public health, and epidemiological journals; 16 participant observations of ACE and two of WE ACT; and 20 interviews with ACE and WE ACT staff, public health practitioners and researchers, and government officials. Because much of the organizing and empowerment work of ACE and WE ACT occurs at an informal community level, it was important to have participant observations that complemented the more direct questioning of a traditional interview process. Interviews and questioning often referenced programs and events that we had observed and allowed us to compare our own observations with the perceptions of participants. The ACE observations were mainly conducted at classes taught by ACE in public schools in nearby Boston neighborhoods. These classes provide basic information on the symptoms of asthma, on how to seek help, and on environmental triggers. They also introduce students to concepts of environmental justice, and offer them opportunities to get involved in community activism. A few observations were made of other public presentations by ACE staff to conferences and workshops. Observations of WE ACT included spending a day in their office and another day with them at a New York area environmental justice meeting. Unreferenced quotes come from our interviews and observations.

The Significance of Asthma in Health and Social Policy

Asthma, like most diseases, strikes lower-income populations and populations of color more than other groups. This difference is very pronounced in the United States, though not in the United Kingdom. Although asthma also affects people across all classes, and is not restricted to dense urban areas, the bulk of media and research attention has been focused on low-income people and people of color because they are disproportionately affected by recent increases. Many people of color now report asthma as one of their chief health problems. From 1980 to 1994, asthma rates among children between the ages of 5 and 17 years increased 74 percent nationally, a figure that more than doubles to 160 percent for children under the age of 4 years (Pew Environmental Health Commission 2000). People with asthma are more likely to be children between the ages of 5 and 14 years, blacks compared to whites, and females (Mannino et al. 2002). In many low-income urban areas, especially communities of color, rates are significantly higher than the national average. While national prevalence of childhood asthma in 1997 overall was 7.8 percent for 1–6-year-olds and 13.6 percent for 6–16-year-olds, black children and poor children were 15–20 percent more likely to have asthma (National Health Interview Survey 1997).

Social movement activism has developed in response to the racial disparities in asthma and the attention to air pollution as a trigger. In its focus on environmental and social determinants, asthma activism challenges the individual responsibility approach. Many well-intentioned public health programs understand the importance of outdoor as well as indoor factors. But they usually feel only able to act on indoor factors due to available resources, political constraints, and the fact that indoor solutions appear to provide rapid health effects. Since this involves parents doing a variety of domestic cleanups, people may be left feeling that they are the primary agents responsible for dealing with the problem. Parents can consequently feel responsible for their children's suffering in spite of domestic cleaning regimens. This type of individual-level solution often obscures the role of corporate pollution and government regulation.

Asthma activism advances the environmental justice approach that originally focused largely on demonstrating race and class differences in toxic exposures and proximity to waste sites (Bryant and Mohai 1992; Bullard 1993; Brown 1995). The environmental justice approach has rapidly become central to US environmental policy and includes a Presidential Executive Order to reduce environmental injustice, as well as Environmental Protection Agency programs and guidelines to do so. Further, environmental justice efforts take on a strong intersectoral approach, linking health to neighborhood development, economic opportunity, housing policy, planning and zoning activities, transportation accessibility, sanitation, social services, and education. In this sense, environmental health is a model for intersectoral approaches to health, since so much can be done to reduce or prevent asthma through non-medical action. The Environmental Protection Agency (EPA), the National Institute of Environmental Health Sciences (NIEHS), the Department of Housing and Urban Development (HUD), and the Centers for Disease Control (CDC) have begun intersectoral approaches, including funding community intervention programs that have explicit anti-racist foundations, and that view social inequality as contributing to the asthma epidemic. Asthma has become perhaps the primary disease in which poor people and people of color have pointed to social inequality and have engaged in widespread political action. The case of asthma demonstrates how environmental justice approaches place ethics and rights issues in the center of health policy.

Political Response to Particulate Matter Science

Unlike other diseases, activists concerned with asthma do not have to fight the government concerning the impact of environmental factors. There is much congruence among activist, public health, and government actors on the acute and chronic health effects of air pollution. This is based primarily on the very large and respected body of scientific evidence that supports correlations between air pollution and health effects. Used by federal and state governments to set national ambient air quality standards, the research body represents one of the strongest in environmental health field. For activists, the credibility and strength of this science are valuable tools when addressing air pollution effects with local, state, and federal governments.

However, government efforts to enact strict air pollution standards have been met by opposition from industry interests that politically challenge the scientific evidence undergirding new air quality standards specifically, as well as the government's right to regulate air pollution more generally. Through both lawsuits and political pressure, industry interests have been able to delay the implementation of new air quality standards suggested by scientific research.

Evidence dating back more than 50 years suggests a link between asthma and air pollution (Amdur 1996). Natural experiments such as the closure of steel mills (Pope 1989) or reductions in automobile traffic (Friedman et al. 2001) have temporarily lowered regional asthma rates and strengthened the links between air pollution and asthma. Recent particulate matter research led the EPA in 1997 to set a new standard targeting air particulate matter larger than 2.5 microns (Dockery et al. 1993).

The US government agency responsible for monitoring air pollution and setting air quality standards, the Environmental Protection Agency (EPA), has only been marginally successful in reducing dangerous particulates and has been the target of multiple lawsuits that seek to either implement or delay more stringent air quality standards. In 1994, the American Lung Association filed suit against the EPA for failing to review the air particulate standards every five years, as required by the Clean Air Act, resulting in the revision of its standards to reduce particulate matter to the 2.5 mg/m^3 level in 1997, from the 1987 standard of 10 microns. Industry representatives who feared high economic costs of reducing the particulate matter in their airborne filed a series of lawsuits against the revisions in 1997. Although initially the federal appellate court ruled against the EPA for unconstitutional delegations of legislative power, the decision was overturned by the Supreme Court in early 2001 (Greenhouse 2001).

The lawsuits also questioned the scientific evidence used to set new particulate matter standards, suggesting that the new standards were not cost effective and that the EPA was relying on hidden data. Although independent analyses rejected these claims and supported the 1997 EPA standards, the result was to postpone the implementation of the new standards until the next five-year review in 2002. In preparation for the review, the EPA installed thousands of air monitors across the country, strengthening the scientific evidence supporting the $PM_{2.5}$ standard (Greenbaum 2000). (For a more extensive discussion of the scientific literature and the conflicts on regulation, see Brown et al. 2003.)

For activists, the inability of the government to effectively implement and enforce air quality standards can be a source of frustration. Yet despite benefiting from the legitimacy of the scientific evidence for particulate matter health effects, the illness experience continues to be framed in individual terms. Public health professionals and activists believe that not enough has been done to treat and prevent asthma.

Applying the Environmental Justice Frame: Alternatives for Community and Environment and West Harlem Environmental Action

ACE began in 1993 as an environmental justice organization based in the Roxbury-Dorchester area of Boston and has since become nationally recognized for its work. One of its earliest actions was a successful mobilization to prevent an asphalt plant from being permitted in Dorchester. ACE had initially expected to focus on issues such as vacant lots, and did not intend to focus on asthma, but a year of talking with the community showed ACE that residents established asthma as the number one priority. ACE believes that to address asthma requires addressing housing, transportation, community investment patterns, access to health care, pollution sources and sanitation, as well as health education. As one staff member notes, "everything we do is about asthma."

West Harlem Environmental Action (WE ACT) was founded in 1988 in response to environmental threats to the community created by the mismanagement of the North River Sewage Treatment Plant and the construction of the sixth bus depot in Northern Manhattan. WE ACT quickly evolved into an environmental justice organization with the goal of working to improve environmental protection and public health in the predominately African-American and Latino communities of Northern Manhattan. They identified a wide range of environmental threats, including air pollution, lead poisoning, pesticides and unsustainable development. WE ACT has continued to grow and expand, extending its reach beyond West Harlem to other Northern Manhattan communities.

Developing a Social Structural, Environmental Justice Approach

It is not easy to develop an environmental justice approach that emphasizes social structural causes of asthma, and to spread that approach to others. Asthma activists have adopted an environmental justice framework that links a discourse of rights and social justice, drawn from the legacy of the civil rights movement, together with mainstream environmental values (Taylor 2000). By drawing on an environmental justice discourse, asthma activists frame the unequal burden of asthma in their communities in terms of inequality, rights, and social justice. For ACE and WE ACT, the environmental justice frame (Capek 1993) is a useful tool for addressing social and environmental causes of asthma.

By linking present conditions to a historical political-economic approach, groups like ACE and WE ACT link the full range of social structural inequalities, including housing, transportation, employment, municipal services, land use, and education. This is the type of approach noted by Pellow (2000). Pellow's environmental inequality model emphasizes the interaction of three methodological and analytical needs: the need to view environmental inequality as a sociohistorical process rather than a discrete event, the need to understand that environmental inequality involves a multiplicity of stakeholders with "shifting interests and allegiances" rather than a simple dyad of victim-perpetrator, and the need to view environmental inequalities as a cyclical process of production and consumption. Pulido (1996: 4–5, 27) views these environmental justice efforts as "subaltern struggles" in which activists are in "direct opposition of prevailing powers" and are challenging "the entrenched and all-encompassing ways in which power relations are constituted and experienced." The central theoretical insight offered by Pulido's approach is that subaltern struggles over environmental issues are never solely about the environment. Subaltern struggles call into question forms of structured inequality and directly challenge these institutionalized forms of domination. Many urban asthma coalitions have developed in recent years to treat, prevent, and educate around asthma. Some of these asthma programs openly talk about the racial and class inequalities in asthma incidence, pointing to poverty, racism, poor living conditions, inadequate sanitation, and unequal access to health services. They call for housing reform, in order to provide better living arrangements that will keep children safe from dust, roaches, and poor indoor air. Many people involved in these programs frame their concerns in terms of environmental justice. Several programs train community health workers; these programs are reminiscent of the 1960s and the early 1970s, when laypeople in the community were taught considerable public health skills in order to have them carry out intervention work in a culturally/racially/ethnically appropriate way (Cohen and Love 2000).

Despite that broad political understanding, most asthma projects focus on controlling indoor environmental factors. In view of the extent of the asthma epidemic, it is understandable that many clinicians, social workers, and community activists want to do front-line work to achieve rapid changes in personal behaviors, which are often effective in reducing asthma suffering. But even if these programs reach a significant fraction of inner-city residents, they cannot prevent outdoor air pollution from remaining hazardous (both outdoors and when it enters the home).

This is where the environmental justice groups come in. They focus on sources of outdoor pollution, and engage in local-level intersectoral political organizing. This includes reducing or eradicating diesel buses, pressing for stronger air quality regulations, and curtailing hazardous plant emissions. While some broad national efforts, such as changing air quality regulations, will take a long time, local changes in public transportation can be relatively rapid, resulting in benefits to the entire population.

Transit Issues

ACE encourages communities to take ownership of the asthma issue and to push for proactive, empowered solutions. Central to this is the role of direct action and education, such as a campaign in which residents identified idling trucks and buses as a major source of particulate irritants. They organized an anti-idling march and began giving informational 'parking tickets' to idling buses and trucks that explained the health effects of diesel exhaust.

Since ACE identifies diesel buses as a problem, they also take up transportation issues more broadly than just air pollution. ACE ran a major campaign targeting local and state government over the allocation of transit resources. Charging "transit racism," ACE argued that the estimated 366,000 daily bus riders in Boston were being discriminated against by the over $12 billion of federal and state money being spent on the "Big Dig" highway project, while the Massachusetts Bay Transit Authority (MBTA) refused to spend $105 million to purchase newer, cleaner buses and bus shelters. In tying dirty buses to higher asthma rates, ACE successfully framed an issue of transit spending priorities into one of health, justice, and racism. In 2000 the Transit Riders' Union, largely created by ACE, got the MBTA to allow free transfers between buses, since the many inner-city residents who relied on two buses for transportation had to pay more than others who had free transfers on subways.

Similarly, WE ACT has identified diesel exhaust as a major factor behind the disparate burden of asthma experienced in their community. Using publicity campaigns such as informative advertisements placed in bus shelters, public service announcements on cable television, and a direct mailing, WE ACT has reached a vast number of community residents and public officials and let them know that diesel buses could trigger asthma attacks. Though their efforts increased public awareness of WE ACT and its efforts to reduce asthma, the media campaign did not lead to a shift in New York's Metropolitan Transit Authority's (MTA) policy toward diesel buses. In November 2000, WE ACT filed a lawsuit against the MTA with the federal Department of Transportation claiming that the MTA advances a racist and discriminatory policy by disproportionately siting diesel bus depots and parking lots in neighborhoods with people of color.

Community Empowerment through Asthma and Social Education

A major component of ACE's education and empowerment efforts is reflected in its Roxbury Environmental Empowerment Project (REEP). REEP teaches classes in local schools, hosts environmental justice conferences, and through its intern program trains high school students to teach environmental health in schools. Classes are designed to educate students about environmental justice, and use asthma as a focal issue. For example, REEP teachers discuss the potential process for siting a hazardous facility in people's neighborhoods, and ask the students why was this being sited there, and what would they do about the siting decision. Through their "know your neighborhood" strategy, they teach students how to locate on local maps the potentially dangerous locations in their area. ACE has helped some of its high school interns get into college as a result of the education they received in the REEP program. ACE also participates in job fairs to help students find good employment prospects. On some occasions, ACE has brought Harvard School of Public Health air quality researchers along with them, to present findings to school audiences. In this way, ACE demonstrates to children in underfunded and understaffed schools how important they are, by having important scientists share their relevant work with them.

WE ACT's Healthy Home Healthy Child campaign reflects a similar community empowerment approach. WE ACT works to address a broad range of issues and does not attempt to separate environmental issues from each other or the community context. The Healthy Home Healthy Child campaign, developed in partnership with the Columbia Center for Children's Environmental Health, works to educate the community on a variety of risk factors including cigarettes, lead poisoning, drugs and alcohol, air pollution, garbage, pesticides, and nutrition. Educational materials, translated both from English into Spanish and from medical terminology into lay language, inform residents about the effects of risk factors and actions they can take to alleviate or minimize those effects. In the case of air pollution, one of the actions that residents can take is to contact WE ACT and become involved in their clean air campaign. WE ACT believes that focusing solely on air pollution can be a disservice to the community and thus it addresses all of the issues raised in the Healthy Home campaign. As with ACE's experience in identifying community issues, WE ACT's Healthy Home Healthy Child campaign began by focusing on specific asthma triggers, but soon expanded to include such concerns as drugs, alcohol, and garbage.

Approaches to Scientists and Academic-Community Collaboration

ACE's use of an environmental justice frame means that the organization is not wedded to the procedures and science of public health. They see that other groups have gotten entangled organizationally in complicated scientific debates over statistical significance and epidemiology that can last many years. At the same time, ACE understands the need for scientific evidence and scientific legitimacy, recognizing the long-term importance of establishing links between air pollution and asthma. ACE's decision to work selectively with science, and to insist on the role of science in empowering community residents, is central to their asthma work. Hence, they use science as a tool in the larger arsenal of political and social movement tactics.

Support from some researchers at the Harvard School of Public Health and the Boston University School of Public Health provides an opportunity for ACE to work with science in its own way. ACE's AirBeat project monitors local air quality and then analyzes the relationship between air quality and medical visits. ACE mobilized researchers and government agencies to install a monitor at their Roxbury office. Community members are also directly involved in the planning and implementation of these studies, as evidenced by the involvement of REEP students in identifying data types to be collected from community clinics. On one level ACE collaborates with scientists to produce quantifiable outcomes they hope will lead to greater understanding of air pollution and asthma. This has resulted in jointly authored articles on air particulate concentrations, published in major environmental health journals. However, AirBeat is useful in other ways as well. ACE derives legitimacy from the involvement of government agencies and scientists in the process, such as the presence of Harvard scientists and the then-EPA Region 1 head John Devillars at the press conference when the air monitor was unveiled.

WE ACT has been much more eager than ACE to work together with university-based scientists. They are partners with Columbia University

School of Public Health in a federally funded project on collaborative academic-community research and advocacy. They have published numerous papers in scientific journals, and in 2002 edited a Supplement of the prestigious *Environmental Health Perspectives* on "Community, Research, and Environmental Justice" (which contained an article by ACE staff members). WE ACT also coordinates conferences that bring together activists and scientists to consider pressing ethical and policy concerns. Both ACE and WE ACT believe they are pushing their scientific allies to be continually more community-oriented in defining problems and designing research and interventions.

Organizing with Environmental Justice Principles

While working with scientific collaborators to improve our understanding of the link between asthma and air pollution may promote stricter federal regulations, ACE and WE ACT are dedicated to improving local environmental conditions. Environmental justice organizations like ACE and WE ACT are rooted in grassroots activism that is very community oriented. Although their work has national implications, ACE's promotion of a new approach to asthma remains expressly local in focus. Like other grassroots environmental justice organizations, ACE believes that if it becomes too nationally focused or involved in too many governmental and academic meetings, it would forsake the individuals in the neighborhood that have granted ACE the efficacy in the first place. ACE is aware that even if there is national implementation of safer $PM_{2.5}$ air quality standards, local injustices will remain, and hence local action will always be necessary. Local action can have national impact based on the accumulation of action and research by citizen-science alliances involving national-level research universities. In influencing the way this science itself is done, the organizations can shape how the findings are presented, and in some cases, the findings themselves. Additionally, limited national networking encourages community-based organizations to use other groups' issues and strategies—ACE borrowed its 'transit racism' campaign from the Bus Rider's Union in Los Angeles, while WE ACT's current challenges to the Metropolitan Transit Authority's bus depot sitings mirror ACE's actions in Roxbury. Thus, strategies are shared, even if there is no national organization.

This environmental justice approach relies on community-level organizing and empowerment to respond to structural factors. But the same approach also has ramifications for internalized self-perceptions of people with asthma, and hence for their illness experience. Part of the rationale for ACE's and WE ACT's efforts to change social perceptions of asthma causation is to simultaneously transform the self-perception of people with asthma. One of the REEP interns wrote an essay in which he characterized the kind of transformation that ACE engenders in people:

> There are things in my environment that truly outrage me. The fact that people have to wait hours for dirty diesel MBTA buses on extremely cold or hot days, the fact that someone I know is being evicted from their home because they can't pay their rent, and the fact that a small child I see everyday has died of asthma in a community where asthma rates are 6 times the state average. These things should not be happening where I live or where anyone lives. Everyone no matter what community they reside in should have the right to a safe and healthy neighborhood. So what is environmental justice is a hard question but I know what it is to me. It is allowing everyone the right to have the best life has to offer from affordable housing to safe neighborhoods and clean air.

Thus, ACE's environmental justice frameworks allow the student to see their individual lived experience in the context of a larger set of structural factors and injustices, and thereby empowers them to participate in community changes, rather than marginalizing and isolating their experiences.

Reframing Asthma and Creating a Collective Illness Experience

As was mentioned earlier, we are not examining how asthma shapes individual illness experience, but rather how activist groups create a collective identity around the experience of asthma. These organizations collectively frame asthma as an environmental justice issue, and therefore transform the personal experience of illness into a collective identity aimed at discovering and eliminating the social causes of asthma. When people view asthma as related to both air pollution and to the living conditions of poor neighborhoods, they reconstruct asthma narratives differently than the narrative reconstruction that occurs with other chronic illnesses. Because asthma is increasingly framed in the language of air pollution and environmental justice, the disparities in asthma suffering are translated into the rhetoric of illness experience. Illness experience in the case of asthma is broader than that of the typical illness narrative. Such narratives typically incorporate perceived causes and effects of the disease with personal perception, work, family, relationships, and schooling. But asthma activists also include the political economic framework surrounding the production of asthma and the political perspectives that situate asthma in terms of housing, transportation, neighborhood development, the general economy, and government regulations. This broader focus on the social and economic factors shaping the illness experience of asthma is reflected in the goals of one ACE organizer:

I think we have to look at how is it that our society has created such disparate environments for people to live in—from the kind of housing you have, to the kind of school you go to, to the kind of vehicle you ride in, to the kind of air that is outside your door. . . . I think that there's huge changes that are way beyond individual lifestyle changes that we need to look at about production of synthetic chemicals that may play a role, or about the way we're designing and building our cities, towns, and whatnot.

This enables people with asthma to place responsibility in part on social structural forces.

The experience of illness plays a major role in the educational programs conducted by ACE and WE ACT. Because ACE, WE ACT, and various academic-community partnerships hold so many educational sessions to make asthma a very public concern, the stigma and denial normally associated with asthma is lessened. A common theme to emerge from qualitative studies of people with asthma is the feeling of powerlessness. Both among children and adults, people with asthma are without a potential cure for the disease and can rely only on management to prevent attacks. For children, managing asthma requires reliance upon their doctors, parents, and teachers, which reduces their sense of individuality and exploration (K. Rudestam et al., "Children's Asthma Experience and the Importance of Place," *Health* 8, 2001: 423–444). Children learn to associate various places with asthma exacerbation, leading many children and their families to associate local environmental hazards with their asthma. When observing a child's asthma attacks, parents themselves may feel powerless to help their child breath normally. Limited access to quality health care also leads parents to feel helpless to reduce their child's asthma suffering. Frequent trips to the emergency room are the norm for impoverished families seeking asthma treatment, resulting in both poor management and the loss of control (Center 2000). Inequalities in health polarize the experience of asthma in terms of agency. For children and their families who cannot afford quality management of the disease, asthma becomes another problem beyond their control, exacerbating the feeling of powerlessness. Not only do they not have adequate access to health care, but they have little control of either indoor or outdoor sources of asthma triggers.

Community groups like ACE and WE ACT work to reframe the illness in terms of the larger illness experience. They feel that the medical establishment has a limited ability to address many of the important factors in the experience of asthma, and see their role as a bridge. One WE ACT organizer recounted the experience many people with asthma go through in a medical setting:

I think that doctors think that there is very little that they can do about [the factors of asthma]. They go through this checklist of risk factors at the beginning of a physical, which now includes "Do you wear seatbelts?" Like different questions assessing individual behavior and risk taking behavior. They focus on things that they feel they can change somehow. So they ask about the indoor environment.

Groups like ACE and WE ACT realize that doctors are often unable to address larger issues than individual behavior, as an ACE activist pointed out:

Even if a kid has really terrible asthma, they're in the hospital, you know, once every two weeks. Sometimes doctors aren't trained to ask "Do you have mold in your home? Where do you live?"

Organizers at ACE and WE ACT also recognize that even if the medical community incorporated questions about the home environment, many other important factors shaping the illness experience would still be neglected. As an ACE staff person noted:

It feels like [asthma] has been taken out slightly from the context of everything else that is happening to people. . . . And I don't think that that is the way that community groups really approach asthma. They see it in the way environmental justice sees it, defining the environment where people live, work, play, and breathe. And so it's the underlying conditions of poverty and social injustice that are contributing to all these things. And no matter whose fault it is, you can't just get rid of cockroaches and expect asthma to go away. For that matter, you can't just put in better buses and expect asthma to go away. It's all got to be approached in a social justice framework.

As the above perspective indicates, public health and transportation interventions can be helpful, but there are nevertheless overarching social inequalities that will continue to yield disproportionate exposure and disease unless the core social structure is altered. In painting this broad picture of the experience of asthma, ACE and WE ACT create the foundation for an environmental justice-based approach to reducing the burden of asthma.

Through the educational programs held by ACE and WE ACT, people with asthma learn to manage their disease while simultaneously beginning to see themselves as part of a collective of people with asthma who understand the importance of external factors beyond their individual homes. By learning that even their indoor exposures through poor housing are a social phenomenon, they see themselves less as individual sick people and more as part of a group that has unfair disadvantages. The environmental justice approach informs these people that they can act to change their social circumstances, and in that sense asthma becomes a stepping point to a politicized view of the world. For example, ACE got state, regional, and federal agencies to place an air monitor in their Roxbury office. They use this monitor for their educational programs in public school and community afterschool programs, showing students the relationships between their results on a pulmonary function test and current levels of outdoor air pollution. The ACE interns and many of the children they teach cannot separate out their experience of wheezing from their knowledge of the harmful effects of diesel exhaust from nearby buses. They cannot think about their inhalers without thinking about the excess of bus depots and trash incinerators located in their neighborhoods.

For a growing number of people and organizations, the experience of illness has transformed asthma from an individual disease into a social movement focused on health inequalities. Their role in building and maintaining this social movement is a growing concern for organizers, as noted by this ACE organizer:

The other part of ACE that's really emerged probably in the past couple of years is our role as movement builders; building an environmental justice movement both locally and nationally. And the leadership development fits under that as well. But it has changed the way we look at our programs. Now we're trying to figure out how we not only take out interns and train them as educators, but train them as organizers.

Based on the illness experience we have described above, we believe that many people with asthma have developed what we term a "politicized illness experience," in which their personal experience of illness, symptoms, coping, and adaptation has become linked with a broad social critique. This critique involves assessing responsibility for the causes and/or triggers of the disease, as well as responsibility for treating and preventing the disease. The use of an environmental justice discourse frames ACE and WE ACT's activism in terms of social justice that has both local and national components. On the local level, ACE and WE ACT are directly involved in improving the living and working conditions of community members who suffer from asthma. By addressing transit issues and other socially structured forms of environmental inequalities, ACE and WE ACT are able to address local environmental problems. At the national level, the organizations have been able to establish collaborative scientific endeavors to improve our understanding of the relationship between asthma and air pollution. These collaborations between activists and scientists also advocate for social justice through their focus on outdoor source of air pollution rather than indoor causes (which places the burden of responsibility on the individual). Thus the politicized illness experience links the local burden of disease together with broader social factors, which in the words of an asthma activist is working toward "building an environmental justice movement both locally and nationally."

Conclusion

As we have shown, a considerable amount of attention to the new asthma epidemic comes from laypeople who are concerned with environmental factors as triggers. Their broad intersectoral approach to asthma includes action in diverse social sectors, such as housing, transportation, and economic development, and is framed in environmental justice terms that emphasize race and class inequities. The environmental asthma activists focus their attention on political and economic action. Although they understand the need for household level attention, they reject the primacy of individual responsibility for asthma control.

ACE and WE ACT exemplify this environmental asthma approach, and define themselves as environmental justice organizations for which asthma activism is only one part of a broader approach. Even though they are not primarily health-oriented, they offer a sociologically informed approach to disease. This type of wide-reaching approach to social health, rather than just medical health, provides an important insight into new ways that lay-driven efforts can reframe social conceptions of health.

This environmental focus on asthma has achieved legitimacy in part because of its health inequalities and environmental justice approach. Because of its express social justice ideology that places issues of ethics and rights in the center of health policy discussion, government officials are pressed to pay attention. Activists' legitimacy was enhanced by not having to struggle for recognition of the epidemic—there was ample attention from medical, public health, and educational institutions and professionals, and there was an excellent science base. In addition, although WE ACT and ACE approached science and scientists differently, these groups have found creative ways to work alongside scientists, while not placing primary emphasis on research.

Asthma has become perhaps the primary disease in which poor people and people of color have pointed to social inequality, and it is a useful class and race indicator of health inequalities. The wide-ranging, intersectoral perspective we see in environmental asthma activism offers lessons for future contested illnesses. In cases of isolated community contamination, the intersectoral approach is difficult to adopt. But as more diseases come to be understood as widespread phenomena linked to modern industrial practices and consumer lifestyles, illness activists stand to learn from the approaches of asthma activist organizations such as ACE and WE ACT.

Further, the growing perspective on social and environmental determinants of asthma fosters a different approach to personal illness experience, what we term a politicized illness experience. We expect this politicized illness experience, together with support from public health and science allies, to lead to concrete results in health policy, especially in terms of health tracking, academic-community collaboration, and stronger air quality regulation. The Trust for America's Health (formerly the Pew Environmental Health Commission) has pointed to asthma as one of the central reasons why the United States needs a national health tracking system, and has garnered much scientific and governmental support for this approach, including recent passage of a health tracking bill in Congress. Innovative academic-community collaborations sponsored by federal grants have developed in recent years as well, with asthma a main focus because there are such strong community organizations available to do joint work with researchers. Last, the growing power of the environmental justice activists, combined with much public health sympathy toward the environmental justice perspective and with a solid science base of particulate researchers, holds the potential to support stronger air quality regulation.

Acknowledgments

This research is supported by grants to the first author from the Robert Wood Johnson Foundation's Investigator Awards in Health Policy Research Program (grant 036273) and the National Science Foundation Program in Social Dimensions of Engineering, Science, and Technology (grant SES-9975518). We thank Rebecca Gasior, Meadow Linder, Rachel Morello-Frosch, and Pamela Webster for their involvement in the larger project from which this research arises. We are grateful to the staff of Alternatives for Community and Environment and West Harlem Environmental Action for granting access to their work.

13

Whose Environmental Justice? An Analysis of the Governance Structure of Environmental Justice Organizations in the United States

Robert J. Brulle and Jonathan Essoka

To be able to satisfy these functions in the sense of democratic opinion and consensus formation, [a social movement organization's] inner structure must first be organized in accord with the principle of publicity and must institutionally permit an intraparty or intra-association democracy to allow for unhampered communication and public rational-critical debate.
—Jürgen Habermas (1962: 142)

The means by which citizens act together to pursue their common interests has long been a topic of intellectual inquiry and practical politics. The important potential role played by civil society in the maintenance, legitimacy, and stability of democratic society has been recently examined by a number of authors (e.g. Skocpol 2003; Barber 1984; Calhoun 1993; Habermas 1984, 1987, 1991, 1996; Putnam 2000; Fiorina and Skocpol 1999; Fung 2003). Civic organizations, based in civil society, are seen as a critical link in translating the impulses from everyday experience into political demands for change (Habermas 1987, 1998). The core idea is civil society forms an autonomous site independent of the market economy and the state, providing citizens with the opportunity to freely associate, develop an ethical life and exercise their citizenship. Thus civic associations form an important site for the creation and maintenance of a democratic society (Skocpol 2003; Clarke 2001). This puts civic associations at the center of the renewal and transformation of social institutions, including the transition to an ecologically sustainable society.

Thus, how environmental movement organizations are governed has important consequences for the viability of this movement. First, to enhance and strengthen the democratic nature of civic life of the communities in which these organizations work, it is important that they have open and participatory structures. A participatory structure enables the community to develop its indigenous leadership capabilities, and increases its ability to meaningfully participate in its own governance. Conversely, as Clarke (2001: 141–142) notes, "to the extent that these are oligarchical, professionalized organizations with weak links to members and gendered leadership structures, the opportunities for developing political identities and skills decline." Secondly, the political capacity of a social movement organization is linked to the organization's ability to mobilize its constituency. As Skocpol (2003) demonstrates, organizations with open and participatory structures are better able to develop committed members, which in turn enhances the mobilization capacity, and thus political power of the group. Conversely, professionally managed, oligarchic institutions have a limited capacity to mobilize their members. Thus, both the mobilization capacity of an organization and the political power of a community are heavily influenced by the structural characteristics of civic associations.

The environmental justice (EJ) movement is generally seen as composed of democratic and participatory organizations. To date, most scholars of environmental justice and social movements have summarily labeled EJ as a grassroots phenomenon, citing among other things its lack of a nationally recognizable structure and its reliance on local groups (Bullard 2000; McAdam et al. 1996; Mahoney 2000; Schlosberg 1998). For example, Cook (1992: 38) contrasts the highly institutionalized and bureaucratic structure of mainstream environmental groups with environmental justice organizations, noting that they are "organized in a highly democratized fashion, and shun top-down hierarchical models." However, this and many other analyses are anecdotal, or are based on case studies of only a few organizations.

One major consideration regarding the effectiveness and potential of the environmental justice movement is the nature of the organizational structure of the groups that make up this movement. The more open and democratic the movement's organizations are, the greater will be its political capacity. The aim of this chapter is to conduct an empirical analysis of the organizational structure of environmental justice organizations.

Democracy, Civic Life, and Political Power

The linkage of democracy and intentional social change is based on the well-founded theoretical formulation developed by Jürgen Habermas.

In *The Theory of Communicative Action* (1984, 1987), Habermas links democratic movement organizations and rational social change. For Habermas (1984), a rational social order is based on providing good reasons for accepting a particular discourse through democratic dialogue. This dialogue forms the basis for rational action by establishing an intersubjective consensus for which valid arguments can be made. Habermas argues that such open and participatory communicative action is vital to the renewal of institutions to meet new circumstances. If this process is blocked, the institutions are unable to adjust to new circumstances. Habermas maintains that Western society's capability for self-correction is systematically blocked by the institutions of the capitalist world economy and the bureaucratic state. Specifically, the learning capability of our society is hindered by the dominance of decision-making criteria based in the institutions of the market and state administrative agencies. The market bases its decisions on the profitability of an activity, without regard to either its social or environmental costs. The decision-making process of the state is based on the political calculus of the governing party, and its attempt to retain power. Both of these institutions are thus based on a limited notion of instrumental reason, and unable to effectively generate creative alternatives. This systematic restriction of communicative action has created a society that is unable to hold these institutions accountable for their actions. One result of this dynamic is the creation of the ecological crisis (Habermas 1984, 1987; Dunlap 1992; Brulle 2000).

Habermas thus sees social movement organizations, being based in civil society, as the agents of rational control over the market and the state. These institutions, since they are based in communicative action, offer a possible means to restore democratic control over the political and economic systems (Habermas 1987). Accordingly, these organizations provide an arena in which an ethical life can be developed and citizenship exercised (Offe 1990; Habermas 1987). This links the resolution of ecological problems to the development of a democratic social order. Since social learning is based on open communicative action in the lifeworld, the enhancement of the democratic capacity of society is a necessary prerequisite for initiation of the actions through which environmental problems could be resolved.

To ensure a process of open and democratic communication in these organizations, their internal structure must be democratic and open. Hence, Habermas (1962: 142) has concluded that the public sphere could "only be realized today, on an altered basis, as a rational reorganization of social and political power under the mutual control of rival organizations committed to the public sphere in their internal structure as well as in their relations with the state and each other." This leads Habermas to specify in the following statement the requirements that these organizations must meet to contribute to an open communicative process:

> To be able to satisfy these functions in the sense of democratic opinion and consensus formation their inner structure must first be organized in accord with the principle of publicity and must institutionally permit an intraparty or intra-association democracy—to allow for unhampered communication and public rational-critical debate. In addition, by making the internal affairs of the parties and special-interest associations public, the linkage between such an intra-organizational public sphere and the public sphere of the entire public has to be assured. Finally, the activities of the organizations themselves—their pressure on the state apparatus and their use of power against one another, as well as the manifold relations of dependency and of economic intertwining—need a far-reaching publicity. This would include, for instance, requiring that the organizations provide the public with information concerning the source and deployment of their financial means. (ibid.: 209)

Skocpol (2003) echoes Habermas's concern. Skocpol argues that the once vital civic life in the United States has undergone a substantial transformation, from large-scale participatory membership organizations to oligarchically managed, professional advocacy organizations. As a result, the quality of civic life and political dialogue has fragmented. Professional advocacy has also diluted the potential for broad-based civic engagement:

> The profound reorganizations (of civic institutions) of the late twentieth century still make it difficult to bridge between national and local activities and discourage the involvement of large numbers of citizens in organized, ongoing civic endeavors. (Skocpol 2003: 251)

As a consequence, the mobilization capacity of civic institutions has declined, and concomitantly, their political power.

One is left with competing images of social movement organizational governance. In the typical view, social movement organizations are seen as "bottom-up" grassroots organizations based in face-to-face social interactions (Hayes 1986; Cohen 1985). Members are presumably recruited through personal networks and face-to-face communication and, at least formally, these groups are democratic and open (e.g. Gould, Schnaiberg, and Weinberg 1996). This view is partially supported by the empirical research on this topic. Minkoff (2003), Edwards and Foley (2003), and Edwards and Andrews (2004) found significant levels of public participation in a number of social movement organizations. Additionally, Brulle (2000) found that several of the major national environmental organizations were grassroots membership organizations with active local chapters and formal participatory structures.

On the other hand, Ellefson (1992: 307) argued that "interest groups are in reality almost always dominated by staff, elected officials, and a small cadre of very active members." Brulle (2000) also found that, despite some democratic organizations existing in the environmental movement, the majority are formal oligarchies with constitutions providing for self-selecting boards and lacking formal participatory mechanisms. Such organizations have been labeled "professional social movement organizations" (Zald and McCarthy 1987) and "astro turf" organizations (Cigler and Loomis 1995) and have been called "protest businesses" (Jordan and Maloney 1997) in which the professional staff dominates the organization and members are treated simply as financial contributors. Drawing on this material and her own research, Skocpol (1999) maintains that these types of professional advocacy organizations have created "a new civic America largely run by advocates and managers without members."

However, Clemens and Minkoff (2004: 163) argue, "there is no necessary trajectory of movement organizations toward goal displacement or institutionalization. Rather the incentives for organizational transformation, growth, decline, and change, derive from a combination of internal and external pressures some of which are more easily overcome than others." This was noted by Clarke (2001: 141), who argued that the governance structures of civic institutions are rather mixed. We agree with Clark, and thus we seek to examine the particular governance structures of the environmental justice movement.

The Structure of the Environmental Justice Movement

The organizations that make up the environmental justice movement are generally perceived to have decentralized structures based on multiple local community groups (Schwab 1994, Bullard 1993). In general, environmental justice groups are seen as small and as based in communities (Schlosberg

1998). There are three relevant analyses of environmental justice organizations that address their structure.

Schlosberg (1998) conducted an in-depth case study of two major environmental justice umbrella organizations. Schlosberg (ibid.: 121) notes that that, unlike the mainstream components of the environmental movement, the environmental justice movement has developed a unique network structure: "What makes environmental justice a movement are the linkages formed beyond the local." He maintains that the network structure creates a stronger environmental justice movement because it "gives the movement many points of attack, positions from which to argue, and tactics to use, while helping to pool resources efficiently" (ibid.). To the extent that this is actually the case, Schlosberg maintains that the environmental justice community embodies many of the characteristics of an open and democratic community, and the increased learning capacity that this entails.

Schlosberg's analysis, though interesting and important, is not definitive regarding the question of democracy and openness within the environmental justice movement. First, Schlosberg overstates the uniqueness of networks to environmental justice organizations. His dichotomization between national organizations and networks of environmental justice organizations is a false one. As shown by the work of network analysts (Emirbayer and Goodwin 1994; Knoke 1990), different discourses form networks of communicative action. These discourses create real communities that work together, and are not a unique characteristic of the environmental justice community. There are many mainstream environmental organizations that have a national scope and have similar network structures, including organizations as varied as Trout Unlimited, the National Wildlife Federation, and the Sierra Club. In addition, these organizations work together in numerous networks in a manner similar to the environmental justice movement. For example, Tober (1989) shows how networks operate within the field of wildlife management. In addition, the empirical case for Schlosberg's findings is not established. Schlosberg's analysis is based on case studies of two environmental justice organizations. In a field composed of several hundred organizations, this makes his conclusions suggestive but not definitive.

The second analysis of the structure of the environmental justice movement is Rios 2000. The objective of Rios's analysis was to assess the overall structure of the EJ movement, based on two competing images. The first image is that of the conventional social movement, based in formal organizations, with a paid staff, external funding support, and engaging in insider political tactics. The other model, based on McAdam's (1982) characterization of an insurgency, is of a movement with an informal organizational structure, lacking financial resources and a dominant leadership, engaging in disruptive protest activities. Based on an extensive analysis of 81 environmental justice groups, Rios found that the environmental justice movement mostly conformed to the conventional social movement model. Specifically, she maintains that her analyses "reflect a movement that has an institutionalized organizational structure, receives nongovernmental funding resources, and uses education and training as activities targeted to attain the movement's objectives. This analysis indicates that the environmental justice movement does not particularly follow the tenets of the political process model of insurgency." (2000: 197)

This analysis undermines Schlosberg's view that the environmental justice movement is distinct from other social movements, or even mainstream environmental movement organizations. Rios's conclusions are further amplified by Brulle's (2000) examination of the bylaws of nine environmental justice organizations. This analysis showed that only a slim majority (56 percent) have a participatory structure. In addition, while the single largest category of economic income is the membership (42.5 percent), a substantial portion (47.7 percent) of economic support comes from foundations or from government grants. Accordingly, these groups have the potential to be influenced by external funding organizations. Thus, Brulle finds that the organizational practices informed by the discourse of environmental justice are mixed, with some participatory organizations, and a high percentage (44 percent) having an oligarchic structure. However, as with the work of Schlosberg, nine EJ groups cannot be deemed a representative sample of the movement. To establish a firm picture of the governance structure of the environmental justice movement, a larger sample of groups is needed.

Analysis of Environmental Justice Organizational Governance

To further examine the governance structure of the environmental justice movement, a list of 140 environmental justice organizations was developed using data from prior research studies, internet website listings and the 2000 edition of *People of Color Environmental Groups* (Bullard 2000). Each organization was contacted via mail, email, and phone, and was requested to provide a copy of the latest IRS Annual Information Return, their annual report, and a copy of their organization's bylaws. Thirty-one (22 percent) of these organizations had become defunct. Out of the remaining 109 organizations, 49 of the organizations (45 percent) provided these materials. (A list of the organizations in the sample is available from the lead author.) Each environmental justice organization was coded for its Form of Governance, following the analyses described by Lipset (1956) and Brulle (2000). The four governance forms used are as follows:

Democracy—Governed by members. Board of Directors and Officers of the Organization are nominated and elected by membership. Policies of the organization can be debated and voted upon by individual members.

Limited Democracy—Governed by mix between Board of Directors and members. Individual members can nominate/elect some of the members of the board of directors or officers of the organization. However, certain aspects of organizational control are specifically delegated to the Board of Directors.

Representative—Members can elect representatives for their local chapter of the organization. These representatives then participate in the selection of the board of directors, officers, and policies of the organization.

Oligarchy—Governed by Board of Directors. The Board of Directors is a self-replicating mechanism and elects the officers of the organization. No provisions for individual member input exist.

The results of the analysis are shown in table 1. As this analysis shows, the preponderant organizational structure of these organizations is oligarchic, with over 60 percent of the environmental justice groups having no provision for individual membership input into the policies and practices of the organization. The remaining 38 percent have some mechanisms for inclusion of the membership in the direction of the organization.

For comparison, table 2 was constructed using data (from Brulle 2000: 250) regarding the forms of governance across the environmental movement for the more mainstream environmental discourses of wildlife management, conservation, preservation, and reform environmentalism, and the recalculated data for the governance of environmental justice organizations.

Table 1

Form of governance	Number of organizations	Percent distribution
Oligarchy	30	61.2%
Representative	6	12.2%
Limited democracy	6	12.2%
Democracy	7	14.4%
Total	49	100%

Table 2

Discursive frame	Percent oligarchic
Wildlife management	33.3%
Conservation	42.9%
Preservation	62.5%
Reform environmentalism	67.7%
Environmental justice	61.2%

As these data show, environmental justice organizations have a governance structure similar to organizations with discursive frames of preservationism or reform environmentalism. Environmental justice organizations also have lower levels of democracy than do organizations based in the discursive frames of wildlife management or conservation. Thus, in comparison with the other components of the environmental movement, environmental justice organizations have a similar preponderance of oligarchic governance structures. However, in comparison with all nonprofit boards, both environmental justice organizations and the environmental movement as a whole have higher levels of democracy. A survey conducted in the mid 1990s by the National Center for Nonprofit Boards found that only 19 percent of nonprofit boards were elected by members. Thus, fully 81 percent of nonprofit organizations at the national level have an oligarchic structure (Moyers and Enright 1997). This is in keeping with Skocpol's finding (2003) that "national public life is now dominated by professionally managed advocacy groups without chapters or members."

This analysis is limited in two areas. First, the sample size of 49 organizations—while the largest sample undertaken of this movement—still leaves many environmental justice organizations unexamined. This analysis is limited to only formally structured environmental justice organizations that actually have written bylaws. As shown by Edwards and Andrews (2003), there is a vast population of local or regional groups that remains unexamined and that operates outside the purview of the IRS and other government entities. Thus, this analysis presents only an initial image, not a comprehensive picture, of the organizational structure of environmental justice movement organizations. The second limitation of the analysis is the reliance on the bylaws of the organization as the sole indicator of the organization's form of government. While this is certainly a relevant indicator, it may biased toward finding more democracies and representative organizations than actually exist. Organizations with officially democratic structures could, in fact, be dominated and controlled by small groups of board members, and/or professional staff members of the organization. The use of bylaws would not reveal this situation. Hence the indicator is unable to distinguish between a formal democratic structure and democratic practices.

Civic Action for Environmental Justice

Our analysis shows that the environmental justice movement's organizational structure is at odds with both its self-assigned image as a democratic and open movement, and the theoretical perspectives on this movement. While there are some limitations to the study, as noted above, there is no empirical evidence that the environmental justice movement lives up to its billing as being primarily composed of democratic and participatory organizations. The majority of environmental justice organizations do not have a democratic structure. Using a very conservative measure of democracy that is based solely on each organization's bylaws, nearly two-thirds of US environmental justice organizations were shown to have an oligarchic structure, and only one-third have some form of membership participation in governance. While this is higher than the overall population of nonprofit organizations in the United States, it is in keeping with the overall characteristics of the US environmental movement.

This finding is important in both theoretical and practical terms. As a theoretical issue, this analysis shows that the existing literature on the structure of environmental groups is highly deficient. It refutes the prevailing and taken-for-granted notions concerning the environmental justice movement that are common within the academic literature. It is not intellectually acceptable to merely accept the self-definition of an organization offered by its leadership without question. As Rucht (1989) noted, a lack of empirical evidence can lead to the "risk that the self-image as grassroots organizations can be too easily adopted by external observers." An empirical analysis of the bylaws and practices of these organizations can be performed, and forms a solid and intellectually defensible basis from which conclusions about the structure of these organizations can be made. This analysis, coupled with the work of Rios (2000), also challenges the supposed uniqueness of the environmental justice movement in comparison with "mainstream" environmental movement organizations. While there are certainly significant differences regarding the demographic characteristics, issue focus, and funding levels between the environmental justice movement and other components of the environmental movement, the governance structures, dependence on foundation funding, the role of professional staff, and tactics to bring about social change are very similar. In fact, on the question of governance, several "mainstream" organizations, including the Sierra Club, the Audubon Society, and the National Wildlife Federation, have open and participatory structures. Arbitrary and constructed dichotomies, such as between the "Group of Ten" and the environmental justice movement obscure the real variation within the environmental movement, and fail to advance our understanding of the dynamics of this movement. Instead, what is needed is a series of careful empirical analyses of the factors that influence variations within nonprofit organizational governance.

This analysis brings to light the disjuncture between the environmental justice movement's self-image and goals and its institutional practices. Environmental justice is a "rights-based" discourse focusing on the democratic participation of all concerned citizens to secure environmental equality. From a practical standpoint, environmental justice groups based in non-representative governing structures fundamentally undermine the ideological premise and legitimacy of this movement. As Schmitter (1983) noted, "many of these groups define their very existence in ways that defy professionalized representation and bureaucratic encadrement. To be organized corporatistically would destroy the very basis of their collective identity." Without some degree of organizational democracy and membership participation in the decision making process of the organization, environmental justice movement groups can end up replicating the type of environmental organizations they most criticize and seek to separate themselves from. Although having an oligarchic organizational structure may not always undermine the grassroots and democratic ideals of the environmental justice movement, it casts a doubt on the organization's legitimacy as an authentic representative of community concerns. The practice of including environmental groups in government decision making is based on the assumption that they are authentic community representatives. Without the presence of a democratic governance structure, this assumption is tenuous at best.

Another practical concern of this analysis is what this implies for the overall ability and effectiveness of the environmental justice movement to generate social learning capable of resolving the problem of environmental degradation. Social learning is dependent on a strong and viable democratic public sphere. Broad-based civic participation and democratic governance cannot be brought about by expert advocacy. Instead, individuals need to actively participate in the creation and maintenance of their civic institutions. The way to institute democratic politics is to practice democratic politics. There is no separation of ends and means in this area. By mobilizing citizens and providing a legitimate and effective representation of their needs, movement organizations are seen as catalysts for the formation of effective political demand for change.

However, if the movement organizations are not authentic community representatives, this limits and compromises the independence of these movement organizations. The mobilization of citizens to create political demand for change can easily be replaced in professional organizations to targeted advocacy activities. Members become seen as something to be managed and as a source of funds solicited via mass mailings. Foundation funding also becomes an appealing source of funding. As the source of funding shifts, the social movement organization is increasingly controlled by external organizations with their own agendas. So instead of serving as an authentic voice of the community, a social movement organization can become subordinated and controlled by external organizations. This can limit the civic capacity and political power of the organization. This in turn limits the potential development of a democratic public sphere, and for social learning.

What does this analysis imply for how environmental justice groups should structure themselves? There is no single way in which this can be done. There are many creative solutions to the problem of democratic participation. What is important is that environmental justice groups take steps to ensure that they are participatory, open, and representative. Here the legal definition of "representative" organization is relevant. In a series of three US Supreme and District Court cases, the criteria for an authentic and representative organization have been developed and given binding legal status in the United States (Brulle 2000). The US Supreme Court has defined a representative organization as one that expresses its members' collective views and protects their collective interests. To qualify as such, there are two criteria that the organization must meet. First, there must be a substantial nexus of control of the organization by the members. Second, the organization must be linked to people who have a direct stake in the outcome (i.e., they represent either the interested or affected parties). Conversely, these two criteria also define what does not qualify as "representative" organizations. Particular expertise or special interest in an area does not define an organization as a representative organization. Thus organizations governed by self-appointed "community representatives," or professional, expert staff do not qualify as authentic representatives of collective interests. In addition, organizations without formal elections and mechanisms to enable membership control of an organization do not qualify as representative organizations. So-called informal mechanisms for membership communication, such as informal communications between members and staff, letter writing, polls, or the fact of financial contributions, do not constitute a representative organization.

What is needed for the continued health and expansion of the environmental justice movement is a broad-based effort to ensure that the organizations of this movement are authentic representatives of the communities in which they are based. In addition, the funders of environmental justice groups need to be more attuned to the governance implications of their funding activities. Their funding strategies can be used to encourage the formation of democratic environmental justice group structures. The Unitarian-Universalist Veatch Program has adopted such an approach and now considers questions of "membership, leadership and governance, strategy and impact when evaluating existing or potential grantees engaged in grassroots organizing" (Faber and McCarthy 2001: 47–48).

The preceding analysis questions the operations but not the motives of environmental justice groups. The environmental justice movement has provided an alternative outlet to give voice to those suffering from the rampant occurrences of environmental injustices. It needs to continue to function in this role. To meet its goals to be an authentic, grassroots, democratic social movement, environmental justice organizations must reflect upon their means of governance and seek to continually expand their democratic responsiveness. Without such reflexivity, the movement could eventually become the non-representational, bureaucratic hegemony against which it now contends. With this reflexivity, it can continue to struggle to meet the high aspirations it has set for itself. As a community, we need this movement to succeed in its quest to create an ecologically sustainable, just, and democratic society.

Acknowledgments

This research is supported by a grant to the first author from the Nonprofit Sector Research Fund, The Aspen Institute, One Dupont Circle NW, Suite 700, Washington, DC 20036.

14

Collaborative Models to Achieve Environmental Justice and Healthy Communities

Charles Lee[1]

The vision of environmental justice is the development of a holistic, community-based, participatory, and integrative paradigm for achieving healthy and sustainable communities for all peoples. The concerns that give rise to the issue of environmental justice have proved to be intellectually daunting and highly resistant to positive change. Achieving the vision of environmental justice will require the articulation of new thinking, new strategies, new tools, new partnerships, and new models for community empowerment and engagement.

This chapter will present some examples of new ways to achieve environmental justice as told from the perspectives of the community or tribal leaders themselves. The first story is from Mary Nelson of Bethel New Life, a faith-based community development corporation in the West Garfield Park neighborhood of Chicago. The story of Harold Mitchell and ReGenesis in Spartanburg is one example of an emerging "second generation" of environmental justice leaders[2] whose leadership perspectives and approaches were forged as a result of a thoughtful critique of previous leadership modalities. Patrick Spears and Bob Gough from the Intertribal Council on Utility Policy (Intertribal COUP) present a vision of incredible power and reach. Their efforts seek to harness the vast wind energy resources of the Northern Great Plains into a strategy for future economic, cultural and community revitalization through the development of sustainable homeland tribal economies. Lastly, Maria Moya and Paula Forbis from the Environmental Health Coalition (EHC) in San Diego talk about complex issues of land use in the Mexican and Mexican-American community of Barrio Logan in San Diego.

A basic purpose of this chapter is to promote a broad national discourse, particularly on the part of environmental justice activists and practitioners, on what it will take to realize the vision of environmental justice and healthy communities. I believe that such a discourse will yield great benefits for distressed communities on a number of levels, not the least of which is the need for community activists to better understand their own communities' assets and act strategically to harness these resources. Moreover, the multi-faceted nature of the problems in such communities will require new paradigms on the part of government, business and industry, and other institutions. Therefore, I initiated a series of community-based, interagency, and multi-stakeholder environmental justice demonstration projects in my role as Chair of the Federal Interagency Working Group on Environmental Justice (IWG).[3] The IWG designated all four cases here to be such projects.

The collective lessons learned from the cases highlighted in this chapter demonstrate that such a dialogue is necessary and worthwhile for the following three reasons:

• Environmental justice advocates and practitioners must develop a conceptual framework that expands the environmental justice discourse to include effective problem solving in addition to compelling problem identification.

• Environmental justice issues are enormously complex, involving many factors and requiring a wide assortment of resources to make a long-term difference in communities that are environmentally, economically, and socially disadvantaged. One challenge for environmental justice groups is harnessing the necessary resources—human, intellectual, technical, social, legal, institutional, and financial—to address these complex issues. Marshaling the necessary resources will require a combination of different people from different backgrounds representing all sectors of society.

• Environmental justice issues have an especially great need for consensus building, negotiation, and dispute resolution skills because they involve highly complex and controversial problems.

Case Studies

The case studies are essentially the stories of the projects as told by the persons who led them, with all the robustness and intricacy associated with complex stories. No single story portrays the entirety of the model that the author believes to be necessary. Rather, all the experiences, insights, and lessons portrayed in this chapter must be incorporated into a larger whole.

The premises of such a collaborative model to achieve environmental justice and healthy communities include the following:

• seeks proactive, strategic, community-based solutions to environmental justice issues, building on community visioning and planning processes

• promotes an asset-building approach[4] to building community capacity and social capital, particularly for disadvantaged and underserved communities

• incorporates consensus building and dispute resolution principles and methods, including the "Mutual Gains Approach to Negotiations"[5]

• establishes multi-stakeholder partnerships to leverage human, organization, technical, and financial resources

• fosters an integrated approach to addressing environmental, health, social, and economic needs

• promotes multi-agency coordination to effectively utilize resources of all relevant federal, state, tribal, and local government agencies

• integrates an evaluation framework and promotes replication of lessons learned and best practices.

One common theme that is explored throughout is that of social capital, a concept defined as the features of social organization such as networks, norms, and social trust that facilitate coordination and cooperation for mutual benefit. A central premise of social capital is that social networks have value. Social capital works through multiple channels, including flow of information, norms of reciprocity (mutual aid), collective action, broader sense of identity, and solidarity.[6]

Communities are rich repositories of relationships and networks, which can be called upon to address problems. For this reason, Mary Nelson emphasizes the idea of asset building and challenges the traditional approach of service providers and funding agencies that primarily focuses on the needs and deficiencies of neighborhoods.

Because environmental justice often involves communities' learning from direct experience and discovering new information and concepts in the process of "doing," I feel strongly that the reader will benefit most by seeing and understanding a construction of reality as viewed through the community leaders' eyes. One of the basic tenets of the environmental justice movement is that people "speak for themselves" and determine their own destinies. Hence, the theory and practice of environmental justice will not emerge from some outside observer, but from within the impacted communities themselves. In constructing the cases, the term "social capital" is never used, until it is "discovered" in the course of the interview with Maria Moya and Paul Forbis toward the end of the Barrio Logan case.

Bethel New Life, West Garfield Park, Chicago

Chicago's West Garfield Park neighborhood has a reputation of "ruin and despair." Hit hard by neighborhood riots during the 1960s, by white flight, and by the abusive practices of absentee slumlords, this community shares the experience of poverty and social discord that characterize many inner city communities. But that's where the similarities stop. The revitalization efforts in this community are like no others. Bethel New Life, Inc.[7] began in 1979 as an effort of the neighborhood's Bethel Lutheran Church. Since its meager beginnings, Bethel New Life has developed more than 1,000 housing units in the West Garfield neighborhood. One of its latest efforts is an effort to build the Bethel Commercial Center, a "green" development on the site of a former brownfield property.[8] This project is an example of what the executive director of Bethel New Life, Mary Nelson, sees as "turning environmental liabilities into community assets and opportunities."

Can you provide some background on the Bethel Commercial Center effort?

Nelson: We got into this whole thing through two experiences. One was finding that one of our sites in an industrial area was a really difficult brownfield site. So, we had to figure out how you turn that liability an economic opportunity. We had to develop some expertise on how to clean it up and bring in new companies that would have jobs for the community. Our second experience was that of protesting the closure of the main transit line that ran through our community, the Lake Street elevated train. In protesting it, several things happened. We discovered this thing called transit-oriented development. We also learned a whole lot more about air quality and the whole environmental piece in this process. Four or five groups on the West Side got together with the suburban mayors and seven townships that this line impacted. Together, we went and put the pressure on the Chicago Transit Authority. We won the battle. Rather than closing it down, they repaired the line and reopened it.

Can you briefly describe your vision for this project?

Nelson: Our vision of the basic redevelopment around the transit stop involves a 23,000-square-foot commercial center, which includes a day care center, employment services, and five storefronts. The building is a smart green building with a living roof, photovoltaic cells, and recycled materials. Energy costs will be about one half of what they normally would be in such a building. Our vision for the community around the transit stop is developing homes that are energy efficient, within walking distance, and where there are green spaces, play areas, and a sense of safety. Through the positioning of the homes, the lighting of the streets, and the greening of the community, we want to instill the whole notion of a "walkable community." Moreover, we envision the brownfield sites and the industrial area around Lake Street around the building as opportunities. We also want to bring in green industries, such as nurseries and landscaping companies. We envision connecting them with our employment center for job opportunities. Lastly, our partnership with Argonne National Laboratory[9] would help us find the most beneficial uses of the vacant industrial sites for the community. It's a big vision.

What partnerships were key to the success of this effort?

Nelson: One thing that got us into more of the technology of the environmental work was Argonne National Lab. For them, it is was taking the esoteric technology they have and applying it in a community setting, while being sensitive to community ownership and community stakeholders. It has been a wonderful partnership that has helped to make some things happen. Another is the Center for Neighborhood Technology and the Neighborhood Capital Budget Group.[10] These evolved into trying to put this really smart green building together. It has taken partnerships with the Chicago Transit Authority and the City of Chicago, including the Department of Environment and the Department of Development and Planning. It has taken partnerships with the state, both their environmental development as well as their economic development initiative. For instance, there is a contract for Commonwealth Edison and the State Department of Commerce and Community Development to do the photovoltaic cells.

There also were some interesting political pieces. Part of our money for the new building came from our state senator, who got it tucked into the state budget as a special project. That takes partnerships with your political leaders in the community. And then, getting a bank to put part of the financing in. We went to three banks before one was willing to make that investment.

How did the community develop this proactive strategy?

Nelson: You've got to put your priorities together. You need to do an asset mapping in terms of looking at what are the possibilities. Who are the folks that should be included? You need to build on the possibilities from the very beginning. In that way, it isn't just collaboration for collaboration's sake. I'm a strong advocate of this sort of asset-based community development. Too many of our communities feel that we're needy communities who don't have any resources and we need everything to come from the outside. This is a bankrupt approach; those kinds of collaborations don't work.

Our collaboration with Argonne has worked because there is, in the people we work with, a strong sense of appreciation of what we, as a community group and as community folks, bring to the table. So then it's really important, I think, for the community folks to look at what are the possibilities here? What are the opportunities here? What do we bring to the table? So, there is a sense of the real partnership and real collaboration that can happen instead of "Oh we need you." Then, it will be a one-sided kind of thing.

What are your views regarding the relationship between protest and problem solving?

Nelson: Once, we were a major part of organizing protests against the Chicago Transit Authority to persuade them to spend $350 million rehabilitating the transit line. Then, it's "What next?" So, here is where you need people who can—or will learn how to—help you turn that liability into an opportunity for jobs and new life and vitality in the community. Here's when you need friends and allies and you need to find the groups who know and ask them for help.

I think there is a role for the protest, and a whole lot of things wouldn't happen if those protests didn't occur. But we've got to have people to find the way to go beyond the protest into the larger program, into long-term beneficial outcomes. I think this environmental stuff is so easily over-whelming because you are up against Goliath. You are little David, and it is very easy to feel isolated, to feel unappreciated, to get worn down. So, I can understand where people who are in the midst of the struggle, at that end of the struggle, have a hard time moving to the next place. They may feel that energy is taken away from them, leaving them more isolated and abandoned. So I can understand that, and all I can say is that, at some point, you need new energy in your group. And envisioning something beyond what we don't want does give new energy and does give sense of new life and purpose and possibility. It is just really exciting stuff!

ReGenesis Revitalization Project, Spartanburg

In the truest sense of the words, Harold Mitchell is a second-generation environmental justice leader. Mitchell took great pains to observe and take lessons—both positive and negative—from how other communities approached their problems. In formulating a set of strategies to fit the needs of an economically distressed African-American community with multiple Superfund and brownfield sites, Mitchell went far beyond merely identify-ing environmental insults to formulating a vision of community rebirth. He then set out to devise proactive strategies to implement that vision.[11] In this sense, Mitchell clearly builds on the community asset-building concepts described earlier by Mary Nelson.

Whereas the story of the ReGenesis Revitalization Project was at one time a testament to a vision of environmental justice and healthy communities that could spring forth only from the hearts and minds of the impacted communities themselves, it is now much more than that. It is now an object lesson about how to turn that vision into reality.

Can you provide some background into the community and the issues that gave birth to the ReGenesis?

Mitchell: It started with my living across the street from a former fertilizer facility[12] in which we noticed a lot of drug activity. In the beginning, I didn't have any idea of environmental problems. That was the farthest thing from my mind. After getting the files on the facility, I found information about the toxics and contaminants present there. I began to look at some of the problems on the street where residents died of the exact same cancers and respiratory diseases. I found about sixteen similar cases on the same street, including my sister who had died many years earlier. That's when a lot of it started to weigh heavily on me. Hey, there's a problem here. It reminded me of when my Dad and my uncle were talking about how every year we would have to change the screens, and everything metal outside was eaten up. They were saying that if this stuff is eating up everything metal, what in the hell was it doing to us?

I didn't even tell my parents about what I had found. I had no idea of environmental justice wording or terminology, or of a movement. I just continued to gather aerial photos and different things on the site. There were discrepancies between what was listed as a clean closure and what I had personally in my possession. That's when I got a visit from this guy from the South Carolina militia. He told me not to go to the state because they were the ones responsible. He also gave me the 800 number for EPA Region 4 in Atlanta. That's how I first got in touch with the EPA, and the first person I talked to there was Cynthia Peurifoy.

Around that time, my Dad went in to the hospital for the same complaints, and he ended up being diagnosed with lymphoma cancer. So, I left a lot of this alone for a while. About a month before he was diagnosed, we went to a conference at Benedict College in Columbia, South Carolina. We saw State Representative Joe Neal and some folks in the environmental justice movement talking about impacted low-income communities. It was kind of like "Well, wait a minute, you're talking about my community!" That's when it hit me that this is bigger than just Spartanburg, this is everywhere. When we got home I showed my Dad what I had. I told him about my sister. He was just blown away. He and my Mom just got real quiet. For the first time, they opened up and talked about that whole situation. I learned about my sister's condition when she was born—her difficulty breathing for the short period before she died.

After I spoke at my Dad's funeral, I decided to pull together some people in the community, because a lot of people there were touched and moved. We had about 75–120 people there, including Mayor Tally.[13] Some of the same people who had told me to leave it alone began to speak up that night about things that they had seen. Some began to stand up and talk about similar illnesses. People didn't realize that others were suffering from similar things. I told them that EPA was planning to do a preliminary site assessment investigation. At that point, I began to get their attention. We had one more meeting in 1997. State Representative Joe Neal and Connie Tucker, the persons from the Southern Organizing Committee for Economic and Social Justice whom I had met at Benedict College, came up and told us that we definitely had identified a problem here and we were going to have to rally together to remedy it.

Well, nothing happened, because this was right around Christmas. We told everyone that we were going to get back together right after EPA came. The same guy from EPA as before—the emergency response coordinator—came. And he came with an attitude, which was that he was sick and tired of black people crying "environmental racism." When he took me around the site, I had a video camera. Everything that he pointed out was totally opposite of what I knew. I could tell that he had never been to the site and only read documents about it. And, he was trying to convince me that it was not a problem.

How did ReGenesis as an organization begin?

Mitchell: When I learned that the EPA was going to recommend that no further action be taken, I called another meeting with the community. Connie Tucker came back. She told us that we needed to mobilize, organize, and stand up and fight because we had the video and the facts. I realized that the first thing we needed to do was to organize the community. There were three separate neighborhoods: the Arkwright community, a low-income African-American neighborhood; the Forest Park community, a middle-income African-American neighborhood; and the Mill Village, a low-income, predominantly white neighborhood. They had never talked or socialized until our two meetings. But at that point, they began to lock arms.

In creating ReGenesis, a lot of people said it was the first time in 20 or 30 years that they felt like they were a part of something in that community. We had some small victories when coming together. We elected the vice-chair of ReGenesis to the City Council. We got a referendum on the Fire Department passed. All the other districts had 90 to 98 percent residential homes, maybe a couple of commercial dwellings, and full-time haz-mat-trained staff. It was totally opposite our situation. So we came together, went to the Council meeting, and passed the referendum. The people felt like "Man, we did something—just coming, just showing up, just being there." That's when we put a video together to go before City Council about the municipal landfill.[14] We went there an hour before council, with our petitions. We were holding up the signs outside. The media had already gotten behind us at that point. The Council decided unanimously that they needed to do whatever possible to deal with this problem. They were expecting us to have some outbursts. But we told everybody: "Nobody is to make any outbursts unless we say so. We don't want to give them the opportunity to say 'Hey, we came to work with them but they were so outrageous.'" So we were not going to give them that excuse. And we came out with another victory. So we had three victories that they could see, just by simply coming together.

How did the Environmental Justice Demonstration Project start, and what role did it play?

Mitchell: In 1999, Jewell Harper from EPA's Region 4 Office first approached us and talked about the concept of the Federal Interagency Working Group on Environmental Justice—the demonstration projects. Jewell had really been helping tremendously with the project and standing up for the community with the state. In the summer of 2000, we were designated to be one of the 15 national demonstration projects. We had the first meeting, in August 2000, when Charles [Lee] came in. Four or five federal agencies talked about the possibility of a community health center, grant opportunities, and technical assistance resources. Charles suggested the organizational structure for the project, which resulted in a mutual agreement between the city, the county, and ReGenesis to coordinate the project together on an equal representation basis.[15] We got all the grants in. We ended up receiving our Community Health Center Grant, the Brownfields and Superfund Revitalization Grants, and our "Weed and Seed" designation.

There are many misconceptions when you say "environmental justice." However, the more we kept the process open, the more those walls began to dissolve. Even the county representative, who was hesitant about talking about something like this, is now our strongest advocate. Now, she makes sure that the community is a major stakeholder at the table, and no decisions are made without the community input. It really was a paradigm shift, not only for the community, but for the local government. By working on communications and addressing the trust factor, we realized everybody wanted the same thing. There were just different ways of how to achieve it.

Can you describe how you utilize visioning processes in the ReGenesis project?

Mitchell: The visioning process grew out of the forums which followed the first meeting of the federal partners. That's when the public and private sectors, including industry, came to the table. We looked at our basic needs. We also looked at what the city had envisioned; things they had sitting on the shelf were some of the exact same things that the community residents were wanting. The county was the same way. It was kind of a thing where, the more you had residents and the Community Economic Development Office talking, the more we realized that we had mutual concerns in terms of housing and crime and just the basic things that shape a community.

We also realized that in order to rebuild a community, you have to rebuild the people. This is related to the whole visioning process, because it cannot be "This is what the city's going to do and that's that." So it became a thing where, as a stakeholder, the community was at the table, shoulder-to-shoulder with the local government in shaping what the community was going to look like. At that point, the City Manager stated that we need a plan. He said: "Harold, it may all be in your head. But for the rest of us, we need to see it on paper."

There were still some doubts regarding how the city should get involved, because of the responsibility and cost of the landfill. The same was true for the county, because they felt that it was going to take a lot more to invest to rebuild this community than what they were ready to commit. So, we as a community went after an appropriation with Senator [Ernest] Hollings, and basically we didn't have everything that a grant writer would say that you needed. We had limited to no resources, but we put on a paper napkin the sketch and design for a three-page request to the senator. We ended up getting $850,000, which was used to do the redevelopment plan and acquire some of the properties.

ReGenesis entered into a formal dispute-resolution process with Rhodia Chemical Company. Based upon this experience, can you share some lessons in the use of dispute resolution?

Mitchell: We learned a lesson from the IMC process when we allowed the attorneys to step in. Once it became a thing of the attorneys, they started representing things that were not our concern, but concerns that would help them in their case. And once we brought the attorney to the table, the other side had to bring theirs. It became a thing of the attorneys talking and dialoguing, and us sitting to the side.[16]

With Rhodia,[17] we felt that we needed to sit down and talk because there had never been a dialogue between the community and the company. There was much animosity and distrust because the company came in disguised as an apartment complex. The guy that purchased the property from the city said that it was going to be apartments, and it ended up as a chemical facility. The community went through the process of a "harmless" fertilizer plant becoming a Superfund site, and a landfill becoming a Superfund site. Now, you have the visual of this "monster" of a chemical plant. So there were a lot of fears off the bat about environmental health and safety.

We almost went down the same road as before with the attorneys. However, it helped us that there was a new plant manager. He invited me to come to the facility. We ended up with a process for a dialogue, including a face-to-face meeting. We decided who we wanted to be a part of the dialogue. We agreed we didn't want either side to bring attorneys. We wanted their decision makers, and we wanted the community.

But we needed a facilitator. At first, we used someone that both the community and the company decided upon. He did not have, however, the proper background and understanding to proper address the issues. So things got on track only when Tim Fields came in.[18] He had more of an understanding. [He] was able to challenge the industry, and then turn around to the community and challenge the community. We found out that the company had no plans of leaving, and there was no way we could force them out legally. Then with the industry, you say that you want to be a good corporate partner, what are you going to do? And that's when some of the hostility and anger kind of dropped.

In less than seven months, there are five full-time employees as a result of the dialogue process. There is an odor patrol committee that has been set up with the community to monitor the facility. We are working with Georgia Tech on the groundwater issues. We just finished the sampling [plan] for their monitoring. And we looked at some of the things that they could do to better the facility itself. One thing was the odor problem. They are looking at putting up a dome over the waste treatment that would minimize the pile odors. They also are considering walls for a beautification buffer, so as to improve the noise and visual factor. They addressed the sound issue themselves because when they came into the community they heard how loud the speaker was. Currently, we're still in the process of looking to see how a coexistence can occur. We are trying to see how they could best coexist with the redevelopment vision of the community.

The ReGenesis Revitalization Project is now on the cusp of Phase 2 of your community revitalization process. Can you describe what is envisioned?

Mitchell: The community had the opportunity to shape the redevelopment plan for all three subdivisions. Part of that was coming out with a wish list of what they would like to see in the redevelopment. We were awarded our community health center, and within the first three months of operation we've seen more than 2,000 patients.[19] We received another appropriation of one million dollars of transportation money to acquire and design a parkway. Again, the community had the opportunity to voice their concerns about roads coming off of a parkway through the community, and the havoc created by traffic running through local streets. In our vision, one goal is to turn a 30-acre textile mill site into a health and wellness park. We are also exploring a sports park.

What, in your opinion, have been your biggest accomplishments and obstacles in this project?

Mitchell: The biggest accomplishment was having the critical foundation elements in place, especially the community and the local government. When we went after grants to benefit the community, they had to flow back through one of the municipalities. If we did not have the relationship, we would have been stalemated. So I think the communication, having the foundation of the right partners there at the table, thinking outside of the box to create and implement. If you have that, the potential of what could happen is unlimited.

The biggest obstacle was the feeling that community people were not smart enough or capable of becoming a stakeholder to intelligently sit down and discuss their vision in a way that we were able to do. We had to fight through the stereotype, the same way that the community had their walls up against the company. In some cases companies and government may have legitimate concerns about communities, especially when it comes to money. Being able to put a [management] structure in place helped to ease their minds.

What, in your opinion, is the importance of being well prepared and having a good plan of action?

Mitchell: That's the big difference, i.e., knowing when to pick up the bat, when to sit down and talk, and knowing how to present your case. You know a lot of times, we have people who are just talking off the top of their heads. I think there's a lot of times when our credibility is called into question, like it is obvious, "he doesn't know what the hell he's talking about." I believe you should go in with all your evidence and state your position. I mean it's not going to work all the time, but you have to start building your stuff from somewhere. Even if you're talking about litigation, you're going to have to convince an attorney that you have a strong case in the first place.

The Intertribal Council on Utility Policy: Northern Great Plains Tribal Wind Energy Development

The first tribally owned wind generator was dedicated on the Rosebud Sioux Reservation in South Dakota on May 1, 2003. This 750-kilowatt wind power turbine, the culmination of an eight-year vision on the part of the Rosebud Sioux Tribal Utility Commission and the Intertribal Council on Utility Policy (COUP), was the first phase of an ambitious plan to harness the wind energy of the Northern Great Plains as a way to create tribally operated sustainable homeland economies.[20] Based upon this initial success, Intertribal COUP plans to build a 30-megawatt wind power generation project at Rosebud and an additional 80-megawatt project across eight reservations on the Northern Great Plains.

The Intertribal COUP's plans took an important step forward when, on August 8, 2003, Secretary of Energy Spencer Abraham announced that the US Department of Energy's Office of Energy Efficiency and Renewable Energy is making $2.2 million available to seven tribes to support the development of renewable energy resources on tribal lands. One of those grants went to the Rosebud Sioux Tribe to begin development of the planned 30-

megawatt wind energy project. The tribe will sell the electricity to provide economic benefits for the tribe and to create jobs for tribal members.

This case focuses on the unique issues of capacity building and collaboration in a tribal context. Under federal law, American Indian and Alaska Native tribes are recognized as self-governing sovereign governments. The elegant and powerful vision guiding this effort is both a product of and a contributor to the concepts of ecological restoration and restorative justice for tribes articulated in this case.

Please provide some background on the tribal wind energy project.

Spears: The Intertribal COUP was established in 1994, and I have served as its president since then. It is a confederation of tribes with a mission of tribal wind energy development.

Gough: The story of the large hydro-power dams on the Missouri River is a prime example of federal development that has brought benefits to the region, but which has continued to wreaked havoc on Indian lands and cultural values. It is said, "If you don't know where the Indian reservations in the Dakotas are, just find the dams and look upstream." The dams, built for regional flood control along with power generation, were purposely located to flood some of the best reservation bottomlands in order to provide benefits to non-Indian communities downstream. For tribes who have had to relocate both the living and the dead, with entire communities including cemeteries forced to seek higher grounds, "flood control" has come to mean that Indian lands get permanently flooded while someone else is in control.

Given the destructive history of hydro-power dams to Indian Country, we look today at a river that has drastically altered both human and natural habitats in order to support barge traffic below the dams. At the same time, we look at the federal hydro-power dams and the power lines that transmit electricity throughout the region, and we see an infrastructure created by the government that crosses and connects all the reservations and happens to stretch across perhaps the richest wind regime in the world. This is the Northern Great Plains, which covers Montana, Wyoming, North and South Dakota, and a little bit of Nebraska and Minnesota. The Great Plains is subject to three major flowages of air, changes in air and atmosphere coming arctic down, the gulf up, and the jet streams in the West. And the Great

Plains is without mountains or forests. The ever-present winds have a constancy that makes the region very suitable for wind energy generation.

That is the vision we put together for this Environmental Justice Demonstration Project. It is a little different than a lot of other environmental justice efforts in the past. We certainly have environmental assault and injustice in the fact that the tribes have suffered the most from the building of the dams and the flooding of their lands.

We were looking for a way of addressing the environmental injustice with a positive proactive stance by saying "How might we use the current situation and infrastructure to meet the tribal aspirations and to develop a sustainable homeland economy?" Wind looks like one the best opportunities for tribes to own and control a technology and produce a premium product—clean, inexhaustible energy—that also can be environmentally benign and economically valuable.

What were some key challenges for capacity building among tribes?

Spears: The capacity building, first of all, must be education on what it takes to develop a project. We do tribal wind outreach groups. Beginning with tribes up here, we've been conducting tribal wind outreach groups. The National Energy Laboratory recognized that. In fact Bob and I have contracts to do this kind of outreach work across the country. In order to be successful, three basic criteria have to be met. You have to have the energy resource, the transmission access, and lastly road access. The tribes must have a basic understanding of these requirements.

The other type of capacity building is in the area of tribal infrastructure. You must do planning, development. and management of wind energy. We have a general plan. Bob just finished drawing up the actual charter for a tribal wind energy authority that can be expanded to do all types of energy-related things, including energy efficiency, audit, and an innovative resource plan that includes all the resources you have. In this way, development can take place in an orderly manner, with a good plan as well as developing the law that it takes to enforce the good environmental protection. In addition, settled commercial and contract law are also critical so a tribe can do business.

Tribes have not been known for business development. However, we have some great success stories out there. The key ingredient was the separation of the business from the tribal government, so that the business is insulated from political risk. It needs the authority to do business, to seek financing, and to look at different ways of returning that benefit to the tribal membership. Lastly, we need to do capacity building upfront in the environmental area, to make sure we are protecting our environment, especially our cultural resources.

What are your views regarding the relationship between problem-identification and problem-solution orientations?

Gough: At least from my reading of the environmental justice literature, what distinguishes this project is the following: Not only have we identified the problems, but we also have latched onto what we think is a really good strategy for solutions. Tribal opportunities for renewable energy development came out of the context of the global climate change national assessment for native peoples. A workshop was conducted with tribes from around the country. Tribes identified all the assaults on their environments that came from a variety of approaches on and off the reservations. We also looked at the things that have real impact on community health. And everyone of the participants, in looking at global warming as well as economic development on the reservation, saw that renewable energy was a "no regret" strategy for building local sustainable economies as well as addressing the larger global warming issues.

We have recognized the problem and we've come up with a solution. I think the agencies we are working with have appreciated that more than just simply just identifying and complaining about a problem and demanding something must be done. We have presented something that we think can be done, and we're ready to do it.

Do you have examples of some innovative partnerships?

Gough: We have just started exploring an initiative with the US Cities for Climate Protection group. There are about 140 cities in the United States that are voluntarily going to meet the Kyoto targets within their jurisdictions, and they were going to do so through energy efficiency and renewable energy. Well, we are looking at what the opportunities would be for tribes to partner with these cities. Tribes can partner and produce some of the renewable energy those cities would then consume. We would look to the federal government as our partners who own and run most of the transmission lines in the West to make sure that we can move tribally based renewable energy to public power systems. Imagine the environmental justice opportunities in partnerships between tribes and cities, uniting rural and urban interests in energy efficiency and clean energy generation, with tremendous economic benefits for all concerned. Our federal treaty partners could help by allowing renewable energy its rightful place on the transmission system, particularly where those lines were built by taxpayers and are owned and operated by the federal government, as is the case throughout the West, where most tribes are located.

Do you have any thoughts about concepts of restorative justice as they relate to your work?

Gough: Tribal customary law seeks to address how you re-establish social harmony as a resolution of problem. All too often, the Western model is focused too narrowly on compensation for injustice or penal punishment for injustice. Those things don't work in the long run. Restoring the tribe as a full partner in the energy economy, for example, goes much farther than mere compensation or an award in dollars for the damage done. Compensation is an important element to help make a community whole, but that just addresses the past and not the future. It is far better for the tribe to be able to participate in future as a full partner, to stand shoulder to shoulder with the other players—WAPA,[21] the Army Corps of Engineers, other government agencies, the coal companies—in managing the river from now on. Tribes have a future and can provide a powerful and respectful voice in future development, to speak on behalf of all of the interests that the tribes have in the Missouri River as the lifeblood of the region.

Do you wish to share some key lessons learned from your experiences?

Spears: One is the need for training. An idea that we are going to talk more about is the Intertribal COUP Sustainable Development Center, a place for tribal leadership to come learn about what it is going to take to sustain us into the future. We seek to address not only how we can contribute to a sustainable economy for our children but also how we can contribute to the overall restoration of the Earth.

When looking at energy issues, we realize that these involve the long-term planning required for investments of millions dollars to energy infrastructures. In addition, we are dealing with agencies and bureaucracies that only respond to crisis or long-term legislation or other types of long-term plans.

It is strategically necessary and effective to engage them in long-term planning. We couldn't do this 20 years ago, but we can do it now.

Environmental Health Coalition: Barrio Logan, San Diego

On September 12, 2002, Barrio Logan residents and the Environmental Health Coalition (EHC)[22] celebrated a monumental victory for public health and environmental justice. Master Plating—a metal plating shop, located near several homes, that had accumulated more than 150 violations of environmental and health regulations—announced that it would shut down. Master Plating was also required to remove equipment, clean and decontaminate the facility, and completely remove all hazardous waste and materials by November 15, 2002. The following case is an example of how the utilization of collaboration and consensus building became a critical addition to a grassroots organizing and legal strategy in the 15-year effort to relocate Master Plating.[23] While all the cases featured in this chapter are examples of social capital, this case mentions the concept explicitly. It is fitting that this is the last highlighted case in the chapter, as the tensions between problem identification and problem solving, as well as confrontation and collaboration, are revealed in sharp relief. In that sense, this case elucidates some important questions regarding the theory and practice of environmental justice.

Can you provide some background about the Barrio Logan community and what led up to the Environmental Justice Demonstration Project?

Forbis: Barrio Logan was historically a residential neighborhood. Historic land-use documents show that zoning was changed with the increase of people of color and low-income residents. The community was targeted for industrial development. Zoning was changed to allow heavy industries to come in and to put in establishments like plating shops, woodworking facilities, auto body shops. So what you have now is a patchwork quilt of land uses, having very detrimental effects on the health of residents as well as aesthetics and all kinds of other issues (like safety).

Barrio Logan residents have been fighting on this issue for quite some time. In 1990 EHC proposed a "buffer zone ordinance." This would have required the gradual separation of these uses. In addition, it would have put in a buffer between heavy industries and residents. At that time industries organized against it. So the city established a task force to study the issue. The task force came back and recommended that, at least, plating shops and chemical storage and distribution facilities be relocated out of the neighborhood. We then went through a process under an EPA Brownfields Grant of trying to relocate Master Plating.

At that time, the city would not use its eminent domain or police powers to shut the facility down. The owner of the property had been made a fair-market-value offer for the property and the city tried to purchase it. But when he refused, the city would not follow that up with any police powers to force the sale. Subsequently, the community started realizing that in order to move forward, more data was needed to support its concerns around air toxics. We approached the county, but it refused to place a monitor in Barrio Logan, saying there were no problems and a monitor wasn't needed. The former head of our Air Pollution Control District has been quoted in the newspaper saying there is no such thing as environmental justice or injustice. That was the local political situation we were confronting.

At the time we approached the California Air Resources Board, they were in the process of developing their environmental justice program. They agreed and placed a toxics monitor in Logan Heights for 17 months and followed up with specific monitoring around the chrome plating shop. It was at the time that the first monitor was placed when the Environmental Justice Demonstration Project was formed. The project grew out of what was becoming a multi-stakeholder process which involved the community, EHC, business interests, the air pollution control folks, EPA, and the California Air Resources Board. The Environmental Justice Demonstration Project grew out of a process where all of these people already had been meeting together around the issues surrounding the chrome plating shop and the air monitoring.

The project established three goals: to reduce emissions and exposure to air toxics, to reduce incompatible land use, and to protect children's health. We established a partnering agreement because we didn't want to begin by debating whether or not there was a problem. Rather, we wanted to start with the question "How are we going to move forward to address it?" So we developed a partnering agreement in which anyone that wanted to be a partner had to sign onto those goals and had to acknowledge that there was an existing problem in the community.

Moya: The community's vision is like that of any residential community—they want to be able to have the same amenities that all of the other communities within San Diego and most of the United States have. They want more than anything to get rid of noxious industry that sits right beside them. High incidence of respiratory problems is a huge issue in the community. There's a huge traffic issue within and around the community. Some of the issues could be addressed. Others, like the freeways that surround the community, could not. But we're working right now on rerouting trucks out of the community. The main street in the community has a high, high traffic rate of industrial trucks because the port is so close to the community. So we're in the process right now of documenting all of the traffic and the emissions with a community group. That's one of the little steps that we're taking towards changing the land-use issue, which is a bigger issue that is going to take a little bit longer to address. We thought that one way of starting this process of making changes and getting to the land-use issue was to resolve the traffic issue. That would lead us, later on, to the bigger land-use issues within the community.

What lessons can you share about your experience with consensus building in the Environmental Justice Demonstration Project?

Forbis: It was really critical to have a facilitator in the early stages of the partnership, to have someone that is seen as somewhat of a neutral party. I think it was also critical to have a community and federal co-lead (EHC and EPA). This gives the community a seat at the table, but also brings the credibility of the federal agencies. Because of that, there was a lot more interest and participation in this effort. This project was viewed as something capable of being really meaningful down the road. In fact, we still have very good participation from the core members of the partnership. As I mentioned, there was this early stage of developing a partnering agreement. It involved talking about the fact that we didn't want this to be a group that was just going to discuss whether or not there was a problem. So it took a while to hammer out that agreement and to get folks on board. We then solicited essentially letters of interest or applications from folks talking about why they believed in the goals of the project and how they could contribute to moving those goals forward. Then the co-leads went through a process by which the partners were selected. And we made a very clear point with all of the groups that any group that couldn't sign onto the goal statement could participate and could observe because these were public meetings. However, they would not be invited to be partners. In the early stages of the partnership that was very critical. The county refused to sign the partnering agreement, but it was really the only entity. We had the major shipyards ready to sign the partnering agreement even though we didn't have the county, which I think was a very interesting political statement. And so we felt like we ended up with a partnership that had a very wide variety of membership ranging from EHC, individual community residents, and the Logan Clinic, to NASSCO and Southwest Marine—some of the major shipyards on the waterfront and major polluters in the area. In addition, there was a whole group of governmental agencies. So I think the role of the facilitator and the partnering agreement in the early stages was really critical to setting the partnership up as something that will be workable down the line.

What was necessary to build the capacity of the community to participate in a process like this?

Moya: What has helped us develop that capacity within the community was the implementation of the original SALTA Project in 1996,[24] which addressed all the issues of the community such as land use, health, and all of that. So when we got to the point of the EJ Demo in 2000 there was quite a number of community residents that were aware of the situation and also were aware of who were the parties important to solving the problems, and had been active on community organizing to stop fumigation[25] at the port. However, two to three years prior to SALTA, it would have been different because not many community members would have understood where the health problems were coming from. Although many of them understood that there was a problem, they didn't know how to put their finger on it. They knew there was a lot of incidences of respiratory problems, but didn't know why. Once we had the trainings and people read about the issues of air pollution and asthma and respiratory illness, they put one and one together. Part of the SALTA training also was to address the role of the government, so they started to understand what was involved in the process of meeting with their representatives. Most of them understood that they had the right to complain and to ask questions and to be heard. That was the beginning of the capacity building for the community.

Were there benefits for the community from the multi-stakeholder collaborative process?

Forbis: One of the other major benefits is giving visibility and credibility to the issues that are important in the community. The partnership involves federal, state, and local government stakeholders as well as industries, community-based groups, and residents. So that's a pretty powerful voice. It's a pretty powerful voice to have behind them when the community puts forward something. There's an example with the Master Plating process. Once the results came back from the Air Resources Board saying that there was a problem with hexavalent chromium in the Barrio Logan community, that information went to the EJ Demo Project. It was very helpful, at that point, to have the partners sitting around the table—ranging from NASSCO to the Logan Clinic and EHC. Everyone was saying that we needed to set up a separate public process to make sure that the data coming out about this is available to the public, available to the community residents, and is going under some scrutiny so that this problem gets resolved in the short term. There was also a lot of political pressure that came from the EJ Demonstration Project in the form of various partners sitting around the table, because all of a sudden this is open to a lot of scrutiny. Whereas if there hadn't been a collaborative group sitting there when the data came to us, it would have been EHC battling the county to get some other process set up. But the way it happened was that all of the partners agreed that a separate process would be a good thing. So the county supervisor (the same county that had refused to sign onto the project) became so concerned that he formed a separate working group on Master Plating that met every two weeks while the monitoring was continuing and the data was coming out. That was a joint project between him and the city council member for the area. So you actually had two politicians from fairly reluctant government bodies meeting with community residents once every two weeks for a period of a couple months. Then the county took very quick action to shut Master Plating down through the court system. So I think it was all of that added visibility, credibility, and scrutiny that really helped. Once that problem was identified, it was resolved within a fairly short process. The add-on to that is that once Master Plating was shut down, it had the visibility on the federal side. EPA Region 9 got the cleanup to happen very quickly with the Emergency Response Team. Had there not been an EJ Demo

Project, had there not been all of these regular meetings together and getting to build these relationships, I think the whole process would have taken a lot longer.

Moya: I want add just a little bit on the personal or the human side. Just the fact that the city and government representatives are sitting at the table at the same level as the community is important. It seems to me that they were better able to understand the complaints that this community has been making for many years. They were sitting with them listening about their kids, how bad their asthma was. It was not only this family in Barrio Logan that has this problem—they met them, they knew them. And that has a lot to do with how things work. For the community members who met with those who should be solving the problems, it became like a little family—not only NASSCO doing this or the Martinezes making a complaint.[26] It was my friend that I sit at the table with once in a while and we talk and I know who she is and I know who the representative is. So that really had built a lot of—I don't know what the word is—more understanding of one another, the way government works, and the way the community's problems are viewed.

You know what the word is: social capital.

Moya and Forbis: That's it exactly.

Talk a little bit about this because we think the Barrio Logan example is a great example of social capital development and its importance for creating the conditions for solving problems.

Moya: I've seen relationships made that were not there before. On the part of the community, there was a lot of resentment and not trusting the government because they had never done anything. For the government entities and even industry, it was just complaint, complaint, complaint all the time, and they were tired of this. That's what I gather from whenever we talk about the issues. But because of the meetings, people were able to hear from one another. I think that started to help each one another understand what the problem was, from the community's perspective or from the government's perspective.

Forbis: For example, from the government side, bureaucrats (folks doing the monitoring) are famous for saying, "Well, in Site Number 1, we have levels of X." And in some of these meetings, I kept correcting them, "No, at the Martinez family house, at the Ocegueda's house. . . . " So it wasn't "Site Number 1" or "Monitor Number 6," these are real people. I think that message got through because, like Maria said, they were meeting with the Martinez family, they know who's there, and they did develop that relationship. So I think there is a lot more credibility that the community residents have and what they're concerned about with these decision makers. And that they just can't be swept under the rug and ignored as just somebody complaining.

How do you react to those who are critical of consensus-based or collaborative decision-making models?

Forbis: We don't view it as having chosen this tactic over others. It seems like this is an important tactic in building power because you are bringing the community to the table. That's assuming that you do not let the process get out in front of the community, and the community's proposals are driving it. But I think there is a fine balance, because you have to also maintain your independence and your ability to, if you need to, sue somebody that is a member of the partnership over an issue on the side. And one thing that we said, in the beginning of the partnership, was that we understood that this does not mean that we would agree on everything with these partners. And this would not mean that we would not take direct action against the partners. It hasn't come up during the time of the partnership, but this is a fine balance, because we still feel that if there was a need to we would do those kinds of direct action. Hopefully, things could be worked out through the partnership, but if not we still have to maintain our independence and our ability to do what community residents would have us do.

One example is that with the Master Plating we actually did have a protest. We had brought the issue before the partnership, and then in that same week, the county was delivering their State of the County Address. We had a big protest out there. And some of the partners joined us. That also was helpful in getting things to move very quickly on Master Plating.

Moya: And then this last year when they had the State of the County address, we were invited to be part of that event by county representatives.

Forbis: So it is one tactic to build power, but the definite caution is "Do not let it be your only tactic." Then, I think, you give your power away.

Do you have any lessons regarding the relationship between problem identification and problem solving?

Forbis: One of the things that community residents need to be very careful about in a collaborative process is not to let the partnerships get out in front of them. They need to remain in the lead; this is one of the things we've been grappling with in the EJ Demo. It can be tricky when very well-intentioned people, if left to their own devices, might come up with solutions or agendas that would be different from those of the community residents. One thing we had to do is to get some of them to back off a little bit and allow the community process to happen. And then to be ready to be responsive and supportive and provide resources when the community process has matured.

I think the problem is that if communities are not identifying a solution, the one that may be imposed upon them might not be the one they would like. In other words, it might not be the one that they would design. I think community residents are in a unique position to be designing what the solution to these problems should look like. There is a lot of capacity building and empowerment that needs to go along with that. But to me, it is critical to at least place solutions on the table as part of the problem identification process. That is essentially how EHC does its work.

What is necessary to address the complexity of environmental justice situations?

Forbis: Because we see environmental justice as a larger social justice issue, we are mindful of the fact that we look at an issue from more than just a strictly environmental perspective. So when I talk about things like the importance of good jobs in the community and the importance of affordable housing in the community, folks are somewhat taken aback because they do not put that in the environmental justice agenda. Because we see the problem as so multi-faceted and more as a social justice problem than just an environmental problem, we do need to form those strategic alliances. We work with labor on some issues, we work with others on affordable housing issues. It is critical because it is all part and parcel to the same social justice agenda. And we are very mindful of the fact that if we pursue a strictly environmental agenda without thinking about the other implications it can have negative impacts, from a social justice side, on the community. In other words, if we just focus on getting incompatible land uses out of the community without any regard to bringing affordable housing in, this community is very much at risk for gentrification. We see it all as one package.

Conclusion

This chapter has sought to facilitate a broad national discourse on what it will take to achieve environmental justice and healthy communities. I hope that these stories will stimulate thoughtful deliberation about the organizing paradigms, policy frameworks, legal, policy, and planning tools, and consensus-building, negotiation, and dispute-resolution tools necessary to make the vision of environmental justice and healthy communities a reality.

The lessons that the Office of Environmental Justice of the US Environmental Protection Agency has gained from these and other projects are now incorporated into a rudimentary environmental justice collaborative model[27] that is the basis for a new grant program, the Environmental Justice Collaborative Problem-Solving Grants.[28] This was announced on May 30, 2003 in a Request for Applications that will lead to the selection of fifteen funded projects in its first year. This emerging environmental justice collaborative problem-solving model is based on the underlying premise that dynamic community leaders, such as those quoted in this chapter, have acted in proactive and strategic ways to coalesce compelling visions of environmental justice and healthy, sustainable communities and to guide collective action to achieve such visions.

This is a very rudimentary model that will mature only when there is a broad and concerted effort to engage with each other on the lessons to be learned and shared.[29] I chose these four cases because each exemplifies some aspects of the vision and proactive strategic thinking necessary to take the theory and practice of environmental justice to the next level. There are many conclusions to be drawn from these and other cases. It is too early to attempt to do so, because the concepts presented in this chapter are extremely new in the environmental justice context and there is neither a large enough experiential base nor a robust enough body of theory associated with them. In addition to support for impacted communities to implement these concepts, there must be a broad national discourse among impacted communities and all sectors of society on the issues and concepts presented here. These are essential to progress toward developing a robust experiential base and a sound body of theory.

There is one conclusion, however preliminary, that merits some mention at this time. Issues of environmental justice are technically complex and value laden, and they deal with controversial matters. They require expertise in navigating complex relationships. It is critical that the movement develop problem-solving, collaboration, consensus-building, dispute-resolution, and negotiation skills. Lack of such skills has led to social capital deficiencies, to an inability to build coalitions, and to a lack of political capital. To move the conversation from a reactive "the glass is half-empty" to a proactive "the glass is half-full" orientation, environmental justice leaders must develop a greater sense of a sense of vision, strategic thinking, and statesmanship. In addition to critically engaging and broadening the perspectives of environmental justice leaders and creating an umbrella large enough to allow engagement with leaders in related areas (e.g. community development and public health), there must be attentiveness to personal growth and transformation as a critical element of human capital development.

I would like to end with a description of recent developments related to the ReGenesis Environmental Justice Demonstration Project in Spartanburg which I believe to be emblematic of the work that this chapter is trying to promote. Now that a lot the visioning work is done and the underlying issues (such as the land-use dispute between ReGenesis and Rhodia Chemical Company) are being resolved, the ReGenesis Project has moved into a second phase of full-scale revitalization.

By the end of 2004, financial commitments from the public and private sectors amounted to nearly $50 million. This included a $20 million Hope VI Revitalization Grant Award from the US Department of Housing and Urban Development to provide for affordable housing. A community health center had already begun operation. In addition, on February 19, 2004 the *Spartanburg Herald-Journal* ran a front-page news story titled "Hope for Blighted Arkwright: Swiss Company Looks to Build Eco-Friendly Plant in Area." Napac Biotechnology AG, producer of environmentally friendly plastics alternatives, announced that it was going to locate a plant in the Spartanburg's Arkwright neighborhood. With an investment of up to

$20 million, the company will build a 95,000-square-foot facility and create more than 70 jobs.

All these developments bring to mind a point I made in August 2003, when the ReGenesis Project held a celebration of its progress to date. The evening's gala celebration began with a presentation about the project's guiding vision of environmental justice and healthy communities. At the conclusion of the event, I said "It is clear to all of us that, even though much had been accomplished already, the best is yet to come."

Notes

1. The views expressed in this article are solely those of the author. No official support or endorsement by the US Environmental Protection Agency or any other agency of the federal government is intended or should be inferred. The author wishes to express his appreciation to Mary Nelson, Harold Mitchell, Patrick Spears, Bob Gough, Maria Moya, and Paula Forbis for agreeing to be interviewed for this chapter. The author cannot express too strongly his profound appreciation and admiration to each of them for the work they do on a daily basis. This chapter, at its very core, is the author's tribute to them for the work that they do. The author wishes to express his appreciation to David Pellow, Miya Saika Chen, Katrina Behrend, and Sabrina Khandwalla for their assistance in taping and transcribing interviews.

2. The present environmental justice movement began in the 1980s and took shape over two decades. The idea of a "second generation" of environmental justice leaders is too complex to cover in this chapter. However, the "second generation" is an idea based on more than merely chronology; it is based on a decidedly different set of prevailing contexts, assumptions, experiences, and guiding visions that form leadership perspectives and approaches.

3. The Federal Interagency Working Group on Environmental Justice was established by Presidential Executive Order 12898. The IWG's membership consists of eleven federal departments and agencies. In 1999, the IWG initiated the process of developing a series of community-based, interagency, and multi-stakeholder demonstration projects. Two rounds, each consisting of 15 such projects, have been announced, the first in May 2000 and the second in March 2003.

4. Asset building is an approach to community development and problem solving that seeks to identify (asset-mapping) and build upon community-based assets such as the skills of local residents, the power of local associations, the resources of public, private, and non-profit institutions, and the physical and economic resources of local places. See John P. Kretzmann and John L. McKnight, *Building Communities from the Inside Out* (ACTA Publications, 1993).

5. The "Mutual Gains Approach to Negotiations" was developed by Lawrence Susskind, a professor at MIT and the president of the Consensus Building Institute.

It calls for a process by which parties with different interests can create value by exploring mutually beneficially options. See www.cbuilding.org.

6. Robert D. Putnam, *Bowling Alone* (Simon and Schuster, 2000).

7. More information can be obtained at www.bethelnewlife.org.

8. Brownfields are properties whose redevelopment is complicated by the presence or potential presence of hazardous substances.

9. Located in the suburbs of Chicago, Argonne National Laboratory is one of the US Department of Energy's largest research centers. It was the first national laboratory, chartered in 1946. Never a weapons lab, Argonne focuses on basic science, energy resources, and environmental management. Among its projects is a unique partnership with Bethel New Life and the neighboring West Garfield neighborhood on weatherization, energy efficiency, environmental cleanup, and recycling issues.

10. The Center for Neighborhood Technology is a Chicago-based non-for-profit organization that provides technical assistance, primarily to citizens' groups, on tools and methods to create and maintain sustainable urban communities. Its URL is www.cnt.org. The Neighborhood Capital Budget Group is a Chicago-based coalition established to empower communities to plan for, participate in, and benefit from the revitalization of the city's neighborhoods by bringing together money and people through budget and policy research and coalition building. Its URL is www.ncbg.org.

11. For his efforts, Mitchell received the EPA's 2002 National Citizen's Excellence in Community Involvement Award and the Ford Foundation's Leadership for a Changing World Award.

12. This refers to the International Minerals and Chemicals Inc. site, now considered a Superfund-caliber site.

13. James Tally was elected mayor of Spartanburg in 1998. The present mayor is William Barnett III, elected in 2002.

14. The Arkwright Dump is the second Superfund site in this area.

15. In order to ensure better coordination, the EPA Region 4 Office was later added as a fourth member of the ReGenesis Revitalization Project Steering Committee.

16. Residents of Spartanburg filed a lawsuit against IMC Global Inc. around issues arising from proximity to the Superfund site. A settlement was reached in 2003.

17. Rhodia Inc. is a large conglomerate that manufactures specialty chemicals. It has operations around the world. Its North America Group has headquarters in Cranbury, New Jersey. Rhodia operates a small facility in Spartanburg that employs 60 people and makes ingredients for home and health care products. Rhodia acquired this facility in 1998.

18. Timothy Fields Jr. is the former Assistant Administrator for Solid Waste and Emergency Response at the US Environmental Protection Agency. He is currently a vice president of Tetra Tech EM Inc.

19. At its dedication ceremony on August 11, 2003, the community health center was officially named the Hollings-Mitchell Community Health Center.

20. See www.nativeenergy.com.

21. The Western Area Power Administration (WAPA) is one of four power marketing administrations within the US Department of Energy whose role is to market and transmit electricity from multi-use water projects. It markets and delivers hydroelectric power and related services within a 15-state region of the central and western United States.

22. See www.environmentalhealth.org.

23. See the fall 2002 special issue of *Toxinformer*, a journal published by the Environmental Health Coalition of San Diego.

24. *Salud Ambiental Latinas Tomando Acción (SALTA)* is an environmental justice and community organizing training manual developed to work with Latino communities on environmental justice issues. It can be adjusted to work with any community organization that is working on social change, community empowerment, and environmental justice.

25. The SALTA Project was active in community organizing efforts, like stopping the use of methyl bromide to fumigate shipments at the port of San Diego.

26. The Martinez family lives next door to Master Plating, only a few feet away. Their story was featured as the cover photo essay for the Rockefeller Foundation's 1999 Annual Report. Five-yea-old Robert Martinez is one of hundreds of children in Barrio Logan who suffer from asthma. He has lived next to Master Plating for most of his life.

27. Environmental Justice Collaborative Model: A Framework to Ensure Local Problem-Solving (EPA 300-R-02-001). Copies are available from www.epa.gov.

28. US Environmental Protection Agency, "Office of Environmental Justice, Environmental Justice Collaborative Problem-Solving Grant Program Request for Applications," *Federal Register* 68 (2003), no. 109: 33934–33942).

29. See Towards an Environmental Justice Collaborative Model: An Evaluation of the Use of Partnerships to Address Environmental Justice Issues in Communities (EPA/100-R-03-001) and Towards an Environmental Justice Collaborative Model: Case Studies of Six Partnerships Used to Address Environmental Justice Issues in Communities (EPA/100-R-03-002). These reports were based on studies conducted by the EPA's Office of Policy, Economics, and Innovation (www.epa.gov/evaluate). In addition, the International City/County Management Association (ICMA) is conducting a study of the IWG demonstration project collaborative partnerships, looking particularly at the community–local government interface.

III

Environmental Justice and the Challenge of Globalization

15

South African Perspectives on Transnational Environmental Justice Networks

Heeten Kalan and Bobby Peek

This chapter, adapted from an interview with David Pellow, represents the personal views of Heeten Kalan and Bobby Peek.

Heeten Kalan

I direct groundWork USA, which is based in Boston. My organization has an interesting history that I would like to relate to you.

In the early 1990s, I started the South African Exchange Program on Environmental Justice (SAEPEJ) as a way of connecting the environmental justice struggles in the United States with those of my home country.

I come to this work with the understanding that governments are talking to each other, multinationals are in constant touch with each other, but the communities that are actually bearing the brunt of corporate and government practices and policies have no vehicles that allow them to talk to each other. So how does a community that is poisoned by Rhone-Polenc in West Virginia talk to a community outside of Johannesburg that is also poisoned by Rhone-Polenc? What vehicles must be created there to ensure this level of networking and communication?

We were running a very small operation when we began in 1993, largely for me traveling to South Africa making connections to the EJ movement here, trying to bridge the roles. I had a vision that we were a switchboard, we were an exchange, we were looking at how to connect people across borders and continents. We took the traditional definition of "exchange" and threw it open. We said it means informational exchange, it means technical assistance exchange, it means people-to-people exchange. Initially, students were approaching me saying "We heard you do exchanges." My response was "Yes, we do, but this isn't about student exchanges, this isn't about you going to another campus; this is about communities and organizations visiting each other and talking to each other." We started off where I would try to get someone from South Africa invited to a conference in the United States and get the conference to pay for their travel. And I would say "Can we add two weeks to this person's visit?" And that way we'd take advantage of the bulk of the expenses, get them to speak at different campuses, get them to speak with different environmental justice groups around the country. SAEPEJ's roots can be traced to my first job out of college, with the National Toxics Campaign Fund (NTCF) in Boston. In 1993, I began exploring the potential of an in-house South African project there.

On my first trip to South Africa for NTCF, I took a bunch of samples that we later tested in the Citizens' Laboratory (housed at NTCF). The samples were of various toxins from a number of sites outside Johannesburg. One of the activists in South Africa commented on a report listing the chemicals that had been found in one of the samples: "The fact that I could actually sit with the company and throw this report down, whether that report was valid or not, sent a strong message to them—a reminder to the company that we can now access this kind of information within a week." There was power just in that, he noted. To be able to say "We're no longer reliant on you to give us information and we have our own way to get information" changed the power dynamic. And granted this was a time where we weren't the only ones doing this. Greenpeace, for example, was playing a very important role around the Thor Chemical case. They had their scientists going to South Africa and testing the mercury level in the Mngeweni River. I see all this as adding capacity to what was already happening in South Africa.

For me there was another side to the exchange. While Americans were trailblazing on environmental justice and had a lot to teach South Africans, South Africans had a lot of organizing knowledge and experience to share with Americans. So for me, as a South African, it was an attempt to really try to establish what I called "an equal two-way exchange." In the early days I pushed hard on the question "What does solidarity organizing mean?" I was convinced that the days were gone when American were organizing because they felt for those poor brown people in South Africa. We were saying "This isn't about that; this is about saying what's in your back-yard, and what's a problem in your backyard is also a problem in South

Africa—that a problem in South Africa is a problem here as well." To drive this home, I used the South African lens to actually look at the United States. I spoke on college campuses and in churches. I would describe West Dallas and have my audience think I was describing a place in South Africa. I tried hard to make these connections and not see them as separate problems. I think US-based activists had to go abroad, and they also had to get put in their place by activists abroad a lot of times. One South African activist was detailing stories of escaping death during the apartheid government and visiting activists were moved and began saying "Wait a minute, OK, my struggle is not number one." I've always said that just because the term "environmental justice" was coined in the United States doesn't mean that the US has a monopoly on the term. People have been doing this kind of work all around the world and may not be calling it environmental justice. The US environmental justice movement has given the rest of us an incredible tool by giving us a language to talk about it, giving us the Principles of Environmental Justice. However, it doesn't mean that you monopolize the issue. We can only get beyond that once you get exposed to the work other people are doing and see the day-to-day harsh realities that people have to face. This happens largely because people get to know each other and people get to talk to each other. I have been on delegations where the US arrogance has been mind blowing. And in South Africa we can be quirky. If you're an American, regardless of your skin color, you're an American. So there were a lot of people, people of color, who would go to South Africa thinking you know "I'm now going to relate to my brothers and sisters," and the South Africans are sitting there saying "I don't know what you're talking about, you're an American!" It's not that there was no affinity, it was just that there's a reality that South Africans wanted to acknowledge. You're an American, you come with many more resources that I have and, quite frankly, that's a difference and we need to acknowledge it; we can't shy away from it. The other very important piece for me is that South Africans—and South Africans aren't the only people to blame here—often brushed the United States with one stroke. One needs to see that the United States itself has its own layers of oppression. You always hear the term "North-South exchanges," right (between people of the Global North and people of the Global South)? What I always wanted to do with these exchanges is connect the South with the South of the North. Clearly there is a South in the North, right? Who are those people who are the marginalized or the oppressed in the North? We have a lot in common with each other, and I think that's an important piece for South Africans to see that "Oh wow, things are not just hunky-dory in the United States, everyone's not living in a home with a white picket fence and has a nice job and weekends off." There is a harsh reality here in the United States. What are the remnants and impacts of slavery? What does it mean to be a Central American immigrant farm worker? What does it mean to be a single mother on welfare? What are those issues, who are those people? For me that became very important. As I spent time in the United States, I realized, as one who had brushed the US with one stroke, that we have allies there and that we need to know who they are and we need to be working with them.

In August of 2003, SAEPEJ, having worked closely with groundWork in South Africa over the years, decided to become an affiliate of groundWork. Thus was born groundWork USA. For me, groundWork USA continued the mission of two-way exchanges by opening an office in the United States.

In some ways, our campaign against Shell International is a good example of how transnational networks, communication, and activism come together. The campaign against Shell International is an effort by a coalition of groups from South Africa, Nigeria, the Philippines, England, the Netherlands, the Salchalin Islands, Curaçao, and the United States. The way we do it is building it slowly; this doesn't happen overnight. We approach our work knowing that if we do the groundwork, in terms of the organizing work, the campaigns will follow, rather than using the campaign to define the work. If we just work off a campaign model, we leave very little behind. The campaign model is, unfortunately, the one employed by the major environmental groups. They don't take the time to build the infrastructure that can actually sustain campaigns over the long haul. We place a lot of emphasis on building the relationships with institutions and individuals, with building good strong solidarity networks with groups and individuals so that when an appeal comes across our desk or if we send out an appeal to one of our partners around a certain campaign, they're not just signing a letter, it's giving the issue more weight than that and we think that, ultimately, we'll all be stronger to deliver on something.

The Shell Campaign allows us to work with other international NGOs like Friends of the Earth as well as local groups who are affected by Shell's operations all over the world. In 2003 we held a big press conference in London with community representatives from South Africa, Nigeria, the Philippines, and the United States. We went to the Shell shareholder meeting as shareholders, and we took up almost all of the space. We're engaging them on a number of different issues, but primarily we are saying "You need to get away from the case-by-case basis, you need to having some global stances and global policies." I gave a talk the other day and someone asked me "What is the community in South Durban asking from Shell? Are they asking to shut the plant down?" And I said they are not asking to shut the plant down. I said actually what they are asking for is something very simple, they're asking to sit down with Shell and jointly work out and agree on a five-year pollution reduction plan. I said that is not asking for a lot. In fact, if you really look at it, that is an incredibly reasonable request. But we're painted as these crazy guys who are trying to shut Shell down and take people's jobs. So I think this sort of campaign is going to build more and more momentum in the next year or two, and they're going to have to take us very seriously because we really are connecting with other people around the world, we're not going to take this any more. It will require creativity and alliances with people from various backgrounds. For example, we are well aware of the contentious divisions between the mainstream white middle-class environmental movement and the people-of-color environmental justice movement in the United States. Some folks might say that a parallel gap has emerged between people-of-color environmental justice groups in the United States and other transnational environmental organizations like the Basel Action Network (BAN), the Global Anti-Incinerator Alliance (GAIA), Greenpeace, and Friends of the Earth—groups that are fighting for international environmental justice. GroundWork has been able to cross this boundary and work with groups on both sides.

I think part of it is that South Africans tend not to approach our political activism from a point of identity politics. Whoever we decide to work with in the United States, I see them as allies. They're our allies. They're people who can help our struggles, they strengthen the work. Over the years, I've realized that to me it hasn't mattered whether folks who step up to the plate and further the struggle in South Africa by providing assistance, research, or whatever are people of color or good solid white folks. Ultimately they have decided to come and serve the cause and the struggle, and the minute we think that either the people of color or the white folks are not doing it on our terms we put a stop to it. As long as folks are willing to say "This is your struggle; I'm willing to help you and support you and be respectful of where you want to take this; I am at your service," we'll work with you.

We need to realize the common ground that links us together. Since the day I heard the term "disproportional impact," I had a huge problem with that. Why? Because I used to (at least quietly or within the circles of the EJ movement) say "So if we had proportional impact, it would be just fine and we were all going to go home? Why are we focusing on disproportional impact? So if it was proportional, we're happy? Is that what we're saying?" And people are saying "No, no, no that's not what we're saying." And so then lets forget this disproportional impact, let's really focus on the core issue. I know for a fact that there are white folks in the South, white folks in Maine, white folks in New Hampshire who are poor as hell getting screwed by big multinational companies. Now are those issues not important to me? Absolutely they are, and they should be because it's the same bloody company that's killing people in South Africa. If I can't make the connection between how paper workers in Maine are treated by a South African paper company and what that company is doing in South Africa, I've closed myself off to this work. I am closing myself off to the strength we can gain by working together. Now, I have my struggles with predominantly white organizations around issues of race, but I'm not willing to throw the baby out with the bathwater, and I'll engage them on those issues and I'll be direct with them on those issues and I'll work with them in pushing for a world that's cleaner and safer for all of us. I can't just wipe them off, because they bring good resources, they bring good knowledge, good experience, and they bring their portion to this. So in the EJ movement, should the women of color now send all of the guys home because they're sexist? And say well "Screw off, we're not going to come talk to you, and should we now draw another line?" I think it's futile and it's problematic. Now, I completely support and agree with how the environmental justice movement has decided to pursue a grassroots-led people-of-color movement. I fully respect it. Who am I to say "No" to that? I think the limitations emerged because the EJ movement has not really debated and articulated how it is going to work and function with its white allies.

With regard to where I think the EJ movement is today, I think the space needs to be created for new leaders; the space needs to be created for new organizing work to emerge rather than people protecting their turf. And I think a national agenda will emerge from the strong local work. But unless it's backed up by local statewide work, a national agenda won't work. I don't think the EJ movement is as strong as it was in 1994–95, but in order to really see this we have to understand the cycle that movements go through. We have to understand this work historically. We also need to measure the EJ movement with a different yardstick, and we have to always remember that this is a very new and young movement. It's not that old, but we compare it to the labor movement, the women's movement, and the civil rights movement. It's young, it's broad in scope, and it's global. So ultimately I think we'll look back and say those were all lessons that make us stronger.

Bobby Peek

I live in South Africa and I work very closely with Heeten, who is based in Boston. In 1999, with two colleagues, we started groundWork as a response to the need for activism around environmental justice issues at a local level. I believe the birth of the EJ struggle in South Africa occurred in 1992 when the EarthLife International Environmental Conference posed the question "What does it mean to be Green in South Africa?" The EJ struggle in South Durban was born on March 25, 1995, when the community protested against the local oil refinery (originally owned by Mobil). The refinery was opening a new unit without two or three pollution-reduction mechanisms. President Mandela came to open the plant and we protested. Mandela invited us to his residence, and we negotiated a settlement. The space that was created at that time led to the birth of the South Durban Community Environmental Alliance.

The communities we at groundWork work with are facing pollution from a number of sources, including oil refineries (Shell, BP, Mobil, Total, Caltex), hazardous waste incinerators and landfills, petrochemical storage facilities, sewage plants, paint manufacturers, acrylic fiber manufacturers, and plastic manufacturers. The incineration of waste is a big issue in South Africa. We have had success at stopping new incinerators and other hazardous land uses from coming in, primarily when we are able to control the framing of the debate and focus it on waste. The government wants to focus on the use of this waste as an alternative energy source, but we reject this view.

People outside of South Africa might think that since the fall of apartheid the environmental justice situation there must be better. However, the realities and legacies of apartheid are still with us. That doesn't change just because in 1994 we have democracy for the first time. Because the areas we are concerned about invariably are inhabited by the poorer (in political and economic mobility) parts of the population, these neighborhoods tend to remain the same. Certain folks move out of those neighborhoods, but generally they remain black.

But at the same time, you have industrial practices ongoing. And there's an infrastructure that the apartheid government set up, with roads, other infrastructure, and industries. Industries go back to these zones, and they continually develop them and affect poor black neighborhoods. Despite the principles of environmental justice guiding our legislation, despite Section 24 of the Bill of Rights of the South African Constitution, there is continual redevelopment and foreign direct investment in these industrial areas, which were developed on principles of environmental racism.

The South African state oil corporation Sasol has bought a facility in Mossville, Louisiana. We have been tracking this case and worked with the residents there. That's what is wonderful about having international activist networks, because sometimes we can go to America and say "We know you've had a bit of experience with this company that's moving here, so can we learn from you?" In the Sasol case, of course, it was the other way around. There was a big multinational out of South Africa, and a community in America is saying to us "Help us. What do you know about this?" I think that was an important part of an exchange process. At another level, we have basic organizing experience to offer. South Africa has a very rich history of good organizing at a local level against apartheid, which the world can learn from, which America can learn from.

Exchanges between the United States and South Africa organized between SAEPEJ (now groundWork USA) and groundWork help people to understand that these things happen globally, and that we can make a difference. That for me was the greatest thing in terms of my EJ awakening. I suddenly realized, in the mid 1990s, that you don't have to live life the way it is—it can be better. You don't have to live next to an industry and suffer pollution, and you can link up globally to fight this injustice.

I think that's what we're trying to do with the exchanges. We take people from South Africa and go to places in America where people have won and have managed to overcome the challenges and get the local communities in South Africa to understand that they can also obtain these victories. These are also technical exchanges where we learn about each other's research as well. The egregious practices of Sasol and Shell provide opportunities to build these activities and support international campaigns.

In terms of where the environmental justice movement is most visible on the Africa continent, there are two or three nodes where it is becoming a big issue. South Africa being one, by virtue of our link during the anti-apartheid with the civil rights movement in the United States, so the language that was appearing in the civil rights movement and around the environmental justice movement during the late 1970s and the early 1980s was something that came to South Africa during the late 1980s and the early 1990s. In terms of other nodes, Cameroon and Nigeria are where there is a lot going on because mainly they are forced to respond to the impacts of the very brutal oil industry. In Cameroon there has been a clear articulation against globalization and corporate power, and I know that people have used the principles of environmental justice in their struggles against the oil industry in Nigeria. Across the continent, major EJ issues include access to basic services, energy needs, healthy food and crops, clean water, labor rights, and various problematic industrial practices. We work closely with people in many nations here, and we are trying to develop an African platform on environmental justice issues. We are working with colleagues and comrades in Mozambique and Swaziland. I also recently met with people from the Copper Belt in Zambia (where mining companies have raped the land and natural resources) and with activists from Angola (which is going to be Africa's biggest crude oil producer in the future), so we are making linkages there in this broad African environmental justice campaign.

In Africa, we work with other NGOs with whom we build an understanding of the struggles we all face. Obviously they have their own linkages to the local communities, so we try to support what they are doing, with solidarity, with advice, with information, and hopefully, in the various countries they play very close local roles so we can start this African environmental justice movement. It's a process in which people must see that they are not alone, and that there are other people who are suffering from similar realities. In South Africa we work with local communities, linking them with and showing them the broad international scenario, providing technical assistance and providing administrative support around their campaigns.

As every activist knows, this kind of work brings its own set of risks. We have come under tremendous political pressure at times. The mayor and the city manager in Durban do not approve of what we're doing. There have been vicious attacks on us in the media. Government has sent the National Intelligence Agency (the old security state police—the equivalent of your CIA) knocking on our door with questions like "What are you doing?" and "Why are you doing it?" And eventually they came to the office and I had a groundWork lawyer and the chairperson of the board sitting with me, and I said "If you're going to talk to me, here's my chairperson, here's my lawyer, talk to me formally. I'm not going to talk to you informally." There is that heavy-handed pressure, which is intimidating enough for some people. I view it this way: "If you want to know what we are doing, sit down, let's talk. I'll talk for ten hours with you, and let you know everything, because there's nothing to hide." So, rather than having a chilling effect on us, I think that incident just motivated us to carry on doing what we were doing, and motivated us to do it in a much more organized way. We let our comrades know that this was going down and to beware of it.

There are numerous obstacles to achieving environmental justice here in my country. One problem with civil society in South Africa right now is that we lost a lot of great leaders to government in the post-1994 period, and for good reason, because obviously, the government needed good people to work with them, a lot of good comrades went into that line of work. A lot of them still continue fighting to the death on the inside, there's no doubt about it. But some of them have become typical bureaucrats, and that's the reality. So we need a strong civil society and people recognize that. Slowly but surely we are building up to its former strength. But I must stress that this is a very slow process, and that's our challenge, to build up this sector.

I think that at one level we might not be facing a black-versus-white issue so much as we are facing a North-versus-South issue, and this is something that comes up so much more often these days. At the World Summit on

Sustainable Development (held in Johannesburg in 2002), it was clear that America's greatest flaw is the feeling that "We know it all." I think that needs to change, and there needs to be a recognition that the South can speak for itself, that the South can put its own agendas on the table, and that the South can create its own policies and can lead those policies. So that needs to change. In terms of how that impacts the global EJ movement, what I'm saying to you is that America needs to sort itself out first—especially in light of the internal difficulties that emerged at the EJ Summit II in 2002—before the balance with the movement in the South will happen. The divisions between North and South make things very difficult in terms of environmental progress. Sometimes when you in the North take one step forward, we in the South tend to take two steps back. With every EJ victory there is some bitterness on the other level, on the other side, and for me, that's the sad reality that is quite painful at times.

We have had a lot of victories but need many more victories still. In terms of basic communication and transportation infrastructure it is sometimes difficult to reach communities here because there are parts of Africa and South Africa that are far more remote to us than Europe and the United States. Until we work at these levels of communication and can get people together at the local level, there's always going to be this arena open for corporate, industrial, or government abuse. Looking at that from that perspective, we have a hell of a long way to go. We've still got decades, even centuries of work ahead of us, so that is scary and alarming and exciting, but we have no choice because we have to do this work.

We have a set of principles of environmental justice but we need laws to give meaning to it, and this means special regulations to protect people who are in what I would call the danger zones. What you need to start doing is developing other industrial zones where we can start afresh from the green fields and start investing upfront in a proper manner. My belief is that if these multinational corporations are genuine about investing in Africa, they will invest long-term in terms of industries with a good environmental performance record. Parallel to this, the other important thing is that, as civil society, we need to work on weakening the corporate influence on the state. How do we chip away at corporate power? That's the main question.

16

The Pen Is Mightier Than the Sword: Global Environmental Justice One Letter at a Time

Paula Palmer

This chapter, adapted from an interview with David Pellow, represents Paula Palmer's personal views.

The main goal of the environmental justice movement is for communities marginalized by race, ethnicity, and poverty to gain political power to effectively protect their health and defend and manage their territories and resources. Over the last 20 years or so, there has been a lot of progress in bringing together activists for human rights, indigenous rights, labor, progressive politics, and environmental protection under the umbrella of environmental justice. The movement has deepened our understanding of our own and others' issues and served as a unifying tool. During the same years, corporate globalization has unleashed increased destruction of ecosystems and cultures, especially in developing countries, pitting the EJ movement against a tremendously powerful alliance of corporate, political, and military forces and making our work even more urgent. We learned we must globalize the movement, and we are still learning how to democratize it—that is, build a movement characterized by equity in a world characterized by growing inequality in resources and power.

Global Response was founded in 1990 as an international citizens' network for environmental activism and education. We work in partnership with other non-governmental organizations (NGOs) at the local, national, and international levels to prevent environmental destruction and support local communities as they defend their rights, traditional territories, and ecosystems.

The organization's founders were environmental activists in Colorado who thought globally and acted locally. In Boulder they spearheaded the protests against the Rocky Flats nuclear weapons plant, created the successful community recycling organization Eco-Cycle, and lobbied for the Clean Air Act, the Clean Water Act, the Endangered Species Act, etc. By the early 1990s, they realized that the success of the US environmental movement had had an unanticipated and undesired outcome: corporations were leaving the United States in search of locations in developing countries where they would be unburdened by environmental regulations. They were setting up operations in the most politically disenfranchised communities, where local people would find it very difficult to defend themselves and their natural resources. The founders of Global Response felt obligated to start acting globally by lending a hand to these communities. They created an organization that would adapt Amnesty International's successful model of citizen letter-writing campaigns to the environmental justice crisis in the developing world.

How Global Response Works

Grassroots organizations and indigenous peoples engaged in struggles for environmental protection and environmental justice can ask Global Response to launch international letter-writing campaigns on their behalf. We choose to work on campaigns where there is a significant environmental threat, strong local organizing, reliable scientific information, and where local people believe that international letters will increase their chances of success. We work with the local organizers to research the issues, develop a letter-writing strategy, and write action alerts that give solid background information and guidelines for letter writing. We issue the alerts by mail and email to our membership in 100 countries, asking our members to write personal letters to decision makers and send them by mail. As letters from all around the world pile up on their desks, corporate and government officials realize that the world is watching and they can't hide their abusive behaviors even in the most remote regions of the world.

Global Response campaigns have a very high success rate. An impressive 44 percent of the campaigns we have undertaken in the last 14 years have achieved their goals. Of course we can't take full credit for these victories—the local communities and organizers earn most of the credit for their courage, creativity, and persistence. But very often the local organizers say they could not have won their battles without the political pressure brought to bear by Global Response letters. We attribute our record of successful campaigns to solid research into the issues, effective partnerships with local and international organizations, and a membership that is committed to letter writing as effective citizen action for social change.

We have celebrated campaign victories in Nicaragua (where we helped the Mayagna indigenous communities stop illegal logging by a Korean multinational), in Costa Rica (where we blocked oil explorations by US companies on the biologically and culturally diverse Atlantic coast), in Ecuador (where we helped stop a Mitsubishi copper mining project in a cloud forest region), in Haiti (where the persistence of Greenpeace, Global Response, and other activists over a 10-year period finally resulted in the removal of toxic ash that had been dumped on a beach by a ship carrying garbage from Philadelphia), in India (where our letters helped persuade a company called P&O Ports to abandon plans to build India's largest industrial port at Dahanu, a region of forests and indigenous peoples), in Mexico (where we helped persuade the Mexican government to cancel permits for hotel construction at X'cacel, the last and best nesting beach for sea turtles on the Caribbean Coast), and in India (where we stopped World Bank funding for construction of medical waste incinerators).

Winning campaigns is not our only goal. We are also building a network of citizens around the world who are learning and practicing the skills of cross-cultural cooperation, global citizenship, and Earth stewardship as they write letters for Global Response. We encourage children, teens, teachers, and families to participate in our campaigns, hoping to instill in them the values of global cooperation for the sake of the planet as a whole.

An Actions Advisory Committee helps me select our campaigns from among the many requests we receive. Committee members include a physician, an international human rights lawyer, a hydrologist, a geologist, an engineer, and a sociologist, all with extensive international experience. They help me evaluate the information we receive from local organizers and conduct further research as needed to develop our written materials on each campaign.

Global Response Campaigns

Here are some brief descriptions of recent Global Response campaigns:

• A coalition of Ghanaian NGOs and communities affected by mining asked Global Response to support their efforts to keep multinational mining companies out of Ghana's protected forest reserves. We directed letters to the president of Ghana and to the CEO of Newmont Mining Company, urging them to enforce and respect Ghana's existing environmental laws, which prohibit mining in the forest reserves. We also collaborated with Project Underground (a US-based NGO) to organize protests inside and outside Newmont's annual shareholders' meetings in 2002 and 2003.

• The Sarayacu indigenous people of Ecuador, who are determined to keep oil companies out of their traditional territories, asked Global Response to write letters to the president of Ecuador and the CEO of Chevron/Texaco. Our letters support the Sarayacu people's right to say No to oil development within their territory, and to pursue their own ideas for culturally appropriate and sustainable economic development alternatives (ecotourism, for example). We also denounced Chevron/Texaco and CGC oil companies' unethical practices of bribery, threats, character defamation, trespassing and physical violence against the Sarayacu community.

• The Machiguenga indigenous people of Peru and a coalition of international organizations including Amazon Watch and Friends of the Earth asked Global Response to write letters urging the US Export-Import Bank not to finance construction of the Camisea Gas Pipeline. This pipeline project threatens the survival of indigenous groups that live in voluntary isolation as well as the Machiguenga communities; its construction and inevitable spills also threaten pristine tropical rainforests and habitat for many endangered species. In our letters we also asked the Bank (whose funds come from US taxpayers) to adopt and implement strict social and environmental standards for all their loans. In August 2003 the Bank dropped the Camisea project from its funding agenda "indefinitely"—a victory that can set an important precedent for Bank policy.

• Indonesian indigenous communities and NGOs and the Rainforest Action Network asked Global Response to write to the CEO of Citigroup, the world's largest private financial institution, demanding that they adopt and implement strict social and environmental standards for their loans. Specifically, we demanded that they stop financing the expansion of palm oil plantations in Indonesia, where companies are destroying rainforest and indigenous farms and villages. In response to public pressure, Citigroup and several other banks published and endorsed the Equator Principles, guidelines for socially and environmentally responsible financial practices. We will continue to press for stronger guidelines to be adopted, but the Equator Principles are a good start.

• Afro-Caribbean and indigenous Bribri communities along Costa Rica's Atlantic Coast asked Global Response to help them convince the Costa Rican government to cancel multinational corporations' permits to explore for oil both offshore and in the lowland tropical rainforests. The Harken Oil Company of Houston retracted its bid to explore inside the Talamanca Indigenous Reserve when it realized that Costa Rica would enforce the International Labor Organization's 169 Convention, which requires a transparent consultation process with potentially affected indigenous communities. The coastal Afro-Caribbean communities waged a multi-faceted campaign that included savvy legal work, grassroots organizing, high-profile public events and media, and international support from Global Response, the Natural Resources Defense Council, and the International Fund for Animal Welfare. After 18 months of campaigning, we celebrated a victory in 2002, when the Costa Rican government rejected the companies' environmental impact studies.

• A coalition of environmental, human rights, and other organizations in Kenya asked Global Response to help them stop a Canadian company's titanium mining project on the Kenyan coast. Kenya's Minister of Environment announced that he had received over 1,000 letters from people all over the world, convincing him to put the Tiomin Resources mining project "on hold" while further environmental and social impact studies could be conducted. In this case, Global Response's letter-writing campaign bought valuable time for the Kenyan groups to get scientific and legal assistance and develop their strategies for defending their communities, forests and marine resources against this threat.

Measuring Success

We measure success in various ways. Of course we hope our letters will contribute toward clear victories where our major demands are met. Over the last 14 years this has actually happened in 44 percent of our campaigns. For Global Response and for the local communities that are fighting for their health and safety, each campaign is considered ongoing until it is won. We frequently issue follow-up action alerts to our members, and we have done as many as six rounds of letters on a single issue.

We have also learned the hard lesson that no victory is permanent, and that the price of victory is eternal vigilance. When valuable resources—especially forests, minerals, and fossil fuels—are present, laws and regulations are frequently overturned, and communities must rise to defend themselves again. This is happening right now in Kenya, where a Global Response letter-writing campaign helped halt a Canadian titanium mining project for three years. Suddenly, in July of 2003, the new environment minister issued a mining license in complete disregard for the community consultation and environmental impact assessment processes that had been negotiated and approved. We initiated another round of Global Response letters on this issue soon afterward, supporting the demands of a coalition of Kenyan NGOs.

Aside from winning and losing in relation to our specific campaign demands, we celebrate other successes. For example, it's a success when we motivate hundreds of teachers and schoolchildren to write letters to save sea turtles, when we publicize in the West the inspiring example of religious leaders in South Korea who marched 195 miles in a continuous series of three steps followed by a bow with knees and foreheads on the Earth in hopes of saving a tidal flat, and when we hear from a member of a grassroots organization "Today you have lifted my spirits."

I think people everywhere are thrilled by true-life victories of the Davids over the Goliaths. To build the movement, we need to inspire people with these success stories and the possibilities they portend for all communities, everywhere.

All our campaigns seem hopeless at the outset, and I am not a very good judge of which ones will succeed. But since so many of them do, it is clearly worth putting all our effort into each one.

Most campaigns have many components—technical/scientific reports, litigation, legislation/lobbying, public protests, media coverage, letter writing, behind-the-scenes meetings—and at the end it is very difficult to calculate the relative effectiveness of each component. The best campaign strategy is to form coalitions where various organizations collectively undertake all of the above tasks. In the letter-writing component of campaigns, the keys to success are articulating clear demands supported by reliable scientific data, addressing them to the appropriate decision maker, pointing out the benefits to the decision maker of taking the desired decisions, and invoking international treaties and conventions.

A major question in each campaign is "Where is the desired change most likely to occur?" Should we aim to influence the corporations (and who within the corporate structure—the CEO? the shareholders? the board of directors?)? Or should we target government offices (the president? a sympathetic cabinet member? a legislative committee?)? Or should we target the international financial institutions that hold the purse strings? How about retail outlets for the product and potential consumers? Coalitions are increasingly focusing campaigns on public and private financial institutions, urging them to adopt environmental and social standards that they would apply to all their loans and underwriting. This strategy has the most potential for raising the environmental and human rights standards in all industries and geographic regions at once.

As we enter our fifteenth year, we at Global Response are increasing our participation in international EJ coalitions, starting with membership in the Amazon Alliance, and hope to help develop coalition campaign strategies to deal with overarching issues like the free trade agreements, the World Trade Organization, extractive industries, international financial institutions, rights of indigenous peoples, etc. We also prioritize campaigns requested directly by grassroots activists in developing countries who may have no other international contacts or partners. We help them find the resources they need to build their campaigns—financial, legal, technical/scientific, media, etc—and help them build citizen participation in their own countries through letter writing and youth activities.

Pros and Cons of Technology

Global Response may be the only activist organization that still asks its members to write personal letters, put them in envelopes, stamp and mail them to decision makers. We have resisted the trend toward model letters, mass emails, and mass postcard campaigns because we believe that personal letters mean more to both the receiver and the sender. We think it is a disservice to suggest that ecosystems can be saved by a click on a website; we think it takes more time and commitment than that. We work to inspire personal commitment in our members, and we encourage personal communication.

But with our small budget, we rely almost entirely on email for communications with local communities and national and international NGOs. It is hard to imagine how we could do this work without email. We are so dependent on it that we can easily forget its limitations.

For example, recently I was corresponding by email to develop action alerts with activists in South Korea. On the morning I was about to print the alerts, I received a phone call from one of the Koreans. "What time is it there?" I asked. "2 A.M.," she said. Alarmed, I thought she must have found errors in our action alert text that needed last-minute correcting. "No," she said, "That's not why I called. I called to hear the voice of someone who is doing so much to help us. I called to say 'Thank you.'" This personal phone call reminded me how much more we are than our words on paper. We know our world and each other through five senses. The more of our senses we engage, the deeper is our experience. We need to create as many opportunities as possible to meet face to face, and to eat, walk, talk, laugh, and sing together. We need to create these opportunities not only because they enrich our work but also because they enrich our lives. Ask anyone who has participated in the World Social Forum or the Rio and Rio + 10 conferences what they remember most, and they will tell you about individuals they met and connected with in a personal way. These heartfelt connections provide the most enduring basis and motivation for our work.

On the other hand, technology does offer us many ways to see and hear each other across time and space, and these virtual encounters save us lots of time and money.

Challenges of North-South Collaboration

In our international coalitions it is also important that decision making and leadership are shared equitably. For example, the Amazon Alliance, a coalition of indigenous organizations and environmental NGOs in the South and the North, undertook major structural, leadership, and budget changes to ensure equality at all levels. We need to build greater equality into all our international alliances.

Most EJ activism is, by definition, local, as communities of color and low-income persons rise up to demand their right to a safe and healthy environment. This is happening in thousands—perhaps millions—of places around the world. The movement usually starts in isolation, but very soon leaders seek out EJ networks for information and assistance of all kinds. The network or movement in each country tends to build locally, then regionally, then nationally. In view of the vast cultural, linguistic, political, and economic differences that must be bridged, it is no surprise that international organizing comes into focus last.

Global awareness and organizing are facilitated by a number of trends too. Indigenous peoples and other ethnic groups increasingly organize their own federations outside national political frameworks. The global economy requires and engenders a global movement against its abuses. And human ingenuity, compassion, and technology make that possible.

When grassroots groups ask Global Response to organize international letter-writing campaigns on their behalf, they often ask if we know of any other communities that faced similar challenges: How did they fight? How did they win? Faced with industrial pollution, people in Louisiana are not likely to ask communities in South Africa to help them develop successful strategies—but South Africa might in fact be an excellent source of effective ideas. We need to make EJ movement strategies and success stories available. One important web-based resource is the Data Base of Successful Strategies and Tactics (dbsst.org), which catalogs successful movements for peace, social justice, environmental protection, and environmental justice.

We can and do win EJ battles at the local level, and we can replicate successful strategies in other communities, but until we address the root causes of environmental injustice there will always be another battle. Looking into root causes brings us face to face with racism, classism, consumerism, corporate globalization, free trade agreements, imperialism, and militarism—realities that can easily overwhelm us. We all need continuing education and conscientization in these areas, but the EJ movement and each organization within it needs to prioritize and focus its work on specific policies and structures where we can have the greatest impact. Right now I believe these are the various arms of corporate globalization—the World Trade Organization, free-trade agreements, and international financial institutions. If US-based EJ leaders are not already involved in the global movement against corporate globalization, they should certainly plug in. Since the US government is the principal architect and military enforcer of corporate globalization—a rogue nation that rejects international conventions on biodiversity, climate change, racism, landmines, arms control, and children's rights—US activists face the tremendous challenge of changing US policies that affect the world at large.

Of course, another powerful way US organizations can become involved in global campaigns for environmental justice is by joining Global Response and encouraging their members to write letters for our campaigns. When a teenager in Louisiana's Cancer Alley writes a letter to help villagers in Ghana protect themselves from gold mine pollution, a connection is made that can grow into global consciousness and lifelong activism.

Tremendous resentment has built up among indigenous peoples against some of the large international environmental organizations for ignoring the presence of indigenous communities in the areas they designate for protection, expecting indigenous peoples to support their pre-established agendas, and blaming indigenous communities for environmental degradation. I saw a lot of this during the years I lived in Costa Rica. From the indigenous peoples' standpoint, the attitudes and behaviors of the missionaries, multinational corporations, government agencies and environmentalists were all about the same, although their goals were different. Environmental organizations have to earn the trust and respect of indigenous communities.

At Global Response we are committed to supporting indigenous peoples' political demands as well as their demands for environmental protection. We become allies in their campaigns with the intention of increasing their chances of success. We don't issue statements on these campaigns without their approval. Our practice is grounded in the principles of participatory action research, community organizing, and non-violence.

Corruption is rampant in the North and in the South; however, governments *can* be persuaded to act in the interests of sustainability and human rights. Activists have to keep a watchful eye on government policies that can be changed by each new incoming administration. That is why we often say that all environmental victories are temporary, though defeats are permanent. In the United States, our democracy is deeply compromised by corporate money and influence at all levels of government, and this undercuts all efforts to legislate for the environment, human rights, civil rights, economic rights, etc. Campaign finance reform must be a high priority here.

A good example of a legislative initiative in the United States that can have broad positive impacts worldwide is the International Right to Know campaign. We are promoting US legislation that would hold US-based corporations to the same standards for transparency in their international operations as in their domestic operations.

The global economy and the technology divide are widening the gap between rich and poor, and the stakes are higher as the planet's nonrenewable resources are being exhausted. The Global South still suffers the legacy of colonialism, and now it is being further exploited by corporate colonialism.

One of the biggest challenges to traditional societies and ethnic communities is the seductive pressure, especially on young people, to assimilate into the global economy and the consumer culture. Traditional societies need to be able to develop—on their own terms—viable, sustainable economies so that their young people don't feel they must make a choice either to sell out and be rich or to maintain their culture and be hungry.

Fortunately, a lot more people are talking to each other now, over all kinds of divides. During the 1970s, when I lived in Costa Rica, biologists from the North came to Costa Rica in droves, all very concerned about how to protect the tropical rainforests. But it never occurred to them to talk with the indigenous and Afro-Caribbean people who lived in the forests, or with the Costa Rican anthropologists and sociologists who worked with these communities. In the last two decades, most of us have been learning how much we have to gain by crossing the divides, expanding the dialogue, widening the circle of our concern, and drawing on the knowledge of the astonishing diversity of human cultures in order to live in peace.

17

Between Economic Justice and Sustainability

Cheryl Margoluis

Though it is widely used, "sustainable development" remains an elusive term. This is not for a lack of definitions, however, as sundry variations exist. The term first became popular when it appeared in *Our Common Future* (the "Brundtland report," issued by United Nations World Commission on Environment and Development), which defined it as "development that meets the needs of the present without compromising the ability of future generations to meet their own needs" (World Commission on Environment and Development 1987). As the term became more popular, more variations on the definition developed. Many now de-emphasize the intergenerational equity aspect, defining it, for example, as "improving the quality of life while living within the carrying capacity of supporting ecosystems" (Dobson 1998: 23). For this chapter, an appropriate definition could be "the need to ensure a better quality of life for all, now, and into the future, in a just and equitable manner, while living within the limits of supporting ecosystems" (Agyeman et al. 2003: 2). In this chapter, I am interested in looking at sustainable development as a merging of movements and at how this has contributed to its unattainable nature.

Sustainable development is an intuitively appealing idea for several reasons. In many ways it embodies the values of the environmental justice and environmental sustainability movements. Thus, the appeal of sustainable development is obvious—it holds the promise of a "win-win" situation (Wunde 2001): communities reap the benefits of development but in a manner that achieves environmental justice and sustainability. But in reality, sustainable development is difficult to attain. Often the social, economic, and environmental goals of a project simply do not overlap enough—and therefore the attainment of one goal does not necessarily contribute to the others. In other cases, the goals are actually mutually exclusive—the achievement of one goal precludes the ability to achieve others. In fact, it may be that there are "inherent contradictions" in sustainable development, and a sustainable society may be an "unattainable utopia" (Robinson 1993). The reality is that sustainable development is based on an assumption—that environmental justice leads to environmental sustainability (Sachs 1995). And while it remains a noble ideal, it is not necessarily a realistic assumption (Redclift 1987; Robinson 1993; Dobson 2003).

Yet each year hundreds of environmental and social organizations aim to achieve sustainable development, with little discussion about instances where social, ecological and economic goals simply do not overlap. But understanding these cases is crucial to our ability to achieve these goals, separately or together. In this chapter I explore the link between environmental justice and environmental sustainability, using a protected area in Guatemala as a case study.

This case study demonstrates the difficulties that can arise when trying to achieve sustainable development when there appears to be little overlap between the goals of environmental justice and the goals of sustainability.

The Alignment of the Causes

While sustainable development as a concept grew out of a number of movements worldwide (such as indigenous rights, environmental protection, and development), my interest in this chapter is the influence of the environmental justice and sustainability movements (particularly with regard to conservation).

Environmental Justice

At this point it is more common to define environmental *injustice*—the notion that "certain minority populations are forced, through their lack of access to decision making and policy-making processes, to live with a disproportionate share of environmental bads [and] suffer the related public health problems and quality of life burdens" (Agyeman et al. 2003: 6)—than to define environmental justice. The environmental justice movement gained momentum, both domestically and worldwide, in the 1980s and the 1990s. Internationally, the movement is more focused on changing patterns of exclusion from the decision-making processes and on discrimination that arises due to class or wealth differences, rather than race. Environmental justice progressed in this arena by way of development projects funded by overseas donors that, in the 1950s and the 1960s, focused on the increase of national Gross Domestic Product (GDP) as a goal. The idea was to increase the use of natural resources in a country, which would increase imports and exports—and therefore increase the well-being of its citizens (Robinson 1993). This approach was largely unsuccessful, however, and most of these projects shifted focus—to large-scale infrastructure projects, rather than to building human capital—eventually moving toward decentralized decision making and more recently to a focus on good governance.

Environmental Sustainability

While sustainability was a recognized concept in certain environmental sectors, such as forestry, it did not become a popular environmental concept until the 1970s and the 1980s. It was originally used to describe the ability of an ecosystem to persist over time. Owing to its rise in popular usage though, sustainability now is in many ways more of a political concept rather than a technical or biological one (Agyeman et al. 2003). In 1972, the Club of Rome published *The Limits to Growth*, which examined the trends of industrialization, rapid population growth, widespread malnutrition, depletion of nonrenewable resources, and a deteriorating environment (Club of Rome 1972). This report is credited with initiating the environmental concern that began to develop in this era. Conservation approaches at this point focused primarily on protected areas. A few years later, however, conservation began to shift in focus from strict protection to a more "human-friendly" approach as people became more sensitive to the social and cultural contexts in which they were working (Sachs 1995; Johnston and Soulsby 2002). In some areas, particularly in developing countries, a strict protectionist approach proved difficult to implement. It was difficult to find large tracts of land without human populations, and even more difficult to establish and maintain protected areas without the support of the surrounding communities. As indigenous groups' rights gained recognition, organizations began working with local communities to develop strategies that could address not only conservation needs but also the needs of the human populations living near the protected areas.

Sustainable Development

Initially, the achievement of sustainable development goals required that organizations specializing in social justice (including human rights, environmental justice, and development) and those specializing in the environment work together, as no one type of organization had all the necessary expertise. Perhaps the best-known example of this collaborative effort involved rubber tappers in Brazil. Chico Mendez, the legendary community activist, realized that his local struggle to empower rubber tappers was fighting for many of the same goals as the international struggle to save the rain forest (Sachs 1995). Human rights and environmental activists worked together with the government to create extractive reserves, which permitted extraction by rubber tappers while otherwise protecting the forest from outside interests. Thus, by uniting in their efforts, activists were able to work on social, economic, and environmental goals simultaneously.

The case of the rubber tappers proved to be inspiring, and most conservation organizations have now incorporated these types of goals into their projects—to such a degree, in fact, that sustainable development is one of the major areas of focus of each of the ten major environmental organizations (Warner 2002). For example, the World Wildlife Fund began working with integrated conservation and development projects in the 1980s, and within a decade half of its budget was devoted to this type of effort (Gutman 2001). This is particularly true of those organizations with an international scope, as "environmental questions in the developing world are so bound up with issues of poverty and distributive justice as to be virtually indistinguishable from them" (Dobson 1998). This relationship between poverty and environmental degradation has been so solidly established that many people now assume there is a causal link between them (ibid.).

The Misalignment of the Causes

It is the assumption that poverty causes environmental degradation, or the related assumption that environmental justice leads to environmental sustainability, that is problematic. The idea is that people who are poor must exploit their resources to unsustainable levels, as they have limited options. If they are provided with alternatives, however, they will choose not to over-exploit resources. Therefore, if there is social, economic, and ecological equity, their decision making will improve and allow them to behave in a sustainable manner (Barrett and Arcese 1995). This assumption, according to Wunde (2001), is what led to such an optimistic outlook on win-win potentials in the Brundtland report and from Rio 1992 (Wunder 2001). Yet there is very little evidence to support it (Brown and Wyckoff-Baird 1992; Southgate 1998; Markandya 2001). In fact, integrated conservation and development projects (ICDPs), which were based on this assumption, have met with mixed results (Barrett and Arcese 1995; Dobson 1998; Redford and Richter 1999; Gutman 2001; Kiss 2002; Dobson 2003; McShane 2003). For example, Scholte (2002) found that the development of an ICDP in Cameroon led to increased livestock pressure and greater pressure on an important species in the area: the kob antelope. Barrett and Arcese (1995) cite an example in the Serengeti where no amount of cash or free meat dissuaded certain groups from hunting lions. Brandon and Wells (1992) aimed to determine the overall efficacy of ICDPs as an approach and found that at 23 sites the projects were facing difficulties in meeting either conservation or development objectives.

As more research has been conducted, this assumption has been increasingly called into question. It has even been suggested that not only does environmental degradation not cause poverty; environmental policies (and conservation activities) may cause poverty (Redford and Sanderson 2002) or at least contribute to social injustice (Johnston and Soulsby 2002). Leach and Mearns (1997) suggest that poor people are often the victims and the agents of environmental destruction. The reality is that the link between poverty and environmental degradation is complex. This makes it unrealistic to assume that social and environmental equity will automatically lead to environmental sustainability.

Stumbling Blocks for Sustainable Development

The link between conservation and development, therefore, is not easily predictable. And when sustainable development projects are based on incorrect assumptions, the incentives created to change behavior are ineffective (Kiss 2002). The reasons for behavior are usually much more complex than is assumed, and therefore organizations working toward sustainable development need to examine the second-order and third-order factors affecting behavior to figure out where an intervention would be most effective.

One reason sustainable development has been so difficult to achieve can be seen in the misalignment of the specific goals of the movements that unite for it. For example, while there are numerous organizations that work for environmental justice, all with different specific goals and audiences, they are all "united in the larger struggle for ecological democracy" (Faber and McCarthy 2003: 46). Or, as Dobson noted (1998: 24), "the environmental justice movement seems, stubbornly, to be much more about human justice than about the natural environment—or, rather, it is only about the natural environment inasmuch as it (the natural environment) can be seen in terms of human justice." The primary goal of the environmental sustainability movement, in contrast, is about the management of natural resources. And while this includes humans and the way that they use resources, the emphasis is on the actual management of the resources. This is a slight but important distinction.

Aiming to achieve both environmental justice and environmental sustainability can therefore often prove to be impossible. Often this is simply a matter of resources; with limited resources, managers have to focus on one goal or set of goals. Trying to achieve both amounts to double the work and resources, rather than an incremental increase. Even more problematic is when the goals of the two movements appear mutually exclusive. For example, Dobson (1998: 241) asks "what if it turned out that, under some circumstances, social and economic inequality was conducive to environmental sustainability?" Though it sounds unfortunate, there are many cases where the exclusion of humans in specific areas is the only way to conserve a larger area or let an area regenerate in order to permit sustainable use in the future. There are also cases where a community must exploit its natural resources in an unsustainable manner to survive—particularly when resources and decision making authority are outside of local control. This situation proves the most challenging for sustainable development activists to reconcile. Sustainability is difficult to achieve in deteriorating environmental conditions (Agbola and Alabi 2003) or areas of poverty, rapid population growth, economic decline, and weak systems of governance, let alone in a situation of conflict and large population movements (Neefjes 1999). The problem is that this situation is common throughout the developing world. The Maya Biosphere Reserve in the Petén, northern Guatemala, demonstrates the complexity of these issues in this situation.

Case Study: The Petén

The Maya Biosphere Reserve in the Petén, northern Guatemala, is home to the largest lowland forest remaining in Central America (2,113,000 hectares), connecting what is referred to as the Maya Forest from Mexico to Belize. The Reserve's importance can be viewed on three levels: globally, regionally, and locally. At the global level, the Reserve retains carbon dioxide and produces oxygen. At the regional level, it regulates the water cycle and helps prevent erosion and sedimentation. Locally, the Reserve provides economic benefits through tourism and sustainable resource use. It also provides a habitat for numerous species of flora and fauna, many of which are endemic or require large home ranges.

Until recently, the Petén was a typical frontier, viewed as an area with ample land and resources for all. It is, therefore, not surprising that people chose to migrate there. Migration was seen as one of the only options for families that were looking for available land or greater economic opportunities, or were seeking refuge from violence in other parts of the country. This migration has drastically changed the demography of the Petén. The population growth rate has been variously estimated at between 4 and 10 percent (Fort and Granada 1999; Shriar 2001). Any of those estimates indicates that the Petén is an anomaly in a country where the total overall population growth rate is closer to 2.9 percent per year (Consejo Nacional de Areas Protegidas (CONAP) et al. 1997). This high growth rate is due not only to the above-mentioned migration, but also to a high fertility rate, estimated to be one of the highest in the country, which in turn is one of the highest in Central America (behind Honduras) (Fort and Grandia 1999).

The high migration and fertility rates have also drastically changed the landscape of the Petén. In 1990, the government created the Maya Biosphere Reserve to protect the ecological processes in the area and to address the needs of the local communities. At that point there were only a few communities living in what is now the Reserve. But as social, economic, and political conditions worsened throughout the country, migration to the Petén increased, and the area outside of the Reserve quickly became cleared and settled. As the population continued to grow and land became scarce, it is not surprising that communities settled within the Reserve as well as outside of it. The area, once undisrupted lowland forest, is now a mosaic of forest and agricultural land.

The Reserve is divided into three different use zones: the Buffer Zone, the Multiple Use Zone, and the Nucleus Zone. The Buffer Zone (4,975 square kilometers, 24 percent of the Reserve) is a 15-kilometer area on the southern edge of the Reserve that, as its name implies, was intended to serve as a buffer for the rest of the Reserve by mitigating impacts from the surrounding human populations. This is the area most affected by the demographic changes, as settlement is not restricted. Before 1986, 13 percent of the 474,440 hectares in this zone were converted from forest into agricultural land. Between 1986 and 1995, another 71,800 hectares in this zone were converted. This means that in just 15 years over 28 percent of the originally protected forest has been lost (Consejo Nacional de Areas Protegidas (CONAP) et al. 1997). The Multiple Use Zone (8,484 square kilometers, 40 percent of the Reserve) is an extractive reserve area that permits numerous sustainable resource activities. Communities are allowed to settle in this zone, provided that they create management plans with CONAP for the area of land that they use. The Core Zone (7,670 square kilometers, 36 percent of the Reserve) contains the most valuable areas, both ecologically and culturally. This is the only area within the Reserve that is set aside for strict conservation purposes and where, for scientific and cultural reasons, human settlements are not permitted. Regardless, estimates indicate that there are over 20,500 individuals living in this zone (Grünberg and Ramos 1998).

The Communities

In order to understand the situation in the Reserve, it is important to first understand the communities that settle there. The communities in the Reserve are often stereotyped as either indigenous keepers of the forest or migrants who are to blame for the destruction of the forest. It is widely accepted that the direct factors that drive deforestation in the Petén are the activities of the local communities—agricultural expansion, cattle ranching, and hunting—as well as activities from outside populations, such as petroleum extraction and timber harvesting. But the proximate factors that drive these activities—lack of technological assistance and local control of resources, skewed land holdings, violence, poor economic conditions, weak and/or corrupt institutions—are often overlooked. The result is that migrants in the area are often blamed for the destruction of the forest. Some believe that the migrants simply lack understanding of the local ecology or a connection to the land that fosters stewardship. In contrast, the "native Peteneros," the Itza, an ethnic Mayan group that migrated south to the Petén from the Yucatan peninsula sometime between 1200 and 1450 A.D., are viewed as "keepers of the forest." Historically the Itza were more dependent on resource gathering than on agriculture, cultivating what many believe to have been a "symbiotic relationship and respect for the forest; this was one of the factors that culturally separated Peteneros from the rest of Guatemalans" (Soza Manzanero 1999: 48). These are simplistic representations of what are complex, dynamic communities. In reality, all communities in the Reserve are fairly recent migrants, as the Reserve was largely depopulated after the fall of the Mayans.

While a great deal of research has been conducted on environmental justice and sustainability as pertaining to indigenous communities, very little has been written on this relationship as it pertains to migrants. Outsiders who want to portray the migrants as either destroyers or stewards often distort this relationship, but the true complexity of the situation arises because they are in fact neither. Understanding this relationship is crucial to the environmental justice and sustainability movements as it is very different than the relationship with indigenous groups. This relationship between the environmental justice and sustainability movements and migrants will become increasingly important as resource degradation, economic hardship, and violence continue to drive migration on a global scale.

The Goals of the Maya Biosphere Reserve

The stated goals of the Maya Biosphere Reserve are to conserve ecological processes in the area (through both preservation and sustainable use) while increasing the well being of the surrounding communities. The primary way to increase well being in the area is to increase access to social services (such as schools and health facilities) or to increase access to social infrastructure (such as roads and markets). In order to achieve these goals and create a sustainable Reserve, the managers (CONAP and several NGOs) have developed two strategies: to relocate communities to areas of lower conservation value, and to have the communities sign agreements with the government that limit their resource use activities in the Reserve. The effects of the two strategies have been mixed.

Relocation

Relocation has been a fairly common approach in environmental justice cases in the United States, typically when a community must be moved to avoid a health hazard that has been created by an outside entity. Relocation in the context of the Reserve is a very different concept. The goal of relocation in the Reserve is to move communities who are currently settled in an area considered to be best suited for other purposes, in this case conservation. A more appropriate comparison might be relocations that result from eminent domain issues in the United States. The primary difference is that most of the households involved in Guatemala do not hold a legal right to their land.

The relocations have been effective in conserving ecological processes in the area through the reduction of the impact on the forest. Impact tends to change proportionately with population (York et al. 2003); this is particularly true in the Petén, where the majority of people are subsistence agriculturalists and resource gatherers. While their activities may have been sustainable at lower population levels, as the number of households grows, so do the resource demands in the area. The relocation of communities has allowed the areas that were cleared for fields to regenerate back into forest. The question is, however, whether this move has also increased the well being of the communities.

Relocation is an attractive option for some families. When relocated, families are moved to parcels of land that are legally titled and available for purchase. They are also offered a low-interest loan from the government to assist in buying the land. Since finding available, legal land and then having the means to buy it are the limiting factors for most families, this "relocation package" can be a welcome opportunity.

But there are other families that do not want to move. Many were displaced from land they previously held, while others fled from the violence of the war—they have worked hard to establish a new life in the Petén that they do not want to give up. Legally, those who settled in the Reserve after its declaration do not have the right to be there. But even without the legal right, is it justifiable to forcibly remove people from their homes? And what about the families who settled before the declaration? What if they do not want to move? Even when families do want to move, the ethics are not clear. Who is entitled to the relocation benefits? Only those families who settled before the declaration of the Reserve? The Reserve's managers do not want to encourage increased settlement in the Reserve by promising this relocation assistance to everyone. But the majority of families moved to the area within the past five years, and thus few families would be eligible if it were a limited offer.

User Rights

The other approach, having the communities sign resource-use agreements with the government, has resulted in mixed ecological impacts and raised a variety of ethical questions as well. One of the main goals of the agreements was to limit settlement in the area and reduce resource use outside of individual land plots. This approach focuses on sustainable use of resources in the same area where regeneration is supposed to occur. Settlement has not decreased, however, and families in general do not respect the resource limitations placed upon them in the agreements. The land in this area is legally titled to the government; it cannot be privately titled. The agreements were also designed to stabilize the communities and increase the level of land tenure security in each household. Realistically, however, the communities cannot own their own land and are restricted in the amount of land that they use. This means that they do not have access to credit, cannot pass their land down to their children, and do not have enough land to give to their children to work when they are adults. In order to limit development within the core zone, health clinics and schools are not permitted. Therefore those families who decided to remain and sign agreements do not have access to these social benefits.

Relocation and agreements of permanence are two of many strategies that could be employed in this situation, but the underlying issue remains the same. The pursuit of both environmental justice and sustainability in the Reserve has been difficult, and thus far neither has been achieved. In fact, to some degree they appear to be mutually exclusive. Successful sustainable development means that resources are used sustainably, and in view of the extent of current degradation in the area some resources would have to be set aside to regenerate. But in order to meet the current subsistence needs of the burgeoning population, additional forest would have to be cleared and additional resources consumed.

Whose Rights?

In the management of areas like the Maya Biosphere Reserve, whose rights should be respected? On one side, the Reserve's managers and ecologists argue that permitting the communities to remain illegally settled allows extensive ecological damage to be done to the Reserve. The communities are slash-and-burn agriculturalists—they need to clear land in order to plant their crops, clearing more land every few years to rotate crops. Due to the shallow and relatively poor soils of the lowland tropics, farmers generally use more land and must rotate their crops more often than in other parts of Guatemala. In addition, just by living in the Reserve, the communities impact the area in less obvious ways. The farmers burn to clear their land— satellite images show that the most clearing and burning are done around the periphery of communities in the Reserve. But the result is out-of-control forest fires that destroy viable forest each year. In addition, the communities hunt and fish in the Reserve. A study by Bauer in a nearby community estimated that families walked a minimum of eight kilometers to hunt (Bauer 2002). Each family cuts wood for the construction of their homes and fences, and gathers wood for fodder. Each family also uses non-timber forest products from the Reserve—xate (*Chamadorea sp*), chicle (resin from *Manilkara zapote*), and allspice (*Pimienta dioica*)—are the most commonly harvested. Therefore the subsistence needs of each family amount to a substantial impact on the Reserve. Most ecologists agree that the Reserve cannot absorb these impacts while continuing to protect—and in some cases allow the recovery of—flora, fauna, and ecological processes. (For satellite images of deforestation trends, see Sader 1999.)

Looking at it from the other side, however, what are the options for these families? Many have been displaced from their land in other parts of Guatemala; many have also suffered greatly from the violence of the war. They have no money, no land, and no family in the area to rely on for assistance. The majority of settlers are subsistence farmers (99 percent in the sample for this research) who rely on the land to support their family. There are few economic alternatives for them—and even if there were, few have the skills necessary to take advantage of them. Most have little or no education—in the sample for this study, the literacy rate for the men—normally much higher than that for women—was only 53 percent. And yet, the social infrastructure does not exist to change this situation. Environmental justice occurs when people do not suffer equally from environmental degradation, but the distribution of environmental goods comes down to the ability to pay—those who can afford protection will buy it; those who cannot will suffer (Dobson 1998). "It is the least politically powerful and most marginalized sectors of the population who are being selectively victimized to the greatest extent by the environmental crisis." (Agyeman 2003: 4) In this case, migrants suffer more due to their inability to find and buy legitimate land outside the protected area. If environmental justice is about who gets what, why, and in what amount, then we have to ask if what these migrants are getting is fair. Does the situation further penalize those who are already marginalized in society? With such population pressures, doesn't it make sense to use the land in a more "economical" manner?

Adding to the complexity of the situation is the fact that there are other rights that must be taken into account. For example, what about the fact that the forest is actually part of a larger ecosystem, the Maya forest, that connects with Mexico and Belize? The Maya forest also provides habitat for large animals, such as the jaguar, which would not survive if the forest were to become further fragmented. And of course consideration must be given to the intergenerational aspect of the situation—the current generation has the responsibility to protect resources for future generations.

How to decide whose rights are to be respected becomes even more complicated if we think about how this decision will be made. While the government of Guatemala is charged with managing the protected areas, the overall direction of the Reserve will be somewhat directed by outside interests. The majority of the organizations working in the Reserve are foreign ones, such as Conservation International, the Nature Conservancy, and the Canadian International Development Research Center. And these organizations receive their financial support, and therefore to some degree their mandates, from donors who are primarily in the global North. Therefore, even though the ideas on social justice and environmental sustainability may be fairly different in developing countries, how these movements progress will be largely dictated by the developed countries. This is an important point to consider as the focus of international organizations changes—from protection, to ICDPs, to ecoregional planning, to the next approach.

What Do We Do Now?

The environmental and social justice movements have both come far enough along to realize that they cannot operate in isolation. Many of the issues that affect one movement also affect the other. But now it appears that the pendulum has swung too far. Many people now assume that there is a casual link between the movements—that environmental justice automatically leads to environmental sustainability. This case study on the Maya Biosphere Reserve demonstrates, however, how complex the issues are, and why this assumption has not held true.

Sustainable development remains an admirable goal. It would truly be a "win-win" situation if environmental, social, and economic goals could be achieved in a single project. And certain types of projects are indeed able to achieve this triumvirate of goals. But it many other cases there is no win-win solution, only a series of tradeoffs (Markandya 2001).

It is important to recognize when sustainable development is not an appropriate goal. Throughout the developing world, communities struggle to meet their subsistence needs, often at the expense of the environment. In such cases, the ability to achieve sustainable development seems doubtful. In fact, just trying to achieve economic, social, or environmental goals alone seems daunting. The Maya Biosphere Reserve offers a clear example of the issues that are faced when the current needs of the community cannot necessarily be satisfied in a manner that also allows for the sustainable development of an area.

The key is to recognize that sustainable development approaches, such as ICDPs, are, like any other conservation strategy, appropriate only under certain conditions. Several studies have begun to analyze this situation and determine what these conditions are. The Biodiversity Conservation Network analyzed 20 ICD projects throughout Asia and the Pacific and found that projects were most successful at achieving both conservation and economic success when they revolved around an already viable enterprise, when the enterprise was linked closely to the local biodiversity, when the stakeholders were a strong, unified body, and when this approach was used in conjunction with other approaches, such as environmental education (Salafsky et al. 1999). Van Schaik and Riksjen (2002) suggest that such projects work when communities are tightly knit and enjoy exclusive access to the resource. Brandon and Wells (1992), in an examination of 23 sites in 14 countries, found that ICDPs may be most successful when the threats to the resource are clear, there is a high degree of dependence on the resource, and adequate alternatives exist. Abbot and Thomas (2001) found that strong rule enforcement, collaboration among governments, donors, and executing agencies, and long-term commitment of financial and technical support were critical.

After narrowing down the conditions under which this strategy is appropriate, organizations must focus on understanding local site conditions well enough to know where their interventions will be most effective (Margoluis and Salafsky 1998). While many projects are designed to address the current situation, it is equally important that the projects also address the root factors that contributed to the situation (Margoluis and Salafsky 1998; Faber and McCarthy 2003). For example, any organization that wants to work on sustainable development in the Maya Biosphere Reserve must address the fact that there are very few functioning social institutions in the area. Most communities function as independent units with little connection to the larger area—in fact, many communities lack internal institutions altogether and exist only as groups of families. This means that coordinating activities in the larger area can be very difficult and time consuming. Yet these institutions can play a vital role in the management of the area. For example, in and around Tikal National Park (also located in the Reserve), local institutions help reinforce the accountability of the park and support small tourism projects in surrounding communities. And Tikal has managed to create a viable protected area that achieves some conservation goals—as well as generate economic benefits for their surrounding communities. Creating these institutions and strengthening them are necessary steps in the management of the park.

In cases where local site conditions are not appropriate for an ICD strategy, organizations must prioritize their objectives and must decide whether their primary goal is conservation or development. This is not to dichotomize the issue and argue that only environmental sustainability or environmental justice can be achieved. But there are inherent tradeoffs between the two, and organizations must prioritize their objectives in order to be effective. Striving to achieve social, economic, and ecological goals equally in a situation where it is not feasible may not be the best use of resources, and trying to do so may mean that no goals are achieved.

In such cases, many organizations are now shifting away from ICD projects and focusing more on development-oriented conservation projects or conservation-with-development projects. These projects still address ecological, social, and economic factors, and they may still achieve both environmental and social justice goals; the difference is that they acknowledge that their primary goals are either environmental or social justice, and they plan accordingly.

Sustainable development may, and perhaps should, remain an ideal for which to strive. But it should not be the basis on which we plan and implement all projects and activities. Sustainable development is based on a series of assumptions that, at this point, are not always necessarily true. For now, we may be more effective in achieving sustainable results in a just manner through more realistic planning and prioritization, and by designing projects that are aimed at addressing the root causes of the complex situations we face today.

18

The Future of Environmental Justice Movements

Robert J. Brulle and David Naguib Pellow

Injustice anywhere is a threat to justice everywhere. We are caught in an inescapable network of mutuality, tied in a single garment of destiny. Whatever affects one directly, affects all indirectly.
—Martin Luther King Jr., Letter from Birmingham Jail, 1963

The network that Dr. King wrote about is the one that links humans in the continual struggle for social justice. In the context of the environmental justice movement, the mutuality that he wrote about has extended beyond the human community to concerns regarding the physical environment and natural systems. All of Earth's living inhabitants are caught in a web of mutual destiny. Humans cannot exist on Earth unless all of the planet's inhabitants—people and animals alike—are provided a just, clean, and sustainable environment in which they can flourish. There is no place where one can go to escape from the global system we have created, or its effects, either on people or species.

We set out in this book to initiate a dialogue among scholars, activists, and practitioners from a range of institutions working in the area of environmental justice. The book breaks new ground by examining the environmental justice movement from a critical yet sympathetic perspective. In this chapter we consider the lessons learned and the path that activists and scholars might tread in the years to come.

Environmental Equality and Justice: Progress or Retreat?

What is the status of the EJ movement at the beginning of the twenty-first century? Part I of the book provides a number of important insights. The analyses presented indicate that this movement has experienced both success and failure.

The movement has achieved numerous local and national successes. EJ activists have been very successful at halting the construction of numerous polluting facilities in communities across the United States. Across several states and nationally, the movement has succeeded in policy making, gaining government agency support, and proposing and passing legislation that addresses EJ concerns in many states. Unfortunately, these laws and policies are limited in reach or are too new to be fully evaluated. In addition, the cultural and institutional growth of this movement has been phenomenal. EJ courses are offered at numerous colleges and universities, government agencies are implementing EJ plans, and foundations continue to fund work by non-governmental organizations in this area. The language of environmental justice has entered the lexicon of public health, corporate responsibility, climate change debates, urban planning, transportation development, and municipal zoning in cities where these issues might never have been considered two decades ago. These are extraordinary accomplishments. However, these successes must be tempered by the following realizations:

• Activists have yet to achieve significant legal victories via Title VI of the Civil Rights Act.

• Movement leaders must still develop a coherent national strategy.

• Structural, political, and economic changes that would produce environmental justice and sustainability have not yet materialized.

What the above suggests to us is that, as several contributors to this volume have stated, despite the EJ movement's radical orientation, the focus on justice and redress through the existing legal system may actually reinforce the very institutional relations that create and maintain environmental injustice. This dynamic demonstrates that it is necessary to reframe environmental justice and to tie its radical analyses of the causes of environmental injustice to its action strategies.

New Strategies for Achieving Environmental Justice

Part II of the book asks what new strategies can move the discourse and action forward in order to better realize the goals of the environmental justice movement. These emerging strategies among EJ activists hold a great deal of promise for the future. They converge around the tensions of working within the system versus outside of the system to achieve local control, autonomy, and meaningful political participation. Whether one is focused on legal or regulatory issues, on food or energy politics, or on public health and pollution reduction, the chapters in part II make a persuasive case for creating innovative practices through existing entities and for developing new institutions apart from traditional ones. We find each approach compelling, and we would argue that a sophisticated EJ vision would incorporate both practices as a way of maximizing power and minimizing tactical inefficiencies.

The chapters in part II push scholars, activists, and policy makers to think in innovative and creative ways about what constitutes environmental injustice and how communities can move toward building greater levels of social capital, food security, legal protections, and autonomous spaces in which new models of environmental justice might be achieved and enjoyed. Departing from mechanistic models of EJ rooted in the equity paradigm, the authors force us to consider not only how communities might repel toxic facilities but also how communities might feed themselves, provide energy, build new systems of governance and decision making while influencing existing ones, and produce and control new knowledge about public health and the environment. This is the next generation of environmental justice theory and action.

Environmental Justice and the Challenge of Globalization

In addition to the task of developing a national agenda for environmental justice in the United States, focusing on transnational and global political economic dynamics is also important. How can the environmental justice movement best address globalization and its impacts on environmental inequality? The EJ movement must be able to combat the excesses of capital in the North if it is to take on the task of battling these forces in the South. Transnational environmental injustices present both parallel and unique challenges to local and national movement efforts.

The chapters in part III offer both hope and caution to activists and others seeking global environmental justice. Although the EJ movement may have formally begun in the United States, it is clear that the need for this kind of activism is a global reality and that, in fact, if the EJM is to survive at all (even in its nation of origin) it must go global. It must go global because the sources and causes of environmental inequality are global in their reach and impact. It must go global because Northern residents and activists have an obligation and a responsibility to the nations and peoples of the South, as Northern corporations and military campaigns wreak social and ecological havoc in Latin America, Africa, Central and Eastern Europe, and Asia. At the same time, because the primary sources of decision-making power reside in the North (corporate headquarters, the International Monetary Fund, the World Bank, the World Trade Organization, and the White House), the movement must also continue to focus energy on these critical (and more proximal) points of access. And while it is clear that the movement has a long way to go with regard to building coalitions across various social and spatial divides, there are tactics, strategies, and campaigns that have been very successful at doing just that for many years. From transnational activist campaigns to solidarity networks and letter writing, EJ action has a growing global face. Even so, as Margoluis cautions, we should always examine our core assumptions about the world and our vision for social change, because when we have multiple goals for our communities, implementing them is sometimes more difficult than we ever imagined.

A Word to EJ Scholars

To our academic colleagues we offer the following thoughts.

First, for future research on environmental injustices, while we believe it is useful to continue documenting the range of problems facing communities of color, we find the advice of Charles Lee and Orrin Williams quite helpful: scholars must balance this approach with a stronger move toward a solution orientation. Bryant (1995), Bullard (2000), and Getches and Pellow (2000) have done this, but they are exceptions. We certainly find wisdom in the idea that, in order to solve a problem, we must first understand it completely, but scholars must begin to take seriously the obligation to propose new directions for society to heal itself and produce more just and sustainable forms of production.

Second, following the advice of several contributors to this volume (Anthony and Kalan and Peek, for example), EJ scholars might consider bringing a stronger social class analysis back into the field. Scholars cannot understand—and policy makers cannot prevent—environmental injustices through a singularly focused framework that emphasizes one form of inequality to the exclusion of others. Environmental injustices affect human beings unequally along lines of race, gender, class, and nation, so an overemphasis on any one of these factors will dilute the explanatory power of any analytical approach and weaken any effort at serious theory building. This becomes clear not from our conversations with scholars, but rather from our conversations with activists, particularly those who have lived and worked in the global South.

Third, it is imperative for EJ scholars to make more significant links between EJ research and the literatures on social movements, environmental sociology, history, and ethnic studies in order to build the field and produce advances in theory. For far too long, EJ studies has existed without engaging in a dialogue with numerous related and relevant fields where clear contributions can be made. Progress has been made in some areas (law, geography, sociology), but we have a long way to go. For example, there can be no complete body of research on this topic without also paying attention to privileged spaces where the rich and powerful responsible for environmental injustices live, work, and play—this is a line of research suggested by a number of disciplinary perspectives. If EJ studies is to move into a position of greater prominence in the academy, its strength may depend on the ability of EJ scholars to engage in a conversation across disciplines that redefines the way those disciplines approach questions concerning not only the environment, but also race/ethnicity, class, gender, and nation.

Fourth and finally, a great deal of environmental justice research represents a uniquely powerful alliance between scholars and community leaders, using innovative methodological approaches to create new knowledge. We would urge EJ scholars to continue developing a rigorous school of thought and technique around the kind of participatory research methods being used around the world in the service of EJ communities. Following advice from Cable et al., scholars should also be aware of the many pitfalls that this kind of approach may involve—a very good reason for codifying and disseminating these ideas and practices. One of the reasons why environmental justice studies is such an important field is because so many scholars doing this work have produced research that has positive impacts beyond the academy. It is our hope that EJ scholars will find ways to systematically instruct future students and scholars in these methodologies so as to build a stronger institutional presence for this kind of work nationally and internationally.

A Word to EJ Activists

In many ways, our counsel to EJ scholars parallels our thoughts for EJ activists, since the two groups are so closely intertwined at times. We began this book with an acknowledgment that we fully support the broad goals of the movement. Having considered our own views as well as the thoughts of many of the movement's leading advocates (including those contributing to this volume), we respectfully offer the following thoughts for future EJ work.

First, the hope of building a coherent national strategy will only be realized if EJ organizations build support and solidarity for their cause at the grassroots. This means engaging in old-fashioned door-to-door organizing and demonstrating direct support for local residents' concerns. While this has been occurring in local communities since the movement's inception, we worry that an effort to build a coherent national agenda may de-emphasize this approach in the near future.

Second, building on the first point, with regard to mobilizing critical resources, since foundation support is unlikely to increase substantially in the near future, we would hope that EJ organizations could build a greater indigenous base of support from within communities and non-governmental organizations (similar to the civil rights movement's resource-mobilization strategy). These resources would emerge directly from the kind of organizing strategy we suggested in the first point above. A healthier mix of indigenous and external resources might prove more effective at sustaining the movement and building power locally and nationally.

Third, the predominant race-based focus on organizing and issue framing has been very powerful and effective, but we hope that it can become more inclusive of class, gender, and nation inequalities in the near future. EJ activists inside and outside the United States have commented on this problem for a number of years. The history of social movements is clear on this: Mass movements have a greater chance of success when they appeal to a broad base of the population. Organizing people against environmental injustices while significant populations also suffering from these insults are excluded (e.g., poor and working-class whites across America) may lead to unnecessary tactical weaknesses and might facilitate interracial resentment. This is a problem that has emerged continuously inside and outside the United States, and EJ activists have been called to account for this approach. We are keenly aware of the need for ownership and control over the movement by a people-of-color majority, but we also believe that this can be achieved with the inclusion of other groups.

Fourth, we sincerely hope that the continued tension between EJ organizations and mainstream environmental organizations can be resolved or at least managed more productively in the coming years. So much energy has been put into these disagreements that one wonders whether much of this is the result of a divide-and-conquer tactic employed by elite institutions. It certainly would not be the first time. We should be clear that the tensions, divides, and disagreements are real and have substantive merit, but it is also certain that these fractures have produced obstacles to the construction of a powerful mass movement that could potentially produce the sort of structural changes associated with the goals of environmental justice. Addressing these divides would also likely facilitate the kind of rethinking we suggested in the third point above. This point is particularly salient at a time when leading mainstream environmentalists are proclaiming "the death of environmentalism" (Shellenberger and Nordhaus 2004).

Fifth and finally, we encourage EJ activists to collaborate with scholars when it is strategic, logical, and productive for them. Just as Charles Lee argues in his chapter, when activists collaborate under a system of respect and power sharing, they can often leverage more resources and create social change more effectively. If activists can exert ownership and control over research and documentation processes, it makes good sense for collaborations with scholars to take root. But, as Cable et al. make clear, activists would do well to always be cautious and vigilant, because any research process is fundamentally a political exercise.

The future of environmental justice movements must consciously link the local with the global, ancient systems of governance with progressive components of present-day legal approaches, grassroots goals with truly democratic organizational decision-making models, consensus building and collaboration with the threat of disruptive direct action, the desire for issue breadth with the need for focus and depth, and peoples' struggles across class, race/ethnicity, gender, and nation. The ideas presented by scholars, activists, and practitioners in this book represent the next generation of EJ thinking and advocacy.

Movements for environmental justice can and must continue to grow stronger, more powerful, more diverse, and more global. As scholars and activists with a keen sense of history and of the fact that social relations and power are constructed and change over time, we end with the hopeful slogan of the World Social Forum: "Another World Is Possible."

References

Abbot, J., and D. Thomas. 2001. Understanding the links between conservation and development in the Bamenda Highlands, Cameroon. *World Development* 29: 1115–1136.

Adam, B. 1998. *Timescapes of Modernity: The Environment and Invisible Hazards.* Routledge.

Adeola, F. 2000. Cross-national environmental justice and human rights issues: A review of evidence in the developing world. *American Behavioral Scientist* 43: 686–706.

Agbola, T., and M. Alabi. 2003. Political economy of petroleum resources development, environmental injustice and selective victimization: A case study of the Niger Delta Region of Nigeria. In *Just Sustainabilities*, ed. J Agyeman et al. MIT Press.

Agyeman, J. 2002. Constructing environmental (in)justice: Transatlantic tales. *Environmental Politics* 11, no. 3: 31–53.

Agyeman, J., R. Bullard, and B. Evans. 2003a. *Just Sustainabilities: Development in an Unequal World.* MIT Press.

Agyeman, J., R. Bullard, and B. Evans. 2003b. Joined-up thinking: Bringing together sustainability, environmental justice and equity. In *Just Sustainabilities*, ed. J. Agyeman et al. MIT Press.

Albrecht, S., R. Amey, and A. Sarit. 1996. The siting of radioactive waste facilities: What are the effects on communities? *Rural Sociology* 61: 649–673.

Almeida, P. 1998. The network for environmental and economic justice in the Southwest: An interview with Richard Moore. In *The Struggle for Ecological Democracy*, ed. D. Faber. Guilford.

Alston, D. 1990. *We Speak for Ourselves.* Panos Institute.

Amdur, M. 1996. Animal toxicology. In *Particles in Our Air*, ed. R. Wilson and J. Spengler. Harvard University Press.

Amenta, E., N. Caren, T. Fetner, and M. Young. 2002. Challengers and states: Toward a political sociology of social movements. In *Sociological Views on Political Participation in the 21st Century*, ed. B. Dobratz et al., volume 10. Elsevier Science.

Amenta, E., D. Halfmann, and M. Young. 1999. The strategies and contexts of social protest: Political mediation and the impact of the Townsend Movement in California. *Mobilization* 4, no. 1: 1–23.

Anderson, R. 1998. *Mid-Course Correction: Toward a Sustainable Enterprise.* Peregrinzilla.

Anderton, D., A. Anderson, J. Oakes, and M. Fraser. 1994. Environmental equity: The demographics of dumping. *Demography* 31: 229–248.

Andrews, R. 1999. *Managing the Environment, Managing Ourselves: A History of American Environmental Policy.* Yale University Press.

Asch, P., and J. Seneca. 1978. Some evidence on the distribution of air quality. *Land Economics* 54: 278–297.

Associated Press (AP). 1989. Johnston campaign funds questioned. *Lake Charles American Press*, July 3.

Astin, A., H. Astin, A. Bayer, and A. Bisconti. 1975. *The Power of Protest.* Jossey-Bass.

Bailey, C., and C. Faupel. 1992. Environmentalism and civil rights in Sumter County, Alabama. In *Race and the Incidence of Environmental Hazards*, ed. B. Bryant and P. Mohai. Westview.

Balshem, M. 1993. *Cancer in the Community: Class and Medical Authority.* Smithsonian Institution Press.

Barber, B. 1984. *Strong Democracy.* University of California Press.

Barrett, C., and P. Arcese. 1995. Are integrated conservation-development projects (ICDPs) sustainable? On the conservation of large mammals in Sub-Saharan Africa. *World Development* 23: 1073–1084.

Barrett, W. 2002. Bad policy, big bucks. *Village Voice*, October 23–29.

Bauer, E. 2002. Untitled, Flores, Guatemala.

Beck, U. 1986. *Risk Society: Towards a New Modernity.* Sage.

Beck, U. 1995. *Ecological Enlightenment: Essays on the Politics of the Risk Society.* Humanities.

Been, V. 1993. What's fairness got to do with it? Environmental justice and siting of locally undesirable land uses. *Cornell Law Review* 78: 1001.

Been, V. 1994. Locally undesirable land uses in minority neighborhoods. *Yale Law Review* 103: 1383–1422.

Been, V. 1995. Analyzing evidence of environmental justice. *Journal of Land Use and Environmental Law* 11: 1–36.

Benda-Beckmann, K. 1995. Anthropological approaches to property law and economics. *European Journal of Law and Economics* 2: 309–336.

Benford, R. 1997. An insider's critique of the social movement framing perspective. *Sociological Inquiry* 67: 409–430.

Benford, R., and D. Snow. 2000. Framing processes and social movements: An overview and assessment. *Annual Review of Sociology* 26: 611–639.

Berkes, F., and C. Folke. 2000. *Linking Social and Ecological Systems: Management Practices and Social Mechanisms for Building Resilience.* Cambridge University Press.

Berry, B., ed. 1977. *The Social Burdens of Environmental Pollution: A Comparative Metropolitan Data Source.* Ballinger.

Black Leadership Forum et al., 2002. *Air of Injustice.* Martha Keating and Felicia Davis.

Blee, K., ed. 1998. *No Middle Ground: Women and Radical Protest.* New York University Press.

Block, D. 2004. Update on Austin community-based research. *Good Food* (newsletter of Chicago Food System Collaborative).

Bloom. J. 1987. *Class, Race, and the Civil Rights Movement.* Indiana University Press.

Blühdorn, I. 2000. *Post-Ecologist Politics: Social Theory and the Abdication of the Ecologist Paradigm.* Routledge.

Bonfil Batalla, G. 1996. *México Profundo: Reclaiming a Civilization.* University of Texas Press.

Boone, C., and A. Modarres. 1999. Creating a toxic neighborhood in Los Angeles County. *Urban Affairs Review* 35: 163–187.

Boyce, J., and B. Shelly. 2003. *Natural Assets: Democratizing Environmental Ownership.* Island.

Braun, B., and N. Castree. 1998. *Remaking Reality: Nature at the Millennium.* Routledge.

Brennan, T., K. Palmer, R. Kopp, A. Krupnick, V. Stagliano, and D. Burtraw. 1996. *A Shock to the System: Restructuring America's Electricity Industry.* Resources for the Future.

Brown, M. 1979. *Laying Waste: The Poisoning of America by Toxic Chemicals.* Pantheon.

Brown, M., and B. Wyckoff-Baird. 1992. Designing integrated conservation and development projects. Biodiversity Support Program, Washington, DC.

Brown, P. 1992. Popular epidemiology and toxic waste contamination: Lay and professional ways of knowing. *Journal of Health and Social Behavior* 33, no. 3: 267–281.

Brown, P. 1995. Race, class, and environmental health: A review and systematization of the literature. *Environmental Research* 69: 15–30.

Brown, P., and E. Mikkelsen. 1990. *No Safe Place: Toxic Waste, Leukemia, and Community Action.* University of California Press.

Brown, P., S. Zavestoski, T. Luebke, J. Mandelbaum, S. McCormick, and B. Mayer. 2004. Clearing the air and breathing freely: Disputes over air pollution and asthma. *International Journal of Health Services* 34: 39–63.

Brulle, R. 1996. Environmental discourse and social movement organizations: A historical and rhetorical perspective on the development of US environmental organizations. *Sociological Inquiry* 66: 58–83.

Brulle, R. 2000. *Agency, Democracy, and Nature: The US Environmental Movement from a Critical Theory Perspective* MIT Press.

Brulle, R., and B. Schaefer-Caniglia. 2005. Money for nature: The role of foundation funding in the US environmental movement. *Mobilization* 6: 133–150.

Bryant, B. 1995a. *Environmental Justice: Issues, Policies, and Solutions.* Island.

Bryant, B. 1995b. Methodological issues: Pollution prevention and participatory research as a methodology for environmental justice. *Virginia Environmental Law Journal* 14, summer: 589.

Bryant, B., and P. Mohai, eds. 1992. *Race and the Incidence of Environmental Hazards: A Time for Discourse.* Westview.

Bryant, R., and S. Bailey. 1997. *Third World Political Ecology.* Routledge.

Bullard, R. 1983. Solid waste sites and the black Houston community. *Sociological Inquiry* 53: 273–288.

Bullard, R. 1990. *Dumping in Dixie: Race, Class and Environmental Quality.* Westview.

Bullard, R., ed. 1993a. *Environmental Racism: Voices from the Grassroots.* South End.

Bullard, R. 1993b. Anatomy of environmental racism and the environmental justice movement. In *Confronting Environmental Racism,* ed. R. Bullard. South End.

Bullard, R. 1993c. Anatomy of racism. In *Toxic Struggles,* ed. R. Hofrichter. New Society.

Bullard, R., ed. 1993d. *Confronting Environmental Racism: Voices from the Grassroots.* South End.

Bullard, R. 1994a. Symposium: The legacy of American apartheid and environmental racism. *St. John's Journal of Legal Commentary* 9: 445.

Bullard, R. 1994b. Environmental justice for all. In *Unequal Protection,* ed. R. Bullard. Sierra Club Books.

Bullard, R., ed. 1994c. *Unequal Protection.* Sierra Club Books.

Bullard, R. 1995. Decision making. In *Faces of Environmental Racism,* ed. L. Westra and P. Wenz. Rowman & Littlefield.

Bullard, R. 1996. The legacy of American apartheid and environmental racism. *St. John's Journal of Legal Commentary* 9: 445–474.

Bullard, R. 1999. Environmental justice challenges at home and abroad. In *Global Ethics and Environment,* ed. N, Low. Routledge.

Bullard, R., and G. Johnson. 2000. Environmental justice: Grassroots activism and its impact on public policy decision making. *Journal of Social Issues* 56: 555–578.

Bullard, R., J. Johnson, and A. Torres. 2000. *Sprawl City: Race, Politics, and Planning in Atlanta.* Island.

Bullard, R., and B. Wright. 1989. Toxic waste and the African American Community. *Urban League Review* 13: 67–75.

Bullard, R., and B. Wright. 1992. The quest for environmental equity: Mobilizing the African-American community for social change. In *American Environmentalism*, ed. R. Dunlap and A. Mertig. Taylor & Francis.

Bullard, R., and B. Wright. 1993. The effects of occupational injury, illness and disease on the health status of black Americans. In *Toxic Struggle*, ed. R. Hofrichter. New Society Publishers.

Burch, William R., Jr. 1976 The peregrine falcon and the urban poor: Some sociological interrelations. In *Human Ecology*, ed. P. Richerson and J. McEvoy III. Duxbury.

Burger, J., E. Ostrum, R. B. Norgaard, D. Policansky, and B. Goldstein. 2001. *Protecting the Commons: A Framework for Resource Management in the Americas.* Island.

Burke, L. M. 1993. Race and environmental equity: A geographic analysis in Los Angeles. *Geographic Information Systems* 3: 44–50.

Bury, Michael. 1984. Chronic illness as biographical disruption. *Sociology of Health and Illness* 4: 167–182.

Byrne, J., and Hoffman, S. 2001 A necessary sacrifice: American Indians and the industrialization of America. In *Environmental Justice*, ed. J. Byrne et al. Transaction Books.

Cable, S. 1984. Professionalization in social movement organization: A case study of Pennsylvanians for Biblical Morality. *Sociological Focus* 17: 287–304.

Cable, S., and M. Benson. 1993. Acting locally: Environmental injustice and the emergence of grassroots environmental organizations. *Social Problems* 40: 464–477.

Cable, S., and C. Cable. 1995. *Environmental Problems/Grassroots Solutions: The Politics of Environmental Conflict.* St. Martin's.

Cable, S., and B. Degutis. 1991. The transformation of community consciousness: The effects of citizens' organizations on host communities. *International Journal of Mass Emergencies and Disasters* 9: 383–399.

Cable, S., D. Hastings, and T. Mix. 2002. Different voices, different venues: Environmental racism claims by activists, academics, and lawyers. *Human Ecology Review* 9, no. 1: 26–42.

Cable, S., and T. Mix. 2003. Economic imperatives and race relations: The rise and fall of the American apartheid system. *Journal of Black Studies* 34: 183–203.

Cable, S., and T. Shriver. 1995. The production and extrapolation of meaning in the environmental justice movement. *Sociological Spectrum* 15: 419–442.

Cable, S., E. Walsh, and R. Warland. 1988. Differential paths to political activism: Comparisons of four mobilization processes after the Three Mile Island accident. *Social Forces* 66: 951–969.

Calhoun, C. 1993. Nationalism and civil society: Democracy, diversity and self-determination. *International Sociology* 8: 387–411.

Camacho, D., ed. 1998. *Environmental Injustices, Political Struggles: Race, Class, and the Environment.* Duke University Press.

Cancian, F. 1993. Conflicts between activist research and academic success. *American Sociologist* 24: 92–106.

Capek, S. 1993. The "environmental justice" frame: A conceptual discussion and application. *Social Problems* 40: 5–24.

Carey, M. 2001. State sets environmental rules. *Weekend Hampshire Gazette,* January 6–7.

Carr, W., and S. Kemmis. 1986. *Becoming Critical: Education, Knowledge, and Action Research.* Falmer.

Carson, R. 1962. *Silent Spring.* Houghton Mifflin.

Castells, M. 1997. *The Power of Identity.* Blackwell.

Center, R. 2000. Poverty, Ethnicity, and Pediatric Asthma in Rhode Island. Senior Honors Thesis, Center for Environmental Studies, Brown University.

Chambliss, W. 1974. The state, the law, and the definition of behavior as criminal or delinquent. In *Handbook of Criminology,* ed. D. Glaser. Rand McNally.

Chang, J., and L. Hwang. 2000. It's a survival issue: The environmental justice movement faces the new century. *Color Lines* 3, no. 2: 1–8.

Charmaz, K. 1991. *Good Days, Bad Days: The Self in Chronic Illness and Time.* Rutgers University Press.

Chavis, B., Jr. 1993. Foreword. In *Confronting Environmental Racisms,* ed. R. Bullard. South End.

Checker, Melissa A. 2002. "It's in the air": Redefining the environment as a new metaphor for old social justice struggles. *Human Organization* 61: 94–105.

Cigler, A., and Loomis, B. 1995. *Interest Group Politics,* fourth edition. Congressional Quarterly Press.

Clarke, S. 2001. The prospects for local democratic governance: The governance roles of nonprofit organizations. *Policy Studies Review* 18, winter: 4.

Cleaver, H. 1988. The uses of an earthquake. *Midnight Notes* 9: 10–14.

Clemens, E., and D. Minkoff. 2004. Beyond the iron law: Rethinking the place of organizations in social movement research. In *The Blackwell Companion to Social Movements,* ed. D. Snow et al. Blackwell.

Club of Rome. 1972. *The Limits to Growth.* Universe Books.

Cohen, J. 1985. Strategy or identity: New theoretical paradigms and contemporary social movements. *Social Research* 52: 663–716.

Cohen, L., and M. Love. 2000. Urban Asthma and Community Health Workers. Presented at annual meeting of American Public Health Association, Boston.

Cole, L., and S. Foster. 2001. From the ground up: Environmental racism and the rise of the environmental justice movement. New York University Press.

Collette, W. 1987. *How to Deal with a Proposed Facility*. Clearinghouse for Hazardous Wastes.

Commoner, B. 1992. *Making Peace with the Planet*. New Press.

Conrad, P. 1987. The experience of illness: Recent and new directions. *Research in the Sociology of Health Care* 6: 1–31.

Consejo Nacional de Areas Protegidas (CONAP), USAID, and F. Peregrino. 1997. El estado de la Reserva de La Biósfera Maya en 1996, Guatemala.

Cooper, C., and C. Warner. 1995. Is old dumpsite toxic? Not very, EPA says. New Orleans *Times-Picayune*, April 4.

Coser, L. 1964. *The Functions of Social Conflict*. Free Press.

Couto, R. 1987. Participatory research: Methodology and critique. *Clinical Sociology Review* 5: 83–90.

Cress, D., and D. Snow. 2000. The outcomes of homeless mobilization: The influence of organization, disruption, political mediation, and framing. *American Journal of Sociology* 105: 1063–1104.

Cromwell, D. 2000. Local energy, local democracy: Are economics and ecology on a collision course? www.ru.org/10-1cromwell.htm.

Cronon, W. 1996. *Uncommon ground: Rethinking the Human Place in Nature*. Norton.

Daugherty, C. 1998. Digging in. New Orleans *Gambit*, November 3.

Davis, C. 1993. *The Politics of Hazardous Waste*. Prentice-Hall.

Delgado, R., and J. Stefancic, eds. 2000. *Critical Race Theory: The Cutting Edge*, second edition. Temple University Press.

DeLuca, K. 1999. *Image Politics: The New Rhetoric of Environmental Activism*. Guilford.

Di Chiro, G. 1998. Environmental justice from the grassroots: Reflections on history, gender, and expertise. In *The Struggle for Ecological Democracy*, ed. D. Faber. Guilford.

DiPerna, P. 1985. *Cluster Mystery: Epidemic and the Children of Woburn*. Mosby.

Dobson, A. 1998. *Justice and the Environment: Conceptions of Environmental Sustainability and Theories of Distributive Justice*. Oxford University Press.

Dobson, A. 2003. Social justice and environmental sustainability: Ne'er the twain shall meet? In *Just Sustainabilities*, ed. J. Agyeman et al. MIT Press.

Dockery, D., C. Pope, X. Xu, J. Spengler, J. Ware, M. Ray, B. Ferris, and F. Speizer. 1993. An association between air pollution and mortality in six US cities. *New England Journal of Medicine* 329: 1753–1759.

Donham, K. 1993. Respiratory disease hazards to workers in livestock and poultry confinement structures. *Seminars in Respiratory Medicine* 14, no. 1.

Dowie, M. 1995. *Losing Ground: American Environmentalism at the Close of the Twentieth Century*. MIT Press.

Downey, L. 1998. Environmental injustice: Is race or income a better predictor? *Social Science Quarterly* 79: 766–778.

Dunlap, R. 1992. From environmental to ecological problems. In *Social Problems*, ed. C. Calhoun and G. Ritzer. McGraw-Hill.

Dunlap, R., and R. Scarce. 1991. The polls—poll trends: Environmental problems and protection. *Public Opinion Quarterly* 55: 651–672.

Eagleton, T. 1991. *Ideology*. Verso.

Ebright, M. 1994. *Land Grants and Lawsuits in Northern New Mexico*. University of New Mexico Press.

Ecologist, The. 1993. *Whose Common Future? Reclaiming the Commons*. New Society.

Edwards, B. 1995. With liberty and environmental justice for all: The emergence and challenge of grassroots environmentalism in the United States. In *Ecological Resistance Movements*, ed. B. Taylor. State University of New York Press.

Edwards, B., and A. Andrews. 2004. The structure of local environmentalism. Presented at American Sociological Association Conference.

Edwards, B., and M. Foley. 2003. Social movement organizations beyond the Beltway: Understanding the diversity of one social movement industry. *Mobilization* 8, no. 1: 87–107.

Ellefson, P. 1992. *Forest Resources Policy: Process, Participants, and Programs*. McGraw-Hill.

Emirbayer, M., and J. Goodwin. 1994. Network analysis, culture, and the problem of agency. *American Journal of Sociology* 99, no. 6: 1411–1454.

Environmental Protection Agency. 1999. Record of Decision Abstracts: Agriculture Street Landfill.

Erikson, K. 1976. *Everything in Its Path: The Destruction of Community in the Buffalo Creek Flood*. Touchstone.

Erikson, K. 1991. A new species of trouble. In *Communities at Risk*, ed. S. Couch and J. Kroll-Smith. Lang.

Escobar, A. 1994. *Encountering Development: The Making and Unmaking of the Third World*. Princeton University Press.

Eskew, G. 1997. *But for Birmingham*. University of North Carolina Press.

Essoka, J., and R. Brulle. 2002. From Urban Problems to Environmental Justice: A Historical Perspective on the Development of Environmental Concern in the Black Community. Unpublished manuscript.

Esteva, G. 1991. Tepito: No thanks, first world. *In Context* 30: 38–42.

Esteva, G. 1997. The meaning and scope of the struggle for autonomy. Presented at annual meetings of Latin American Studies Association, Guadalajara.

Esteva, G., and M. Prakash. 1999. *Grassroots Postmodernism: Remaking the Soil of Cultures*. Zed.

Evans, D., M, Fullilove, P, Shepard, C. Corbin-Mark, C. Edwards, L. Green, and F. Perera. 2000. Healthy Home, Healthy Child campaign: A community intervention by the Columbia Center for Children's Environmental Health. Presented at annual meeting of American Public Health Association, Boston.

EWG (Environmental Working Group). 2004. Obstruction of Justice. www.ewg.org.

Executive Office of the President, Office of Science and Technology Policy. No date. Climate Change: State of Knowledge.

Faber, D., ed. 1998. *The Struggle for Ecological Democracy: Environmental Justice Movements in the United States*. Guilford.

Faber, D., and E. Krieg. 2001. Unequal exposure to ecological hazards: Environmental injustices in the Commonwealth of Massachusetts. Northeastern University.

Faber, D., and D. McCarthy. 2001. *Green of Another Color: Building Effective Partnerships between Foundations and the Environmental Justice Movement*. Northeastern University Press.

Faber, D., and D. McCarthy. 2003. Neo-liberalism, globalization and the struggle for ecological democracy: Linking sustainability and environmental justice. In *Just Sustainabilities*, ed. J Agyeman et al. MIT Press.

Feagin, J., and C. Feagin. 1986. *Discrimination American Style: Institutional Racism and Sexism*, second edition. Krieger.

Feagin, J., and M. Sikes. 1994. *Living with Racism: The Black Middle-Class Experience*. Beacon.

Fendrich, J. 1993. *Ideal Citizens: The Legacy of the Civil Rights Movement*. State University of New York Press.

Ferree, M., and F. Miller. 1985. Mobilization and meaning: Toward an integration of social psychological and resource perspectives on social movements. *Sociological Inquiry* 55: 38–61.

Fiorina, M., and T. Skocpol. 1999. *Civic Engagement in American Democracy*. Brookings Institution Press.

Fischer, F. 2000. *Citizens, Experts, and the Environment: The Politics of Local Knowledge*. Duke University Press.

Fisher, K. 1998. Locating frames in the discursive universe. Sociological Research Online 2, no. 3.

Fisher, W. 1984. Narrations as a human communication paradigm: The case of public moral argument. *Communication Monographs* 51: 1–23.

Foreman, C. 1998. *The Promise and the Peril of Environmental Justice*. Brookings Institution.

Fort, M., and L. Grandia. 1999. Population and the environment in the Petén, Guatemala. In *Thirteen Ways of Looking at a Tropical Forest*, ed. J. Nations. Conservation International.

Foster, J. 1994. *The Vulnerable Planet: A Short Economic History of the Environment*. Monthly Review Press.

Foster, J. 1998. The limits of environmentalism without class: Lessons from the ancient forest struggle in the Pacific Northwest. In *The Struggle for Ecological Democracy*, ed. D. Faber. Guilford.

Foster, S. 1998. Justice from the ground up: Distributive inequities, grassroots resistance, and the transformative politics of the environmental justice movement. *California Law Review* 86: 775.

Foucault, M. 1977. *Discipline and Punish*. Penguin.

Frazier, E. 1957. *Black Bourgeoisie: The Rise of a New Middle Class in the United States*. Collier, 1962 reprint.

Freeman, A., III. 1972. The Distribution of Environmental Quality. In *Environmental Quality Analysis*, ed. A. Kneese and B. Bower. Johns Hopkins University Press.

Freire, P. 1993. *Pedagogy of the Oppressed*, twentieth-anniversary edition. Continuum.

Freudenberg, N. 1984. *Not in Our Backyards: Community Action for Health and the Environment*. Monthly Review Press.

Freudenberg, N., and C. Steinsapir. 1992. Not in our backyards: The grassroots environmental movement. In *The US Environmental Movement, 1970–1990*, ed. R. Dunlap and A. Mertig. Taylor and Francis.

Frey, R. 2001. The Hazardous waste stream in the world system. In *The Environment and Society Reader*, ed. R. Frey. Allyn and Bacon.

Frey, R., T. Dietz, and L. Kalof. 1992. Characteristics of successful American protest groups: Another look at Gamson's strategy of social protest. *American Journal of Sociology* 98: 368–387.

Friedman, M., K. Powell, L. Hutwagner, L. Graham, and W. Teague. 2001. Impact of changes in transportation and commuting behaviors during the 1996 Summer Olympic Games in Atlanta on air quality and childhood asthma. *Journal of the American Medical Association* 285: 897–905.

Fung, A. 2003. Associations and democracy: Between theories, hopes, and realities. *Annual Review of Sociology* 29: 515–539.

Gabe, J., M. Bury, and R. Ramsay. 2002. Living with asthma: The experiences of young people at home and at school. *Social Science and Medicine* 55: 1619–1633.

Gamson, W. 1975. *The Strategy of Social Protest*. Dorsey.

Gamson, W., B. Fireman, and S. Rytina. 1982. *Encounters with Unjust Authority*. Dorsey.

Garry, V., et al. 1996. Pesticide appliers, biocides, and birth defects in rural Minnesota. *Environmental Health Perspectives* 104: 394–399.

Gaventa, J. 1993. The powerful, the powerless, and the experts: Knowledge struggles in an information age. In *Voices of Change*, ed. P. Park et al. Bergin and Garvey.

Gerlach, L., and V. Hine. 1970. *People, Power, Change: Movements of Social Transformation*. Bobbs-Merrill.

Getches, D., and D. Pellow. 2002. Beyond "traditional" environmental justice: How large a tent? In *Justice and Natural Resources*, ed. K. Mutz et al. Island.

Ghai, D., and J. Vivian. 1992. *Grassroots Environmental Action: Participation in Sustainable Development*. Routledge.

Gibbs, L. 1982. *Love Canal: My Story*. State University of New York Press.

Giugni, M. 1998. Was it worth the effort? The outcomes and consequences of social movements. *Annual Review of Sociology* 24: 371–393.

Gladen, B., et al. 1998. Exposure opportunities of families of farmer pesticide applicators. *American Journal of Industrial Medicine* 34: 581–587.

Gladwin, T. 1987 (originally published 1980). Patterns of environmental conflict over industrial facilities in the United States, 1970–78. In *Resolving Locational Conflict*, ed. R. Lake. Rutgers Center for Urban Policy Research.

Gledhill, J. 2000. *Autonomy and Alterity: The Dilemmas of Mexican Anthropology*.

Godleski, J. 2000. Mechanisms of Particulate Air Pollution Health Effects. Presented at annual meeting of American Public Health Association, Boston.

Goodman, D., T. Stukel, and C. Chiang-Hau. 1998. Trends in pediatric asthma hospitalization rates: Regional and socioeconomic differences. *Pediatrics* 101: 208–213.

Gordon, C., and J. Jasper. 1996. Overcoming the NIMBY label: Rhetorical and organizational links for protestors. *Research in Social Movements, Conflict, and Change* 19: 159–181.

Gottlieb, R. 1993. *Forcing the Spring: The Transformation of the American Environmental Movement*. Island.

Gottlieb, R. 2001. *Environmentalism Unbound: Exploring New Pathways for Change*. MIT Press.

Gould, K., A. Schnaiberg, and A. Weinberg. 1996. *Local Environmental Struggles: Citizen Activism in the Treadmill of Production*. Cambridge University Press.

Green, J. 1999. The spirit willing: Collective identity and the development of the Christian Right. In *Waves of Protest*, ed. J. Freeman and V. Johnson. Rowman & Littlefield.

Greenbaum, D. 2000. Interface of science with policy. Presented at annual meeting of American Public Health Association, Boston.

Greenhouse, L. 2000. EPA's authority on air rules wins Supreme Court's backing. *New York Times*, February 28.

Greenleaf, R. 1972. Land and water in Mexico and New Mexico, 1700–1821. *New Mexico Historical Review* 47: 85–112.

Griffiths, J. 1986. What is legal pluralism? *Journal of Legal Pluralism* 24: 1–50.

Grünberg, G., and V. Ramos. 1998. Base de datos sobre población, tierra y medio ambiente en la Reserva de la Biósfera Maya. CARE, CONAP, Petén, Guatemala.

Guha, R. 1989. Radical American environmentalism and wilderness preservation: A Third World critique. *Environmental Ethics* 11: 71–83.

Guha, R. 2000. *These Unquiet Woods: Ecological Change and Peasant Resistance in the Himalaya*, revised edition. University of California Press.

Gutman, P. 2001. Forest Conservation and the Rural Poor: A Call to Broaden the Conservation Agenda. World Wildlife Fund.

Habermas, J. 1962. *The Structural Transformation of the Public Sphere: An Inquiry into a Category of Bourgeois Society*. MIT Press, 1989.

Habermas, J. 1984. *The Theory of Communicative Acti*on, volume 1: *Reason and the Rationalization of Society*. Beacon.

Habermas, J. 1987. *The Theory of Communicative Action*, volume 2: *Lifeworld and System: A Critique of Functionalist Reason*. Beacon.

Habermas, J. 1991. A Reply. In *Communicative Action*, ed. A. Honneth and H. Joas. MIT Press.

Habermas, J. 1996 *Between Facts and Norms: Contributions to a Discourse Theory of Law and Democracy*. MIT Press.

Habermas, J. 1998. *The Inclusion of the Other: Studies in Political Theory*. MIT Press.

Haines, H. 1984. Black radicalization and the funding of civil rights: 1957–1970. *Social Problems* 32: 31–43.

Halcli, A. 1999. AIDS, anger, and activism: ACT UP as a social movement organization. In *Waves of Protest*, ed. J. Freeman and V. Johnson. Rowman & Littlefield.

Hall, B. 1992. From margins to center? The development and purpose of participatory research. *American Sociologist*, winter: 15–28.

Hall, S. 1982. The rediscovery of ideology: Return to the repressed in media studies. In *Culture, Society and the Media*, ed. M. Gurevitch et al. Methuen.

Halweil, B. 2003. This old barn, this new money. *WorldWatch*, July-August: 24.

Harden, M. 2002. The Fight for Healthy and Safe Communities: Uncovering EPA's Anti-Civil Rights Agenda. National Black Environmental Justice Network.

Hart, S. 1996. The Cultural Dimension of Social Movements: A Theoretical Reassessment and Literature Review. *Sociology of Religion* 57: 87–100.

Harvey, D. 1999. Considerations on the environment of justice. In *Global Ethics and the Environment*, ed. N. Low. Routledge.

Harvey, D. 2000. *Spaces of Hope*. University of California Press.

Hayes, M. 1986. The new group universe. In *Interest Group Politics*, ed. A. Cigler and B. Loomis. Congressional Quarterly Press.

Health Consultation. 1997 Review of Health Outcome Data for the Agriculture Street Landfill Site, New Orleans, Louisiana, Cerclis No LAD981056997. 10-22-97, October 22.

Hicks, G., and D. Peña. 2003. Community acequias in Colorado's Rio Culebra watershed: A customary commons in the domain of prior appropriation. *University of Colorado Law Review* 74: 101–195.

Higgins, R. 1993. Race and environmental equity: An overview of environmental justice issues in the policy process. *Polity* 26, no. 2: 281–300.

Hird, J. 1993. Environmental policy and equity: The case of Superfund. *Journal of Policy Analysis and Management* 12: 323–343.

Hirsch, E. 1990. Sacrifice for the cause: Group processes, recruitment, and commitment in a student social movement. *American Sociological Review* 55: 243–254.

Hirsh, R. 1999. *Power Loss: The Origins of Deregulation and Restructuring in the American Electric Utility System.* MIT Press.

Hoar, S., et al. 1986. Agricultural Herbicide Use and Risk of lymphoma and soft-tissue sarcoma. *Journal of the American Medical Association* 256, no. 9: 1147–1147.

Hofrichter, R., ed. 1993. *Toxic Struggles: The Theory and Practice of Environmental Justice.* New Society.

Hoogvelt, A. 1997. Globalization and the postcolonial world: The new political economy of development. Baltimore: Johns Hopkins University Press.

Horton, M., and P. Freire. 1990. *We Make the Road by Walking: Conversations on Education and Social Change.* Temple University Press.

Hsu, K. 2000. Boston will get $1.9 million to prevent asthma. *Boston Globe,* February 24.

Hunn, E. 1999. The value of subsistence for the future of the world. In *Ethnoecology,* ed. V. Nazarea. University of Arizona Press.

Hynes, H. 1989. *The Recurring Silent Spring.* Pergamon.

Instituto del Libro. 1986. Wa'apin man: La historia de la costa talamanqueña de Costa Rica, según sus protagonistas. Instituto del Libro, Ministerio de Cultura, Juventud y Deportes, San José, Costa Rica.

Jacobson, C. 2000. *Ties That Bind: Economic and Political Dilemmas of Urban Utility Networks, 1800–1990.* University of Pittsburgh Press.

Janicke, M. 1990. *State Failure: The Impotence of Politics in Industrial Society.* Pennsylvania State University Press.

Jasper, J. 1997. *The Art of Moral Protest.* University of Chicago Press.

Jasper, J. 1999. Recruiting intimates, recruiting strangers: Building the contemporary animal rights movement. In *Waves of Protest,* ed. J. Freeman and V. Johnson. Rowman & Littlefield.

Johnson, K. 2001. Critics of power generators sue, citing threat to environment. *New York Times,* February 8.

Johnson, V. 1999. The strategic determinants of a countermovement: The emergence and impact of Operation Rescue blockades. In *Waves of Protest,* ed. J. Freeman and V. Johnson. Rowman & Littlefield.

Johnston, E., and C. Soulsby. 2002. Gaining ecological legitimacy: The development of sustainability consciousness in the flow country, Northern Scotland. *Local Environment* 7: 81–95.

Jones, N., R. Kinsman, J. Dirks, and N. Dahlem. 1979. Psychological contributions to chronicity in asthma patient response styles influencing medical treatment and its outcome. *Medical Care* 17: 1103–1118.

Jordan, Grant, and W. Maloney. 1997. *The Protest Business? Mobilizing Campaign Groups.* St. Martin's.

Kairys, David, ed. 1998. *The Politics of Law: A Progressive Critique,* third edition. Basic Books.

Kaptein, A. 1982. Psychological correlates of length of hospital stay and rehospitalization in patients with acute, severe asthma. *Social Science and Medicine* 16: 725–729.

Kasper, A., and S. Ferguson, eds. 2000. *Breast Cancer: Society Shapes an Epidemic.* St. Martin's.

Keating, M., and F. Davis. No date. Air of Injustice. Pew Charitable Trust.

Keith, L. 2001. California making environmental justice tenet of air policy. Associated Press, December 14.

Kimbrell, A., ed. 2002. *Fatal Harvest: The Tragedy of Industrial Agriculture.* Island.

Kiss, A. 2002. Making biodiversity conservation a land use priority. In *Getting Biodiversity Projects to Work,* ed. T. McShane and M. Wells. Columbia University Press.

Kitschelt, H. 1985. Political opportunity structures and political protest: Antinuclear movement in four democracies. *British Journal of Political Science* 16: 57–85.

Klandermans, B. 1984. Mobilization and participation: Social psychological expansions of resource mobilization theory. *American Sociological Review* 49: 583–600.

Klinenberg, E. 2002. *Heat Wave: A Social Autopsy of Disaster in Chicago.* University of Chicago Press.

Knoke, D. 1990a. *Organizing for Collective Action: The Political Economies of Associations.* Aldine de Gruyter.

Knoke, D. 1990b. *Political Networks.* Cambridge University Press.

Krauss, C. 1989. Community struggles and the shaping of democratic consciousness. *Sociological Forum* 4: 227–239.

Krieg, E. 1998. The two faces of toxic waste. *Sociological Forum* 13: 3–20.

Kroll-Smith, J., and Floyd, H. 1997. *Bodies in Protest: Environmental Illness and the Struggle Over Medical Knowledge.* New York University Press.

Kubal, T. 1998. The presentation of political self: Cultural resonance and the construction of collective action frames. *Sociological Quarterly* 39: 539–554.

LaBalme, J. 1987. *A Road to Walk: A Struggle for Environmental Justice.* Regulator.

LaDuke, W. 1999. *All Our Relations: Native Struggles for Land and Life.* South End.

Landry, B. 1987. *The New Black Middle Class.* University of California Press.

Larson, A. 2001. Environmental/Occupational Safety and Health. Migrant Health Issues monograph 2.

Lathan, A. 1993. Dollie Burwell: Standing up for what's right. *Audubon Activist* 7, May: 8.

Latour, B. 1998. To modernise or ecologise? That is the question. In *Remaking Reality*, ed. B. Braun and N. Castree. Routledge.

Lavelle, M., and M. Coyle. 1992. Unequal protection: The racial divide in environmental law. *National Law Journal* 15: S1–S12.

Lavelle, M., and M. Coyle. 1993. Unequal protection: The racial divide in environmental law. In *Toxic Struggles*, ed. R. Hofrichter. New Society.

Lawson, S., and C. Payne. 1998. *Debating the Civil Rights Movement, 1945–1968.* Rowman & Littlefield.

Lazaroff, C. 2000. No title. Environmental News Service, February 11.

Leach, M., and R. Mearns. 1997. Poverty and the environment in developing countries: An overview study. ESRC Society and Politics Groups, Overseas Development Administration, London.

Lee, C. 1992. Toxic waste and race in the United States. In *Race and the Incidence of Environmental Hazards*, ed. B. Bryant and P. Mohai. Westview.

Lester, J., D. Allen, and K. Hill. 2001. *Environmental Injustice in the United States: Myths and Realities.* Westview.

Levidow, L. 1992. The eleventh annual meeting of the International Association for Impact Assessment. *Capitalism, Nature, Socialism* 3: 117–124.

Levine, A. 1982. *Love Canal: Science, Politics, and People.* Lexington Books.

Lewis, J., and M. D'Orso. 1998. *Walking with the Wind: A Memoir of the Movement.* Simon & Schuster.

Lewis, S., and D. Henkels. 1998. Good neighbor agreements: A tool for environmental and social justice. *Social Justice* 23: 1–18.

Lipset, S., M. Trow, and J. Coleman. 1956. *Union Democracy.* Free Press.

Lipsitz, G. 1998. *The Possessive Investment in Whiteness: How White People Profit from Identity Politics.* Temple University Press.

Lomax, L. 1963. *The Negro Revolt.* Signet Books.

Lorde, A. 1984. *Sister Outsider.* Crossing.

Louisiana Department of Natural Resources, Office of Conservation. 1999. Declaration of Emergency, Amendment to Statewide Order No. 29-B (Emergency Rule) May 29].

Low, N.,, and B. Gleeson. 1998. *Justice, Society and Nature: An Exploration on Political Ecology.* Routledge.

Lundell, C. 1937. *The Vegetation of the Petén*. Carnegie Institution.

Lynd, S., and A. Lynd, eds. 1995. *Nonviolence in America: A Documentary History*. Orbis Books.

Maher, T. 1998. Environmental oppression. *Journal of Black Studies* 28: 357–367.

Mahoney, V. 2000. Environmental justice: From partial victories to complete solutions. *Cardozo Law Review* 21:361–414.

Mannino, D., D. Homa, L. Akinbami, J. Moorman, C. Gwynne, and S. Redd. 2002. Surveillance for asthma—United States, 1980–1999. *Morbidity and Mortality Weekly Report* 51, March 29: 1–13.

Margoluis, R., and N. Salafsky 1998. *Measures of Success: Designing, Managing and Monitoring Conservation and Development Projects*. Island.

Markandaya, A. 2001. Poverty alleviation and sustainable development: Implications for the management of natural capital. Workshop on Poverty and Sustainable Development, University of Bath and World Bank, Ottawa.

Martínez-Alier, J. 1999. Environmental justice (local and global). In *The Cultures of Globalization*, ed. F. Jameson and M. Miyashi. Duke University Press.

Marx, K. 1964. *The Economic and Philosophic Manuscripts of 1844*. International Publishers.

Maslow, A., and Psychological Films Inc. 1968. *Maslow and Self-Actualization*. Psychological Films.

Matthews, D., and J. Prothro. 1966. *Negroes and the New Southern Politics*. Harcourt Brace & World.

McAdam, D. 1982. *Political Process and the Development of Black Insurgency, 1930–1970*. University of Chicago Press.

McAdam, D. 1983. Tactical innovation and the pace of insurgency. *American Sociological Review* 48: 735–754.

McAdam, D., J. McCarthy, and M. Zald. 1996. Introduction. In *Comparative Perspectives on Social Movements*, ed. D. McAdam et al. Cambridge University Press.

McAdam, D., and R. Paulsen. 1993. Specifying the relationship between social ties and activism. *American Journal of Sociology* 99: 640–667.

McCann, M. 1994. *Rights at Work: Pay Equity Reform and the Politics of Legal Mobilization*. University of Chicago Press.

McCann,, M. 1998. Social movements and the mobilization of law. In *Social Movements and American Political Institutions*, ed. A. Costain and A. McFarland. Rowman & Littlefield.

McCarthy, J. 1996. Constraints and opportunities in adopting, adapting and inventing. In *Comparative Perspectives on Social Movements*, ed. J. McCarthy et al. Cambridge University Press.

McCarthy, J., and M. Zald. 1973. *The Trend of Social Movements in America: Professionalization and Resource Mobilization*. General Learning.

McCarthy, J., and M. Zald. 1977. Resource mobilization and social movements: A partial theory. *American Journal of Sociology* 82: 1212–1241.

McFarland, A. 1998. Social movements and theories of American politics. In *Social Movements and American Political Institutions*, ed. A. Costain and A. McFarland. Rowman & Littlefield.

McNamara, W. 2002. *The California Energy Crisis: Lessons for a Deregulating Industry*. PennWell.

McShane, T. 2003. The devil in the detail of biodiversity conservation. *Conservation Biology* 17: 1–3.

Meadows, D. 1972. *The Limits to Growth*. Universe Books.

Meadows, D., D. Meadows, and J. Randers. 1992. *Beyond the Limits: Confronting Global Collapse, Envisioning a Sustainable Future*. Chelsea Green.

Medoff, P., and H. Sklar. 1994. *Streets of Hope: The Fall and Rise of an Urban Neighborhood*. South End.

Meier, A., and Rudwick, E. 1966. *From Plantation to Ghetto: An Interpretive History of American Negroes*. Hill and Wang.

Melosi, M. 1985. *Coping with Abundance: Energy and Environment in Industrial America*. Temple University Press.

Melosi, M. 2000. Environmental Justice, Political Agenda Setting, and the Myths of History. *Journal of Policy History* 12: 43–71.

Melucci, A. 1989. *Nomads of the Present: Social Movements and Individual Needs in Contemporary Society*. Temple University Press.

Merrifield, J. 1989. *Putting Scientists in Their Place: Participatory Research in Environmental and Occupational Health*. Highlander Center.

Merry, S. 1988. Legal pluralism. *Law and Society Review* 22: 869–896.

Meyer, D. 1999. Civil disobedience and protest cycles. In *Waves of Protest*, ed. J. Freeman and V. Johnson. Rowman & Littlefield.

Milton, K. 1996. *Environmentalism and Culture Theory: Exploring the Role of Anthropology in Environmental Discourse*. Routledge.

Mirowsky, J., and C. Ross. 1981. Protest group success: The impact of group characteristics, social control, and context. *Sociological Focus* 14: 177–192.

Mitchell, R., A. Mertig, and R. Dunlap. 1992. Twenty years of environmental mobilization: Trends among national environmental organizations. In *The US Environmental Movement, 1970–1990*, ed. R. Dunlap and A. Mertig. Taylor and Francis.

Mohai, P. 2002. Race and environmental voting in the US Congress. *Social Science Quarterly* 83: 167–189.

Montague, P. 2002a. Rebuilding the movement to win. *Rachel's Environment and Health News* no. 744, February 14.

Montague, P. 2002b. White privilege divides the movement. *Rachel's Environment and Health News* no. 745, February 28.

Morland, K., et al. 2002a. Neighborhood characteristics associated with the location of food stores and food places. *American Journal of Preventive Medicine* 22(1).

Morland, K., et al. 2002b. The contextual effect of the local food environment on residents' diets: The atherosclerosis risk in communities study. *American Journal of Public Health* 92: 1761–1767.

Morris, A. 1981. Black Southern student sit-in movement: An analysis of internal organization. *American Sociological Review* 46: 744–767.

Morris, A. 1984. *The Origins of the Civil Rights Movement*. Free Press.

Moyers, R., and K. Enright. 1997. *A Snapshot of America's Nonprofit Boards*, 1997 edition. National Center for Nonprofit Boards.

Mpanya, M. 1992. The dumping of toxic waste in African countries: A case of poverty and racism. In *Race and the Incidence of Environmental Hazards*, ed. B. Bryant and P. Mohai. Westview.

Muir, S., and T. Veenendall. 1996. *Earthtalk: Communication and Empowerment for Environmental Action*. Praeger.

Mutz, K., G. Bryner, and D. Kinney. 2002. *Justice and Natural Resources: Concepts, Strategies, and Applications*. Island.

Nash, J. 2001. *Mayan Visions: The Quest for Autonomy in an Age of Globalization*. Routledge.

National Health Interview Survey. 1997.

National Research Council. 1999. *Our Common Journey: A Transition towards Sustainability*. National Academies Press.

Neefjes, K. 1999. Ecological degradation: A cause for conflict, a concern for survival. In *Fairness and Futurity*, ed. A. Dobson. Oxford University Press.

Newfield, J. 1966. *A Prophetic Minority*. New American Library.

News-Star. 1994. Agencies do battle over plant. February 5.

Nicholson-Choice, M. 2000. The many faces of environmental justice. *Florida Bar Journal* 74: 5–50.

Novotny, P. 2000. *Where We Live, Work, and Play: The Environmental Movement and the Struggle for New Environmentalism*. Praeger.

NRDC (Natural Resource Defense Council). 2004, www.nrdc.org/water/pollution/ffarms.asp.

Nye, D. 1998. *Consuming Power: A Social History of American Energies*. MIT Press.

Oberschall, A. 1973. *Social Conflict and Social Movements*. Prentice-Hall.

O'Connor, J. 1991. Conference Papers on Capitalism, Nature, Socialism. CNS/CPE Pamphlet 1.

O'Fallon, L., and A. Deary. 2002. Community-based participatory research as a tool to advance environmental health sciences. *Environmental Health Perspectives* 110: 155–161.

Offe, C. 1990. Reflections on the institutional self-transformation of movement politics: A tentative stage model. In *Challenging the Political Order*, ed. R. Dalton et al. Oxford University Press.

Oliver, P., and H. Johnston. 2000. What a good idea! Frames and ideologies in social movement research. *Mobilization* 5: 37–54.

Oppenheimer, M. 1964. The Southern student movement: Year 1. *Journal of Negro Education* 33: 396–403.

Park, L., and D. Pellow. 1996. Washing dirty laundry: Organic-activist-research in two social movement organizations. *Sociological Imagination* 33, no. 2: 138–153.

Partridge, E. 1996. Environmental justice and "shared fate": A contractarian defense of fair compensation.

Pastor, M., J. Sadd, and J. Hipp,. 2001. Which came first? Toxic facilities, minority move-in, and environmental justice. *Journal of Urban Affairs* 23: 1–21.

Pattillo-McCoy, M. 1999. *Black Picket Fences: Privilege and Peril among the Black Middle Class*. University of Chicago Press.

Peet, R and M. Watts. 1996. *Liberation Ecologies: Environment, Development, Social Movements*. Routledge.

Pellow, D. 1994. Environmental justice and popular epidemiology: Symbolic politics, hidden transcripts. Presented at annual meeting of American Sociological Association, Los Angeles.

Pellow, D. 1999. Framing emerging environmental tactics: Mobilizing concensus, demobilizing conflict. *Sociological Forum* 14: 659–683.

Pellow, D. 2000. Environmental inequality formation: Toward a theory of environmental injustice. *American Behavioral Scientist* 43: 581–601.

Pellow, D. 2001. Environmental justice and the political process: Movements, corporations, and the state. *Sociological Quarterly* 42: 47–67.

Pellow, D. 2002. *Garbage Wars: The Struggle for Environmental Justice in Chicago*. MIT Press.

Pellow, D., and L. Park. 2003. *The Silicon Valley of Dreams: Environmental Injustice, Immigrant Workers and the High-Tech Global Economy*. New York University Press.

Peña, D. 1992. The "brown" and the "green": Chicanos and environmental politics in the Upper Rio Grande. *Capitalism, Nature, Socialism* 3: 79–103.

Peña, D. 1997. *The Terror of the Machine: Technology, Work, Gender, and Ecology on the US-Mexico Border*. University of Texas Press.

Peña, D. 1998. *Chicano Culture, Ecology, Politics: Subversive Kin*. University of Arizona Press.

Peña, D. 1999. Cultural landscapes and biodiversity: The ethnoecology of watershed commons. In *Ethnoecology*, ed. V. Nazarea. University of Arizona Press.

Peña, D. 2002. Endangered landscapes and disappearing peoples? Identity, place, and community in ecological politics. In *The Environmental Justice Reader*, ed. J. Adamson et al. University of Arizona Press.

Peña, D. 2003a. The scope of Latino/a environmental studies. *Latino Studies* 1: 47–78.

Peña, D. 2003b. The acequia watershed commonwealth. In *Natural Assets*, ed. J. Boyce and B. Shelly. Island.

Peña, D. 2003c. Identity, place, and communities of resistance. In *Just Sustainabilities*, ed. J. Agyeman et al. MIT Press.

Peña, D. 2003d. Autonomy, Equity, and Environmental Justice: Lessons from the Experience of Participatory Watershed Management. Provost's Lecture Series on Race, Poverty, and the Environment, Brown University.

Peña, D. 2005. *Mexican Americans and the Environment: Tierra y vida*. University of Arizona Press.

Peña, D., and J. Gallegos. 1993. Nature and Chicanos in southern Colorado. In *Confronting Environmental Racism*, ed. R. Bullard. South End.

Peña, D., and R. Martínez. 1998. The capitalist tool, the lawless, and the violent: A critique of recent Southwestern environmental history. In *Chicano Culture, Ecology, Politic*, ed. D. Peña. University of Arizona Press.

Peña, D., and R. Martínez. 2000. Upper Rio Grande Hispano Farms: A Cultural and Natural History of Land Ethics in Transition. Final report prepared for National Endowment for the Humanities. Rio Grande Bioregions Project, Department of Anthropology, University of Washington, Seattle.

Peña, D, and M. Mondragon Valdez. 1998. The "brown" and the "green" revisited: Chicanos and environmental politics in the Upper Rio Grande. In *The Struggle for Ecological Democracy*, ed. D. Faber. Guilford.

Pevar, S. *The Rights of Indians and Tribes*. Southern Illinois University Press.

Pew Environmental Health Commission. 2000. Attack Asthma Report.

Phipps, T., and P. Crosso., eds. 1986. Agriculture and the Environment: An Overview. Agriculture and the Environment Annual Policy Review (RFF 3-31).

Pimental, D., and H. Lehman. 1993. *The Pesticide Question: Environment, Economics and Ethics*. Chapman and Hall.

Pimentel, D., et al. 1992. Environmental and Economic Cost of Pesticide Use. *Bioscience* 42, no. 10: 750–760.

Piven, F., and R. Cloward. 1979. *Poor People's Movements: Why They Succeed, How They Fail*. Vintage Books.

Pope, C. 1989. Respiratory Disease Associated with Community Air Pollution and a Steel Mill, Utah Valley. *American Journal of Public Health* 79: 623–628.

Price, M. 2003. Baton Rouge Bus Boycott: Background. www.lib.lsu.edu/special/exhibits/boycott/index.html.

Pulido, L. 1996. *Environmentalism and Economic Justice: Two Chicano Cases from the Southwest*. University of Arizona Press.

Pulido, L. 1998. Ecological legitimacy and cultural essentialism: Hispano grazing in Northern New Mexico. In *Chicano Culture, Ecology, Politics*, ed. D. Peña. University of Arizona Press.

Pulido, L. 2000. Rethinking environmental racism: White privilege and urban development in southern California. *Annals of the Association of American Geographers* 90: 12–40.

Pulido, L., S. Sidawi, and R. Vos. 1996. An archaeology of environmental racism in Los Angeles. *Urban Geography* 17: 419–439.

Putnam, R. 2000. *Bowling Alone*. Simon and Schuster.

Quinney, R. 1974. *Criminal Justice in America*. Little, Brown.

Rabe, B. 1992. When siting works, Canada-style. *Journal of Health Politics, Policy, and Law* 17: 119–142.

Rawls, J. 1971. *A Theory of Justice*. Belknap.

Rawls. J. 1995. *Political Liberalism*. Columbia University Press.

Rechtschaffen, C., and E. Gauna. 2002. *Environmental Justice: Law, Policy, and Regulation*. Carolina Academic Press.

Redclift, M. 1987. *Sustainable Development: Exploring the Contradictions*. Routledge.

Redford, K., and B. Richter. 1999. Conservation of biodiversity in a world of use. *Conservation Biology* 13: 1246–1256.

Redford, K., and S. Sanderson. 2002. Contested relationships between biodiversity conservation and poverty alleviation. Presented at Conference for Society for Conservation Biology, Canterbury.

Riccardi, M. 2001. Judge Threatens to Halt Work on Queens Power Plants. *New York Law Journal*, February 26.

Rios, J. 2000. environmental justice groups: Grass-roots movement or NGO network? *Policy Studies Review* 17, no. 2/3: 179–211.

Roberts, J., and M. Weiss. 2001. *Chronicles from the Environmental Justice Frontline*. Cambridge University Press.

Robinson, J. 1993. The limits to caring: Sustainable living and the loss of biodiversity. *Conservation Biology* 7: 20–28.

Robnett, B, ed. 1998. *African-American Women in the Civil Rights Movement*. New York University Press.

Rodríguez, S. 1987. Land, water, and culture in Taos. In *Land, Water, and Culture*, ed. C. Briggs and J. Van Ness. University of New Mexico Press.

Rodríguez, S. 1989. Art, tourism, and race relations in Taos: Toward a sociology of the art colony. *Journal of Anthropological Research* 45: 77–99.

Rodríguez, S. 1994. The tourist gaze, gentrification, and the commodification of subjectivity in Taos. In *Essays on the Changing Images of the Southwest*, ed. R. Francaviglia and D. Narrett. Texas A&M University Press.

Rosaldo, R. 1989. *Culture and Truth: The Remaking of Social Analysis*. South End.

Rucht, D. 1989. Environmental movement organizations in West Germany and France: Structure and Interorganizational relations. *International Social Movement Research* 2: 61–94.

Rudestam, K. 2001. The Important of Place: Asthmatic Children's Perceptions of Inside and Outside Environments. Senior Honors Thesis, Center for Environmental Studies, Brown University.

Sachs, A. 1995. Eco-Justice: Linking Human Rights and the Environment. WorldWatch paper 127.

Sader, S. 1999. Deforestation trends in northern Guatemala: A view from space. In *Thirteen Ways of Looking at a Tropical Forest*, ed. J. Nations. Conservation International.

Salafsky, N., B. Cordes, J. Parks, and C. Hochman. 1999. Evaluating Linkages between Business, the Environment, and Local Communities: Final Analytical Results from the Biodiversity Conservation Network. Biodiversity Support Program.

Sanches, J., and G. Mayorga. 1991. Taking Care of Sibö's Gifts: An Environmental Treatise from Costa Rica's KéköLdi Indigenous Reserve. San José, Costa Rica: Asociación de Desarrollo Integral de la Reserva Indígena Cocles/KéköLdi.

Sanches, J., and G. Mayorga. 1993. *Vías de Extinción; Vías de Supervivencia: Testimonios del pueblo indígena de la Reserva KéköLdi, Costa Rica*. Editorial Universidad de Costa Rica.

Sandweiss, S. 1998. The social construction of environmental justice. In *Environmental Injustices, Political Struggles*, ed. D. Camacho. Duke University Press.

Sassen, S, 1998. *Globalization and Its Discontents: Essays on the New Mobility of People and Money*. New Press.

Schlosberg, D., 1998. *Environmental Justice and the New Pluralism: The Challenge of Difference in Environmentalism*. Oxford University Press.

Schmitter, P. 1983. Democratic theory and neocorporatist practice. *Social Research* 50, no. 4: 851–884.

Schnaiberg, A. 1980. *The Environment: From Surplus to Scarcity*. Oxford University Press.

Schnaiberg, A., and K. Gould. 1994. *Environment and Society: The Enduring Conflict*. St. Martin's.

Scholte, P. 2002. Immigration: A potential time bomb under the integration of conservation and development. *Ambio* 32: 58–64.

Schwab, J. 1994. *Deeper Shades of Green: The Rise of Blue-Collar and Minority Environmentalism in America*. Sierra Club.

Schwartz, J. 2000. Fine particulate air pollution: Smoke and mirrors of the '90s or hazard of the new millennium? Presented at annual meeting of American Public Health Association, Boston.

Sears, M. 1997. Epidemiology of childhood asthma. *Lancet* 350: 1015–1020.

Shabecoff, P. 1990. *Earth Rising: American Environmentalism in the 21st Century.* Island.

Sharp, G. 1980. *Social Power and Political Freedom.* Sargent.

Shellenberger, M., and T. Nordhaus. 2004. The death of environmentalism. Presented at meeting of Environmental Grantmakers Association.

Shepard, P., M. Northridge, E. Mary, S. Prakash, and G. Stover. 2002. Preface: Advancing environmental justice through community-based participatory research. *Environmental Health Perspectives* 110, no. 2: 139–141.

Sherkat, D. 1998. What's in a frame? Toward an integrated social psychology of social movements. Presented at annual meeting of International Sociological Association, Montreal.

Shinkle, P. 1998. Uranium plant plan dropped. *Baton Rouge Advocate*, May 13.

Shiven, V. 1999. Ecological balance in an era of globalization. In *Global Ethics and Environment*, ed. N. Low. Routledge.

Shriar, A. 2001. The dynamics of agricultural intensification and resource conservation in the buffer zone of the Maya Biosphere Reserve, Petén, Guatemala. *Human Ecology* 29: 27–48.

Shuman, M. 2000. *Going Local: Creating Self-Reliant Communities in a Global Age.* Routledge.

Shutkin, W. 2001. *The Land That Could Be.* MIT Press.

Silverstein, H. 1996. 1996. *Unleashing Rights: Law, Meaning, and the Animal Rights Movement.* University of Michigan Press.

Skocpol, T. 2003. *Diminished Democracy: From Membership to Management in American Civic Life.* Oklahoma University Press.

Smart, C. 1989. *Feminism and the Power of Law.* Routledge.

Snow, D. 1992. Master frames and cycles of protest. In *Frontiers in Social Movement Theory*, ed. A. Morris and C. Mueller. Yale University Press.

Snow, D. 2004. Framing processes, ideology, and discursive fields. In *Blackwell's Companion to Social Movements*, ed. D. Snow et al. Blackwell.

Snow, D., and R. Benford. 1988. Ideology, frame resonance, and participant mobilization. *International Social Movement Research* 1: 197–217.

Snow, D., and R. Benford. 1992. Master frames and cycles of protest. In *Frontiers in Social Movement Theory*, ed. A. Morris and C. Mueller. Yale University Press.

Snow, D., and R. Benford. 1999. Alternative types of cross-national diffusion in the social movement arena. In *Social Movements in a Globalizing World*, ed. D. della Porta et al. Macmillan.

Snow, D., E. Burke Rochford Jr., S. Worden, and R. Benford. 1986. Frame alignment process, micromobilization and movement participation. *American Sociological Review* 51: 464–481.

Snyder, D., and W. Kelly. 1979. Strategies for investigating violence and social change: Illustrations from analyses of racial disorders and implications for mobilization research. In *The Dynamics of Social Movements*, ed. M. Zald and J. McCarthy. Winthrop.

Soja, E. 1997. *Post-Modern Geographies: The Reassertion of Space in Critical Social Theory*. Verso.

Soule, J., D. Carre and W. Jackson. 1990. Ecological impact of modern agriculture. In *Agroecology*, ed. C. Carroll et al. McGraw-Hill.

Southgate, D. 1998. *The Economics of Land Degradation*. World Bank.

Soza Manzanero, C. 1999. Economic perspectives in the Maya Biosphere Reserve. In *Thirteen Ways of Looking at a Tropical Forest*, ed. J. Nations. Conservation International.

Spiertz, H. 1998. Water rights and legal pluralism: Some basics of a legal anthropological approach. Presented at annual conference of International Association for the Study of Common Property, Vancouver, BC.

Staggenborg, S. 1988. The consequences of professionalization and formalization in the pro-choice movement. *American Sociological Review* 53: 585–606.

Steedly, H., and J. Foley. 1979. The success of protest groups: Multivariate analysis. *Social Science Research* 8: 1–15.

Steinberg, M. 1998. Tilting the frame: Considerations on collective action framing from a discursive turn. *Theory and Society* 27: 845–872.

Stevis, D. 2000. Whose ecological justice? *Strategies* 13: 63–76.

Stoecker, R. 1999. Are academics relevant? Roles for scholars in participatory research. *American Behavioral Scientist* 42, no. 5: 840–854.

Stoecker, R., and E. Bonacich. 1992. Why participatory research? *American Sociologist*, winter: 5–14.

Strand, K., et al. 2003. *Community-Based Research and Higher Education*. Jossey-Bass.

Stretesky, P., and M. Hogan. 1998. Environmental justice: An analysis of superfund sites in Florida. *Social Problems* 45: 268–287.

Sweeney, J. 2002. *The California Electricity Crisis*. Hoover Institution Press.

Szasz, A. 1993. *Ecopopulism: Toxic Waste and the Movement for Environmental Justice*. University of Minnesota Press.

Szasz, A., and M. Meuser. 2000. Unintended, inexorable: The production of environmental inequalities in Santa Clara County, California. *American Behavioral Scientist* 43: 602–632.

Taft, D., and P. Ross. 1969. American labor Violence: Its causes, character, and outcome. In *Violence in America*, ed. H. Graham and T. Gurr. Praeger.

TallBear, K. 2001. Racializing tribal identity and the implications for political and cultural development. Presented at Indigenous Peoples and Racism Conference, Sydney.

Tarrow, S. 1993. Cycles of collective action: Between moments of madness and the repertoire of contention. *Social Science History* 17, no. 2: 281–308.

Tarrow, S. 1994. *Power in Movement: Social Movements, Collective Action and Politics.* Cambridge University Press.

Tatum, J. 2000. *Muted Voices: The Recovery of Democracy in the Shaping of Technology.* Lehigh University Press.

Taylor, B. 1995. *Ecological Resistance Movements: The Global Emergence of Radical and Popular Environmentalism.* State University of New York Press.

Taylor, D. 1989. Blacks and the environment: Toward an explanation of the concern and action gap between blacks and whites. *Environment and Behavior* 21: 175–205.

Taylor, D. 1993. Minority environmentalism in Britain. *Qualitative Sociology* 16: 263–295.

Taylor, D. 1997. American environmentalism: The role of race, class and gender in shaping activism, 1820–1995. *Race, Gender and Class* 5: 16–62.

Taylor, D. 2000. The rise of the environmental justice paradigm: Injustice framing and the social construction of environmental discourses. *American Behavioral Scientist* 43, no. 4: 508–580.

Taylor, V., and N. Raeburn. 1995. Identity politics as high-risk activism: Career consequences for lesbian, gay, and bisexual sociologists. *Social Problems* 42: 252–273.

Taylor, V., and N. Whittier. 1992. Collective identity in social movement communities: Lesbian feminist mobilization. In *Waves of Protest*, ed. J. Freeman and V. Johnson. Rowman & Littlefield.

Thompson, D. 1963. *The Negro Leadership Class.* Prentice-Hall.

Thu, K., et al. 1997 A control study of the physical and mental health of residents living near a large-scale swine operation. *Journal of Agricultural Safety and Health* 3, no. 1: 13–26.

Tilly, C. 1978. *From Mobilization to Revolution.* Addison-Wesley.

Tilly, C., L. Tilly, L., and R. Tilly. 1975. *The Rebellious Century, 1830–1930.* Harvard University Press.

Tober, J. 1989. *Wildlife and the Public Interest: Nonprofit Organizations and Federal Wildlife Policy.* Praeger.

Turner, R., and D. Wu. 2002. Environmental Justice and Environmental Racism: An Annotated Bibliography and General Overview, Focusing on US Literature, 1996–2002. Unpublished.

United Church of Christ Commission for Racial Justice. 1987. *Toxic Wastes and Race in the United States.*

United Nations Environment Program (UNEP). 2001. Living in a pollution-free world a basic human right. Press release 01/-49, Nairobi, April 27.

United States Council on Environmental Quality (CEQ). 1971 State of the Environment.

United States Environmental Protection Agency (EPA). 2004. EPA Office of the Inspector General, Evaluation Report: EPA Needs to Consistently Implement the Intent of the Executive Order on Environmental Justice, March 2004.

United States General Accounting Office. 1983. Siting of Hazardous Waste Landfills and Their Correlation with Racial and Economic Status of Surrounding Communities. Government Printing Office.

VanderLindin, J. 1989. Return to legal pluralism. *Journal of Legal Pluralism* 28: 149–157.

van Schaik, C., and H. Rijksen. 2002. Integrated conservation and development projects: Problems and potential. In *Making Parks Work*, ed. J. Terborgh et al. Island.

Visgilio, G., and D. Whitelaw, eds. 2003. *Our Backyard: A Quest for Environmental Justice*. Rowman & Littlefield.

Wackernagel, M., et al. 1996. *Our Ecological Footprint: Reducing Human Impact on the Earth*. New Society.

Wallach, L., and M. Sforza. 1999. *The WTO: Five Years of Reasons to Resist Corporate Globalization*. Seven Stories.

Waller, M., and M. Bird. No date. Strengths of First Nations Peoples.

Walsh, E. 1997. *Don't Burn It Here*. Pennsylvania State University Press.

Walsh, E., and R. Warland. 1983. Social movement involvement in the wake of a nuclear accident: Activists and free riders in the TMI area. *American Sociological Review* 48: 764–780.

Walsh, E., R. Warland, and C. Smith. 1993. Backyards, NIMBYs, and Incinerator Sitings: Implications for Social Movement Theory. *Social Problems* 40: 24–38.

Warner, K. 2002. Linking local sustainability initiatives with environmental justice. *Local Environment* 7: 35–47.

Wenz, P. 1988. *Environmental Justice*. State University of New York Press.

Westra, L., and P. Wenz, eds. 1995. *Faces of Environmental Racism: Confronting Issues of Global Justice*. Rowman & Littlefield.

White, H. 1992. Hazardous waste incineration and minority communities. In *Race and the Incidence of Environmental Hazards*, ed. B. Bryant and P. Mohai. Westview.

Williams, G. 1984. The genesis of chronic illness: Narrative reconstruction. *Sociology of Health and Illness* 6: 175–200.

Wilson, W. 1987. *The Truly Disadvantaged: The Inner City, the Underclass, and Public Policy*. University of Chicago Press.

Wing, S., et al. 2000. Environmental injustice in North Carolina's hog industry. *Environmental Health Perspectives* 108: 225–331.

Wood, S., and J. Gilbert. 2002. Returning African American farmers to the land: Recent trends and a policy rationale. *Review of Black Political Economy*, spring: 43–64.

Woolcock, A., and J. Peat. 1997. Evidence for the increase in asthma worldwide. *Ciba Foundation Symposia* 206: 122–134.

World Commission on Environment and Development. 1987. *Our Common Future*. Oxford University Press.

Wunde, S. 2001. Poverty alleviation and tropical forests: What scope for synergies? *World Development* 29: 1817–1833.

York, R., E. Rosa, and T. Dietz. 2003. Footprints on the earth: The environmental consequences of modernity. *American Sociological Review* 68: 279–300.

Zald, M., and J. McCarthy. 1987. *Social Movements in an Organizational Society*. Transaction.

Zhang, A. 2002. *The Origins of the African-American Civil Rights Movement, 1865–1956*. Routledge.

Zimmerman, R. 1993. Social equity and environmental risk. *Risk Analysis* 13: 649–666.

Zinn, H. 1965. *SNCC: The New Abolitionists*, second edition. Beacon.

Zweigenhaft, R., and G. Domhoff. 1991. *Blacks in the White Establishment: A Study of Race and Class in America*. Yale University Press.

About the Authors

David Naguib Pellow is an activist-scholar who has published widely on environmental justice issues in communities of color. His books include *The Silicon Valley of Dreams: Environmental Injustice, Immigrant Workers, and the High-Tech Global Economy* (with Lisa Sun-Hee Park; New York University Press, 2002), *Garbage Wars: The Struggle for Environmental Justice in Chicago* (MIT Press, 2002), and *Urban Recycling and the Search For Sustainable Community Development* (with Adam Weinberg and Allan Schnaiberg; Princeton University Press, 2000). He is an associate professor of ethnic studies at the University of California at San Diego, where he teaches courses on social movements, environmental justice, globalization, and race and ethnicity. He has served on the President's Council on Sustainable Development and on the boards of several community-based organizations dedicated to improving the living and working environments for people of color, immigrants, and low-income persons.

Robert J. Brulle is an associate professor of environmental policy in the School of Environmental Science, Engineering, and Policy at Drexel University. His research focuses on the US environmental movement, on critical theory, and on public participation in environmental policy making. He is the author of several articles in these areas and of *Agency, Democracy, and Nature* (MIT Press, 2000). He has also taught at Goethe University in Frankfurt, at the University of Uppsala, and at George Mason University.

Carl Anthony is an internationally recognized advocate for environmental justice and sustainability. Currently a program officer with the Ford Foundation, he is a co-founder and a former executive director of the Urban

Habitat Program, a former president of Earth Island Institute in San Francisco, and a former chair of the Berkeley Planning Commission.

Robert Benford is a pioneer in the study of social movements, a professor of sociology at the University of Illinois at Carbondale, and president of the Midwest Sociological Society.

Phil Brown is a professor of sociology at Brown University and an expert on the sociology of illness, environmental sociology, and public health.

Bunyan Bryant is the director of the Environmental Justice Initiative of the University of Michigan School of Natural Resources and Environment.

Sherry Cable is an associate professor of sociology at the University of Tennessee and an expert in anti-toxics and environmental justice movement activism, with a particular focus on working class and poor communities in the Southeastern United States.

Jonathan Essoka is an environmental engineer with the US Environmental Protection Agency. His doctoral research focused on the effects of brown-fields revitalization projects on communities of color.

Holly D. Gordon is an attorney with Communities for a Better Environment in Oakland.

Keith I. Harley is a professor at Kent College of Law and an attorney in the Environmental Law Program of the Chicago Legal Clinic, Inc.

Donald W. Hastings is a professor of sociology at the University of Tennessee at Knoxville. His research interests include environmental sociology, applied demography, and sociology of sport.

Elaine Hockman is an adjunct assistant professor at the School of Natural Resources and Environment. She also manages the Research Support Laboratory at Wayne State University.

Heeten Kalan is the director of groundWork USA (formerly the South African Exchange Program on Environmental Justice) in Boston. He has been an international environmental justice activist for more than ten years. He is also a program officer for environmental justice at the New World Foundation in New York.

Charles Lee is Associate Director for Policy and Interagency Liaison in the US Environmental Protection Agency's Office of Environmental Justice. Before working at the EPA, he created the environmental justice program of the United Church of Christ Commission for Racial Justice.

Theo Luebke is a high school teacher. His work centers on collaborations among scientists, schools, and communities.

Joshua Mandelbaum is a former National Rural Health Development Partnership Truman Fellow. He currently advises Governor Tom Vilsack of Iowa on health policy.

Cheryl Margoluis is a graduate student at Yale University's School of Forestry and Environmental Studies. She studies the impacts of different community forest management strategies on tropical ecosystems in Central America.

Brian Mayer is a doctoral candidate in the Department of Sociology at Brown University. His research examines the formation of coalitions and alliances between labor and environmental organizations.

Sabrina McCormick is a doctoral candidate in the Department of Sociology at Brown University. Her main interests are the environmental sociology, medical sociology, and the politics of development.

Tamara Mix is an assistant professor in the Department of Sociology at Oklahoma State University. Her research interests include environmental sociology, inequality, and social movements.

Paula Palmer is the executive director of Global Response, an international network for environmental action and education. A long-time social and environmental justice activist, she has worked to link the struggles of communities in the global North and South. Her books include *What Happen* and *Taking Care of Sibö's Gifts.*

Bobby Peek is the director of groundWork South Africa, an environmental justice campaigning organization. He works with international and local non-governmental organizations and people throughout Africa and the global South. In 1998 he received the Goldman Environmental Prize.

Devon G. Peña is a professor at the University of Washington and an activist who has worked for years among land grant communities in southern Colorado. He is the author of *Chicano Culture, Ecology, Politics.*

Timmons Roberts is a professor of sociology and the director of the Mellon Program in Environmental Science and Policy at the College of William and Mary. He is the author of *Chronicles from the Environmental Justice Frontline* (with Melissa Toffolon-Weiss) and *Trouble in Paradise.*

Julie Sze is an assistant professor in American studies at the University of California at Davis. Her forthcoming book on the history of environmental justice activism in New York City is under contract with The MIT Press. It looks at the intersection of planning and health, especially through the prism of asthma, and at changes in garbage and energy systems as a result of privatization, globalization, and deregulation.

Nicholas Targ is counsel to the Office on Environmental Justice of the US Environmental Protection Agency. He also teaches environmental law and environmental justice as an adjunct professor at the Howard University School of Law.

Melissa Toffolon-Weiss is an affiliate assistant professor of health sciences at the University of Alaska at Anchorage. Her research interests include the anti-toxics movement and other public health issues.

Orrin Williams is a veteran social justice activist based in Chicago. He was the principal organizer of the Midwest/Great Lakes Environmental Justice Summit in May 1996. He now directs the Center for Urban Transformation.

Stephen Zavestoski is an assistant professor of sociology and environmental studies at the University of San Francisco. His research focuses on environmental health and the use of the Internet as a tool for enhancing public participation in environmental politics.

Urban and Industrial Environments: The Series

Steve Lerner, *Diamond: A Struggle for Environmental Justice in Louisiana's Chemical Corridor*

Jason Corburn, *Street Science: Community Knowledge and Environmental Health Justice*

Peggy F. Barlett, ed., *Urban Place: Reconnecting with the Natural World*

David Naguib Pellow and Robert J. Brulle, eds., *Power, Justice, and the Environment: A Critical Appraisal of the Environmental Justice Movement*

Index